ANKE RICHTER is a columnist and reporter. Before she immigrated with her family to New Zealand, she worked in newsrooms and TV productions in Hamburg and Cologne. Her investigative and personal features are published in *Die Zeit, Spiegel, FAZ, taz, New Zealand Geographic, North & South, The Spinoff, Canvas* and others. She has written three previous books that were published in Germany.

D1474946

CULT TRIP

TRIP

ANKE RICHTER

HarperCollins*Publishers*

This book contains descriptions of rape, sexual assault and child sexual abuse. Unless full names are mentioned, first names have been changed and identities disguised.

Reproduction of the poem 'Come to the Edge' on page vii: From *New Numbers* by Christopher Logue, Jonathan Cape, London, 1969. Copyright © Christopher Logue. Reprinted with permission.

Patti Smith quote on page vii: From the article 'Patti Smith: Straight, No Chaser', by Nick Tosches, *CREEM*, September 1978.

HarperCollins*Publishers*
Australia • Brazil • Canada • France • Germany • Holland • India
Italy • Japan • Mexico • New Zealand • Poland • Spain • Sweden
Switzerland • United Kingdom • United States of America

First published in 2022
by HarperCollins*Publishers* (New Zealand) Limited
Unit D1, 63 Apollo Drive, Rosedale, Auckland 0632, New Zealand
harpercollins.co.nz

A catalogue record for this book is available from the National Library of New Zealand

ISBN 978 1 7755 4203 2 (pbk)
ISBN 978 1 7754 9234 4 (ebook)

Cover design and front cover illustration by Hazel Lam, HarperCollins Design Studio
Back cover image by shutterstock.com
Author photograph by Emma Wallbanks
Typeset in Adobe Garamond Pro by Kelli Lonergan
Printed and bound in Australia by McPherson's Printing Group

For my father, Harald Richter, who dedicated his life to reconciliation and repairing injustice.

Come to the edge.
We might fall.
Come to the edge.
It's too high!
COME TO THE EDGE!
And they came
And he pushed
And they flew.

Christopher Logue

—

We need a new cosmology. New gods.
New sacraments. Another drink.

Patti Smith

Prologue

In 2019, I attended the annual conference of the International Cultic Studies Association (ICSA) in Manchester. Of 200 attendees, I was the only New Zealander – and apart from a film team, also the only reporter. A range of people connected to the cult world were there: not just therapists, academics and experts, many of whom had their own experience of cults, but also survivors of cultic abuse, bolstered by their support people and families.

Among them was the world's first male supermodel, Hoyt Richards. I met him before the doors to the Holiday Inn conference room had even swung open. A well-dressed middle-aged man with dazzling white teeth, Hoyt's blond Hollywood good looks and confident smile didn't seem to belong to a suffering cult survivor. But back in the 1980s, when he was posing with Cindy and Naomi for celebrity photographers, Hoyt was under the total control of a UFO doomsday cult called Eternal Values. Throughout his twenties, he gave them all his earnings – about US$45 million – but sued them to the ground after he finally managed to extricate himself. Today, he is a public speaker who warns about cultic influence, as well as an actor and filmmaker.

After three days with 90 sessions, ranging from ISIS to magical thinking, I met the American again outside on the hotel deck.

'I love this supportive environment,' he said.

No one looked down on him or questioned his sanity because the Princeton graduate once believed that an extraterrestrial would save his life. 'Crazy' is a blunt generalisation that the conference folk reject for characterising people in cults.

Hoyt was on a mission to erase the myth of why people end up on the cult conveyer belt: that it happens only to others who are weak and dumb. That's dangerous, he explained, because most people wouldn't consider themselves susceptible. He had that stereotype about typical cult followers in his mind, so he thought that couldn't be him. That mindset contributed to him becoming one.

'Even when I was in it, I could not see it. I was that person, and everyone can be it,' he told me. 'There is no profile.'

Hoyt's words have since become my accessway into the world of cults – a secretive and sometimes scary territory that left its marks on me.

Before my curiosity curdled to concern that brought me to the anti-cult conference, I had become somewhat of a semi-professional sex cult tourist: a journalist researching spiritual groups while wondering what was in them for me personally.

In 2017, I spent a week undercover in an OM house in San Francisco. OM, or Orgasmic Meditation, had taken Silicon Valley by storm. It's a fifteen-minute mindfulness ritual where a practice partner strokes a woman's genitals in a precise pattern. In 2001, a Californian start-up called OneTaste began building this trademarked and supposedly revolutionary technique that promises to increase female pleasure. I joined them for an introductory weekend session for a German newspaper feature. The women who ran the OM course wore high heels and cocktail dresses, and the male staff sported black t-shirts bearing the slogan 'Powered by Orgasm'. Their sales pitch was aggressive, their charm seductive, and their expertise in all matters erotic impressive. Our clothes stayed on.

At night, I slept in a suburban commune of OMers, a villa with chandeliers and golden taps in the black-tiled bathrooms. I had my own room, but all the others shared double beds with a flatmate, sometimes on a weekly rotation. It was deliberate so that 'all your shit comes up', as one young tenant explained to me. She was exhausted from the volunteer work she was doing for OneTaste while saving up for an expensive master class. The fridge was stocked with kale, and the Wi-Fi password was 'orgasm123!'.

After San Francisco, I went to Holland to visit TNT (The New Tantra). Started by an eccentric Australian, the organisation had become popular in Europe. I found their course liberating but also unethical and gross. In intimacy exercises that went beyond anything I had ever experienced, we were pushed out of our comfort zones, with drugs and alcohol in the mix, and publicly ranked at the end. Those who made the cut, marked by a wristband and new name, were the attractive and unquestioning ones. A year later, TNT was exposed as a hardcore sex cult sailing under the banner of personal growth. There were reports of physical, verbal and sexual abuse in the inner circle.

Also in 2018, the FBI began investigating OneTaste in San Francisco for prostitution and labour exploitation. The company stopped all classes and moved their business online, while in urban centres around the world, burgeoning OM houses folded. Thousands of people who had believed that they were part of a good thing, who gave their time and skills, their money and energy to these organisations, felt duped and disillusioned. But some became even more entrenched in their defence of the leaders. What had started as innocent and exciting, attracting bright, ambitious members of society with a hunger for connection and growth – because those are the ones that cults want as members, not the broken and dispossessed ones – led to cult carnage and trauma. And this wasn't even the tip of the iceberg. Keith Raniere, the head of the American personal development cult NXIVM who had his initials burned into the skin of women in his inner circle, was arrested and sentenced to 120 years in prison in October 2020. One of his top soldiers, Alison Mack, was a successful Hollywood star. She was sentenced to three years' imprisonment.

From social media echo chambers to sports clubs, we are tribal beings, dependent on connection through a shared purpose. But in an increasingly secular society, traditional religion has lost its place. In its stead has popped up the self-help movement, there to meet and monetise a need that is as old as humankind itself: to understand who we are deep inside, and to make sense of this complicated world. For some, it's about finding their soul on a spiritual path; for others, it's a new technique from an inspirational coach that helps them be their best in their job.

Whatever the pursuit, it usually comes with its own subculture, denomination or lineage. Nothing about these movements, their members and their motivations is innately wrong; there are myriad excellent reasons for stepping out of the maelstrom of a materialist society, wanting to create a world that is more egalitarian, more kind, or more sustainable. Pioneers, activists, revolutionaries and visionaries have always paved the way for social change and higher awareness, from Jesus of Nazareth to Mahatma Gandhi and Greta Thunberg.

But when charismatic leaders turn their followership into parallel societies that look like safe havens in an insane world but cause harm, we call them cults. It's a controversial term among experts. Academics prefer to label them as 'high-demand groups', or even more neutrally, 'new religious movements'. But despite the loaded and multi-layered meaning – a 'cult song' describes a Beatles classic, not a chant at the Hare Krishna temple – I will stick to the term in this book. Its more sinister meaning is fitting to describe conglomerations on the fanatical fringe where people wilfully manipulate some of the most altruistic human traits, usually with disastrous consequences.

When twisted and exploited, the earnest love for an ideal or for a teacher can turn the strongest, brightest person into a mess. Best intentions can bring out the worst. It doesn't need a NXIVM branding iron to create cult slaves. It doesn't even need a public figurehead, as the digital mega-cult QAnon demonstrated during the Covid pandemic.

Although the shape can vary, the pattern remains the same. Michael Jackson's hold on the star-struck families whose children he sexually abused is not that different from the grooming of girls in the Children of God. Hugh Hefner essentially ran a cult at his Playboy Mansion that left many broken. Multi-level marketing companies for essential oils operate on seductive techniques similar to radical political and religious splinter groups. Militant jihadists and neo-Nazis have more in common than they think. It's not about the content, the product, the faith, or the look, but the power structure, the group mind, and the players.

An orange robe and a wacky UFO belief don't make someone a cult leader. Neither does a strange-looking building where people worship make it a cult – nor a remote piece of land where they all live together. A distinction needs to be drawn between cults and intentional communities, of which Aotearoa New Zealand has the highest number per capita in the world. Communes and small communities belong to our national identity.

New Zealand has always been a place of new beginnings, first for early Polynesian explorers. Pre-urbanisation, Māori lived together on and around the marae (meeting house), and for around a million Māori and Pasifika today, communal living is in their ancestral DNA. Later came the first British settlers, and then, in the 1940s and '50s, thousands of refugees from World War II arrived, all of whom made the antipodean islands their safe home. From the '70s onwards, European hippies landed, wanting to get as far away as possible from overpopulation or nuclear disaster in the northern hemisphere. This haven for immigrants became a fertile ground for escapists and utopians, who often chose the most beautiful parts of the country for their new home.

Today, some eco-communities like Tui or Riverside, both in the top of the South Island, still thrive after four decades. They offer a sustainable and socially nourishing alternative to nuclear-family housing, and they are not what this book is about, as much as I'm drawn to them. Ever since I spent a year at a boarding school in England, I dreamed of communal living and joining a kibbutz for a while. Rural or urban communes are communities of people with idealistic goals, choosing to share their resources. It's only when their self-determination flips to destructive persuasion, internally or externally, that we see a cult in the making or in full swing. Although many cults are run by malignant narcissists who would do anything to get their needs met, the cultification is not always obvious – each step is typically innocuous, but in its sum, it can be horrific.

When folk poet James K. Baxter retreated to the upper reaches of the Whanganui River in 1968, his social experiment of simple living at Jerusalem inspired many others to follow him to Hiruhārama, as he called his new home. They lived as a family and shared their food, their clothes, their dreams and hopes. A young woman who joined the commune later described how they danced together, cooked together, laughed and wept, and hugged each other a lot. She was eighteen when James K. Baxter raped her on a bunk bed. The charismatic leader and literary icon was also a serial sexual abuser. The dark underbelly of Hiruhārama was not exposed until 2019.

Sexual abuse is a mainstay of cults. According to cult expert Dr Janja Lalich, 40 per cent of women in cults have experienced it. In closed-off groups, sex and money, the strongest forces driving the world, become means of power and control. Sexuality is either amplified, suppressed or distorted.

If the word 'cult' is debatable, then 'sex cult' is an even murkier term. It is more commonly used in a mocking pop-culture context than in cult studies; not even Wikipedia has a definition for it. Online dictionaries describe them as cults in which 'unrestrained sexual activity is central to worship and ceremonies', which misleadingly suggests orgies with naked women sprawled on altars. Far from the truth. Recently exposed organisations like NXIVM, MISA (Movement for Spiritual Integration into the Absolute) or OneTaste are not in the news for unrestrained sex between adults, but for their criminal and coercive tactics. 'Sex-trafficking cults' would be more apt.

The salacious connotation associated with sex cults tends to hurt those who have suffered in them. It doesn't capture the rape and subjugation of women, or the abuse and neglect of children, or the trauma and exploitation of their members. Instead, it implies that everyone is a fun participant in these activities, fuelled by their libido or blind love for the guru.

In the cults that I have mainly researched over the last ten years – the former therapy cult Centrepoint, the tantric cult Agama Yoga, and the fundamentalist Christian cult Gloriavale – this wasn't the case for everyone. The pressure to be promiscuous and sexually available can be just as abusive as the punishment of natural urges and desires, as happens in many high-control groups that enforce celibacy. But in all the cults explored in this book, sexuality plays a central role. Charismatic leaders like Hopeful Christian of Gloriavale and Bert Potter of Centrepoint had more in common besides being convicted paedocriminals. They defined what their people's sex life should look like, how it should be done, how often and with whom.

I hope that my own journey from enthusiastic participant to critical observer helps to explain why former members fell under the spell of cults. I also hope that those who are emerging from them feel heard and seen, not shamed. Everyone is susceptible to cult conversion – the millions of people around the world who were pulled down rabbit holes into conspiracy theories during the Covid-19 pandemic are now living proof of this vulnerability. To help them come out takes the same skills as helping someone exit from a closed group: listening, compassion, understanding and love.

If we stopped seeing cults as catchments for weirdos, but instead as microcosms of oppression, each their own little *Animal Farm* full of ordinary creatures, then we might become more aware of the institutionalised harm done in the name of religion or politics, from paedophile priests to the racist brutality in state care and offshore detention camps. *Cult Trip* unpacks these hard-to-spot dynamics by giving a voice to those who've sunk deep into the mire of cults or were born or raised in them: victims, perpetrators, or both.

To find those survivors, some of whom have never spoken to a journalist before, I didn't have to look very far.

PART 1

The Lost Tribe of Albany

Chapter 1

A tropical shower pours down on Byron Bay. The afternoon sky has turned dark. It's late summer 2012, and I'm standing on the first-floor balcony of the Byron Community Centre, hot and sweaty from dancing. I stretch my arms out into the rain. Cold drops kiss my skin.

This, I think, *is how I always want to be.*

It's a promise to myself. Or a prayer. I slow my breath down and wipe the rain over my face. People laugh and cheer somewhere, and music pumps in the room behind me where I have just been jumping about. Something happened for me during the ecstatic dance session while I met other eyes and open smiles around me. I'm on a euphoric high from this energy orgy, without any stimulants in my system – not even a coffee.

My inner cynic, a stowaway wherever I go, has vanished. I feel so incredibly alive – connected to the world like never before. 'Vibrating' is the word they use at this festival, called 'Taste of Love', at which I arrived the day before. A week earlier, I wasn't sure if I would last at a trans-Tasman get-together of tantric teachers, sexual healers and shamanic practitioners. It is held annually in the heart of the Rainbow Region in Australia, a part of north-eastern New South Wales colonised by the flower-power generation who turned it into a tie-dyed cliché full of crystal shops. It's not really my scene. I don't speak New Age, I married a doctor, and as a journalist who trades in facts, I'm by default sceptical of anything esoteric. Ask me my star sign and I give you an eye-roll. My spiritual journey – another term that makes me cringe – has not expanded much beyond meditation and yoga classes. Now I'm in this antipodean Vegas of commercialised spirituality, attending 'sex and consciousness' workshops for a magazine assignment. I will write it under a pseudonym.

The stage in the main hall is decorated with a purple velvet sofa, frou-frou lamps and other boudoir paraphernalia. A dozen talks on the stage revolve around orgasm and ecstasy of the natural kind. Drugs and booze are taboo, and the festival plus this whole world has its own language. I learn that 'conscious' does not mean coming out of a coma but being emotionally aware, or 'present' – another favourite. By lunchtime, I've grasped that female ejaculation is the 'nectar of the Gods' and the anus a portal for 'dark divinity'. A woman named Jessica Galactic Butterfly holds a workshop full of deep exhalation sounds. In another room, the Youth Speak forum hosts a panel about sex education that demands young people need more knowledge than just rolling condoms over bananas. It's brave stuff.

As my reservations fade, I make curious contact with the crowd around me who are predominantly clad in flowing silks and purple cotton. I begin to throw words like 'transformation' and 'energy' into my conversations. In the break, I browse a stall that sells delicate 'pussy purses' made from pink satin, complete with a little pearl. Other conferences offer golf tournaments for a social event; this one has a Lover's Mask ball with outrageous sexy costumes, and as the opening act, the practice of deep eye-gazing in a big circle. When I leave at midnight, I'm intoxicated by what the shiny happy people here call 'life energy'. Something clicked. There's nothing to mock.

My first and unsuccessful attempt at neo-tantra – the westernised, body-focused appropriation of ancient tantra teachings – was fifteen years ago, in a bleak gym hall in Hamburg. I was reluctant to hug total strangers on the spot. It seemed forced and artificial. I quit the group after the first exercise, repulsed by a guy in a sweaty t-shirt next to me who was rolling his hips to Enya-style music while moaning loudly – this was just after breakfast. *How do these people do it*, I wondered, *letting themselves go like this?*

Here I am, fifteen years later, letting myself go like this. Making sounds, rolling my hips to music, unblocking my 'kundalini energy' – and not embarrassed at all. Instead of yuck, it feels yum. The next morning, I almost forget to put clothes on before crossing the road to the beach for an early swim. Two days in neo-tantra land, and my inhibitions dissolve like sand in the waves.

The highlight of the last day is a pouchy bald man who looks like a friendly vacuum-cleaner salesman. He has published a picture book about 'yonis' – the Sanskrit and New Age term for women's genitals. He specialises in 'body de-armouring' to help women experience energetic full-body orgasms. We get a demonstration with the blonde conference organiser acting as guinea pig. She takes off her sarong and lies naked on a table in the middle of the auditorium, her eyes closed. When she goes into a kind of trance, the sexual healer starts to move his hands not on, but above, her body, like a magician, occasionally touching pressure points on her throat or knees. She soon heaves and moans, her body shivers, and she clearly comes. Over a hundred people watch in silence with utter reverence. There are no sniggers, no heavy breathing. It feels dignified, not dodgy. What makes sex sacred is not the incense, soft background music or candles. It's your full attention.

Without any indoctrination, coercion or sneaky recruitment, Taste of Love gives me my first taste of infatuation with a new tribe – a word I've never used before in that context. I quickly adopt 'tribe' into my vocabulary until, years later, it feels conflicting and even repulsive. But on that hot and sweaty summer weekend, when I hug, laugh, dance and exhale into 'Omm', my internal shift on the rain-soaked balcony becomes a reference point. I've experienced what thousands of people do when they begin to get hooked by a teacher or group: a feeling of a distinct before and after, of not wanting to be my old boring self anymore, a sense of tapping into something profound. It's like falling in love – with so much potential.

The spiritual festival with its sexy vibe is also my unintentional entry into cult journalism.

On my last day, I'm sipping iced chai in the sunlit courtyard of the Byron Community Centre when Angie Meiklejohn approaches me. The fellow New Zealander is short and curvy, with incredibly blue eyes and a mane of brunette curls. We're both in our forties, and now sparkling from our soul wash. Angie has come from Wellington where she makes a living by giving sensual naked massages. It sounds like sex work, but she tells me it is 'healing' for her clients with intimacy issues. Her directness is disarming. When I leave the closing session to catch my plane back to Christchurch, I see Angie in a tantric yab-yum position – a term I just learned. She sits cross-legged on a guy's lap, embracing him while gazing deep into his eyes. Both look radiant. I don't know it yet, but I've just met the person who will open the door to a historical tribe far more extreme than any of the gentle seekers floating around me.

—

A few months later, I see Angie again in New Zealand, where she's running Snuggle Parties. These are not actual parties; there's no dancing or drinking. They start off as consent workshops where you practise how to state your boundaries, express a 'yes' or a 'no' – a helpful tool for any interaction followed by non-sexual conscious touch exercises.

I can't convince my old friends to come along to this. They recoil as if I had mentioned a '70s-style key party. I don't blame them for thinking that I'm a bit weird. I had the same reservations when I first dipped my toes into this new field, but I have since found some treasures behind the barrier of apprehension and judgement.

After the Snuggle Party, Angie tells me that she always experiences an instant 'No!' reaction when someone approaches her romantically.

'I could not trust my body and its signals for years and years. I was completely shut down, sexually, emotionally,' she says while stacking mattresses. 'I was actually abusing myself.'

It's hard to imagine this voluptuous woman in a clinging low-cut dress, who just led a group for two hours, as self-harming. She looks me straight in the eye.

'I lived in a kind of sex cult when I was young, you know.' Her frankness is the same as back in the Byron Bay courtyard. 'At Centrepoint.'

I've heard the name somewhere before. An item about a cult leader who had died was on the news months earlier: Bert Potter. He looked like a potato farmer to me. No Rolls-Royce or fancy robes. Certainly no sex appeal. But the 86-year-old had been the founder and spiritual leader of Centrepoint Community in Albany since 1977. When I first set foot in New Zealand in 2001, his 'free love' and therapy community had just been shut down after a lengthy court battle. A decade earlier, it was raided for drug manufacturing and child sexual abuse allegations. Eight men, including the spiritual leader, his wife and a top-ranking woman went to jail. Other convictions followed.

The parents and children of Centrepoint – most of them white middle-class – weren't on the public radar again until briefly in 2010 when Massey University published the study 'A Different Kind of Family'. It revealed that every third child among the hundreds who lived at the community in its 22 years was likely to have been sexually abused and that half of the teenagers became sexually active early on. Bert Potter, a former pest-control salesman turned self-proclaimed therapist, was unrepentant right to the end of his life and never apologised to his victims.

But the villain at the centre of Centrepoint doesn't interest me as much as those who enabled him, who lived with him, who slept with him, who loved or hated him. When I first met Angie in Byron Bay, Potter was still alive. When we meet again, he is dead. Angie says she can only talk about Bert Potter now because he's gone.

I wonder about what happened to her in that place, and to the thousands of people who passed through the Albany site in its two decades, including many psychology professionals. In New Zealand's small, close-knit community, every adult in Aotearoa must be only a couple of degrees separated from someone who has been there at some point. So where are they now? Everyone who was convicted has a family. How did they cope afterwards?

Surely this disturbing chapter of New Zealand's social history should be written down. I wonder why no one has done it yet. If those who were there could share their stories, it might help the collective healing. It's daunting, but I'm optimistic.

The same year, I'm back in Berlin for a visit. I regularly travel to Germany to see friends, family and editors I work for. The city is a haven for explorers of all cultural, political and sexual orientations; Germans take their freedom of expression very seriously. One evening on a night out, I end up in a semi-industrial loft in Wedding. Ropes are dangling from the ceiling, mattresses stacked along the walls. Schwelle 7 is an edgy space for bodywork, dance and workshops.

A bald man in a baggy cotton singlet introduces himself as Andreas and asks where I'm from.

'New Zealand,' I answer.

'Oh, really!' He is surprised and delighted. 'I've been there. A long time ago.'

'Where did you go?'

Not that I really care that much. A play-fight with oil is about to begin on a black tarpaulin at the back of the room and I don't want to miss it.

'You probably wouldn't know the place,' says Andreas. 'It doesn't exist anymore. The name was Centrepoint.'

My fascination with the greased-up wrestlers shifts in a split second. It turns out that Andreas, formerly from East Germany, is a counsellor who was interested in polyamory, which means openly loving more than one person and having multiple relationships, with everyone's agreement. Today, it's a much-discussed way of having more honesty and sexual freedom, but without affairs, secrets and family break-ups.

Andreas had been inspired by a promotional talk, two decades ago, held by a Centrepoint representative near Berlin. He decided to visit the little commune for his research, two years after it had created a media storm down under because of the raids and arrests. The Berliner was completely oblivious to any of this; it was before the internet. He didn't know much about New Zealand but had always dreamed of going there. His English wasn't very good because he grew up behind the Wall.

In February 1994, a Centrepoint couple picked up Andreas and his travelling partner at Auckland airport and took them to Albany, where they were going to stay for six days. Andreas didn't know that the man who greeted him had been in jail for indecently assaulting a child.

'It was an amazing place, really,' he tells me.

He sounds like he's still taken with it: the lush green valley with native bush and quaint huts, and the never-ending concert of cicadas in the evenings. His first taste of Aotearoa and its largest alternative community was intriguingly beautiful.

The visitors from overseas were invited to help themselves in the kitchen. They were surprised that the food wasn't organic. Ecological sustainability wasn't a priority, but everyone was friendly and relaxed. The lounge had big cushions where people lay around in each other's arms.

'It all seemed very loving and inviting. So laid-back.'

Andreas interviewed some Centrepoint members about spiritual leadership and open relationships. He was interested in how they managed communal and individual possessions, how it all worked.

'So ... what about the sexual abuse?' I finally ask him, trying to hold back the unease that creeps up inside me. 'After all, Bert Potter was in jail at the time. You must have known about the charges and convictions. Did that not bother you?'

Andreas shrugs. 'The way it was explained to me there ... well, they said that some of the children had seen adults

20

having sex and were later told by counsellors that this was sexual abuse. It was all turned around by the police to damage the community.'

His eyes shift around while he smiles apologetically. 'The allegations sounded like fabrications to me, blown up by the media.'

This narrative seems to sit more comfortably with him than bursting the bubble of his little Kiwi utopia. Eighteen thousand kilometres away from Albany, I'm speaking to the first person I've met with a positive view of Centrepoint. Whenever I mentioned my interest in this topic to someone in my second home, their face went into a pinch that meant 'ouch' or 'yuck'. Eyes never lit up like Andreas's do when he hears the name of his favourite place at the other end of the world. The majority of people, despite never setting foot in Centrepoint, are disgusted or embarrassed by it. At the other end of the spectrum are idealists who don't want to see communal living become tainted by ugly facts.

Andreas promises to give me something to kick-start my research, so I meet him for a coffee at the Hackesche Höfe the next day. He arrives by bike and reaches for his cigarettes, then hands me a book that has been out of print for over twenty years. A red paperback, heavy and glossy. Under the title *Inside Centrepoint*, Bert Potter in a homespun jersey smiles on the front cover, arms crossed. People wearing colourful clothes stand in circles behind him, beaming. I can't wait to open it.

Andreas wishes me luck. 'I just don't trust what outsiders say,' he says. 'Let me know when you meet the people who actually lived there and what they think now.'

He points at the author's photo at the back of the book before he mounts his bike. The handsome man's name is Len Oakes. 'Maybe start with him. He was their historian.'

I browse through *Inside Centrepoint*. Something in me could easily fall in love with how the place presented itself. The black-and-white 1980s photos of wholesome, happy people working together on their own land depict the spirit of alternative antipodean living. My favourite picture, which reminds me of the Taste of Love festival, shows a suntanned, dark-haired woman with a beautiful make-up-free smile and a bare apple bottom. She wears only a striped apron while she carries buckets.

The book evokes more nostalgia, with babies being born, laughing children on trampolines, group therapy sessions, working bees in gumboots, and endless birthday parties. With an average of 150 people living there, at its peak nearly 300, Centrepoint had several celebrations each week. 'To them,' it says on the first pages, 'Centrepoint is not an experiment, it is home.'

The book covers everything from the legal wrangles with the council to the leavers, the opposition, health issues, and 'What kind of person joins Centrepoint?' – I'm asking myself the same question. What strikes me is how normal they all look. How likeable. Despite the occasional unassuming nudity in the book, the Centrepointians don't come across as obvious hippies or radicals of any sort – not even seductively dressed, considering they were labelled a 'sex cult'. They look more like a large bohemian family on an endless outing that includes shared meals, communal sleeping arrangements and an occasional sojourn in old buses.

The only spanner in the works for me is the presence of 'Bert', as he is referred to throughout the book. The first chapter is entirely devoted to the man himself, his humble beginnings and incredible growing popularity.

Written by Bert Potter's loyal in-house academic Len Oakes to counter the public hostility the community had increasingly faced – and to dispel accusations by former members who had made allegations about the sexual violation of children – *Inside Centrepoint* was an excellent piece of PR. It was published in 1986, still a few years away from everything that would later surface, tainting and destroying the community forever.

Oakes calls this idyll north of Auckland a 'communal psychotherapy cult'. He means it as a friendly term, more tongue-in-cheek, nothing sinister. 'Bert is a modern guru,' he states. It reads as a plea for tolerance, for the acceptance of diversity in beliefs, relationship models and lifestyles. It seems so honest and likeable. Oakes is even candid enough to mention a sexual innovation by Bert Potter called 'blowing off'. The technique – loudly blowing with pressed lips on a woman's clitoris – is described half ironically in palatable detail as a 'subtle art' that must have intrigued readers: 'It takes a man time to learn the skill, but it takes a woman no time at all to learn to enjoy it.'

Back in Christchurch, I mention to a neighbour that I'm researching Centrepoint.

'Hey, I've got a funny story for you,' he says with a sly grin, leaning against his truck.

Years ago, he met someone on a building site who lived at Centrepoint as a boy. 'Get this: at one time, these kids had to do this oral sex thing on some of the women. To learn it. The ladies were all lying there in a row, legs spread open.'

His grin now feels a bit off to me.

'It was really noisy, so they made the kids wear earmuffs to concentrate better. Imagine that!'

I'm trying not to.

'And that was a funny story for him?' I ask.

The builder shrugs his shoulders. 'Well, I guess he wanted to shock the guys when he told us, really. But hey, at least he could talk about it.'

It's unlikely that I will ever find this boy with his earmuffs. But there must be others who might talk about it now. Even if it's not that funny.

Len Oakes is listed as a therapist in Melbourne. I call his number and leave a message. He calls me back within a day to say: 'I have never spoken to any journalist from New Zealand, and I never will.'

He is friendly, articulate, and cautious. Len makes it perfectly clear how little he thinks of his home country, its parochial mentality and prejudiced media that he suffered for far too long. He left Auckland forever in 1991, 'when the shit hit the fan'. He had testified for Bert Potter in court, claiming that the drugs they all took were only placebos as part of a psychological experiment. Then he was out and over to Australia.

'So why are you talking to me, then?' I ask.

'Because you're not from New Zealand,' he replies. 'You're an outsider.'

In November 2012 I'm on a plane to Melbourne to meet my first insider. Len picks me up in his car and takes me to his house, a white bungalow in Carlton. We cross the backyard and go straight to his office, past some neatly raised veggie beds. Len and his wife met at Centrepoint and have adult children, but I never meet her; she is resting up before a hospital visit the next day.

Len is in his early sixties, charming and sophisticated. He makes us a cup of tea, carefully warming the teapot with hot water first. Everything is going to be off the record. He finds me too focused on the topic of sexual abuse, whereas I

24

find him to have a blind spot about it – something I noticed when I read his other cult publications.

Len, an authority on all things Centrepoint and a psychologist himself, shows no interest in reading the Massey study about the Centrepoint children, which strikes me as odd since it has been published for two years and can be downloaded online. But he started an online forum for former Centrepoint members called STT, short for 'Spending Time Together' – the Centrepoint euphemism for having a spontaneous quickie. He offers to point me in the direction of some old friends who could add a new perspective, if I in return could be more 'open-minded'.

We meet again in the city the next day before he visits his wife in hospital. He hands me the CD of his recordings as a blues musician. It's called *Imperfect Gentleman*. This isn't my last gift from him. When I arrive back home, I find a whole manuscript in my email inbox. 'Divine' is the unpublished memoir of his life by Bert Potter's side, free for me to use. It's a compelling read that takes me deep into the inner workings of a psycho-cult and to the extreme fringe of the sexual liberation and human potential movement of the early 1980s.

I didn't expect this generosity. The doors are opening, and I have already struck gold behind the first one. I don't yet see the cesspools that lie behind the others.

Chapter 2

In early 2013, Angie is back in Christchurch and staying at my house. She is fasting that week, so I make her a celery and apple juice. She takes a sip and cracks a smile.

'I've been sober for eight years now! Not a single drink.'

I didn't know she had been an alcoholic.

'Yes, and a prostitute, and then almost killed myself.'

The shocked look on my face about her revelation almost makes her laugh. Before we head to bed, she uses the toilet next to the bathroom while I brush my teeth but she leaves the door open so we can still talk. It doesn't bother her one bit.

'Oh, poppet,' she says, laughing at me. 'I lost all those hang-ups back then. They were forever breaking down our boundaries.'

In the morning, we sit down for our interview session in my home office. I can't think of a better first interviewee: emotionally intelligent, articulate and self-reflective, never embarrassed, no questions taboo. She says she had another dream of Centrepoint last night. It happens often lately.

The Meiklejohn parents split up when Angie was ten. Jane Stanton, her mother, gave birth to her when she was only eighteen, then had three more children. Jane had missed out on so much. She wanted to have lovers, but Angie's father wasn't up for that. Shortly after the separation, Jane and the kids visited Centrepoint for the first time, just to have a look.

Angie remembers that it was pouring with rain and there was mud everywhere. The toilet was scary, just a wooden frame with a plastic sheet across the front. 'I was wondering if someone could just walk in.'

The little girl wandered around by herself for a while and then started looking for her mother, who was nowhere in sight. At one point, Angie opened a door somewhere. She was looking into a room full of naked and half-naked people. She didn't understand what was going on. Everyone was lying on cushions, cuddling, and her mum was somewhere in there. Angie shakes off the weird, blurry memory. 'So hard to remember.'

Around that time, she was raped by a fourteen-year-old boy. He was the son of her mum's boyfriend and young Angie had crawled into his bed one night when they were all staying at his place. When she told her mother, Jane didn't believe her. Not long after, as a young teen, Angie became sexually active herself and started to drink. The boys wanted her, she was fun and liked to party. But she was shipped between her parents and social care, went to five different schools in fifth form, was suspended, and got in trouble with the police. She shaved off all her hair, was made a ward of the state and lived in a social welfare home.

'Punk rocker and fully fledged alcoholic at fifteen,' she says. 'Angry, lonely and desperate for someone to love me.' She looks down, choking on these words for a bit.

Her mother, who was on a benefit, was as lost as she was, while also being bashed around by violent boyfriends. Angie was living on the streets by then, eating what people left on their McDonald's trays in Queen Street. Her mum was suffering from an undiagnosed bipolar disorder while also getting into rebirthing and 'Loving Relationship Training'.

'She was looking for love, for support and acceptance,' says Angie.

A community with therapy sounded like the solution, where they could all be together, and the children kept safe. When her mother suggested another visit to Centrepoint, Angie came along to have a look.

'I thought it'd be interesting, after all those years.'

In the 1970s, for those seeking new ways of living and relating to others, Aotearoa was a backwater steeped in puritan Anglo-Saxon values. The sexual liberation movement and social upheavals that were sweeping the world from London to New York had only lightly touched sleepy cities like Auckland and Wellington. Bert Potter, who was big on the self-improvement techniques of popular writer Dale Carnegie, had returned from a visit to the very centre of the human potential movement, the experimental Esalen Institute in California. There, he was given an injection of new therapy styles based on the teachings of Wilhelm Reich and Fritz Perls, such as gestalt and encounter groups that were very different to traditional psychotherapy.

The cutting-edge 'growth work' made Bert Potter popular with clients and social services alike when he set himself up as a therapist in Campbells Bay in Auckland – without any academic background. He became especially known for 'unblocking' women who couldn't orgasm. His Shoreline Human Awareness Trust saw many medical students pass through the seven-day workshops. A professor of psychiatry at Auckland Medical School was a trustee. Everyone was drawn to Bert Potter.

Bert had also stayed at the ashram of Indian guru Rajneesh, or Bhagwan, who later rebranded himself as Osho. The Kiwi aspired to become like him, waking people up and revolutionising the world. The infamous mystic in Pune, India, advocated letting children be around their parents when they have sex so that they grow up seeing it as beautiful and sacred. He claimed it would also inoculate them against sexual abuse.

In New Zealand, Potter's group of followers and devotees grew. Their philosophy emphasised openness and intimacy; promiscuity was encouraged, sex seen as natural and free – the fewer barriers between people, the more authenticity and love could grow. The first child within the group was born while everyone watched and celebrated the occasion. It marked the start of the communal experiment, and the search for land began. On 28 January 1978, 25 adults and 17 children moved into an old Albany farmhouse surrounded by 30 acres of bush. The group bought a wing of a Salvation Army hostel, which was transported there. They erected tents, then a sprawling village with car crates – reused wooden shipping containers. They cleared the bush and started planting strawberries and kūmara. Their commune was born.

In 1980, TVNZ broadcast a fly-on-the-wall documentary about Centrepoint that showed birthing scenes and New Zealand television's first full-frontal nudes. But what was outrageous at the time also became the community's public debut, attracting criticism as well as curiosity.

More babies were born, more land bought, and businesses developed: paper-making, printing, hat-making, silk garment-making, pottery. Resident numbers grew, with around 150 adults, children and long-term visitors by the mid-1980s. Centrepoint held workshops that were open to outsiders, and it set up a counselling centre in the city.

While growing in popularity as well as controversy, the community came under official attack because too many people lived on the property. A legal battle with the Takapuna City Council began that would last for years. The council evicted them, and the 'lost tribe of Albany', as the press called them, was homeless for eighteen months. Before Christmas 1983, the community packed up and moved into rented factories, then slept in shopping malls, on a marae, in buses and barns. They staged a sit-in at the council offices and risked mass arrests. The much-publicised nomadic odyssey ended with a victory in the High Court in June 1985: they were granted the right to have 224 people living on site. Everyone could finally go home – except Bert, who was in hospital with pneumonia brought on by sleeping in a draughty barn. The episode was stressful for the community and had also cost ratepayers around a hundred thousand dollars in court proceedings.

Centrepoint was now recognised as a charitable trust with a spiritual leader. They were officially classified a religion, which the community mainly did for tax reasons. The council granted building permits, and the commune's next phase began. Centrepointians built a 25-metre swimming pool and two tennis courts. They turned swamps into parkland and bought an additional goat-breeding farm. They took over an abortion clinic in the city. Centrepoint workshops were *en vogue* with psychology students and academics alike, who flocked there on weekends. This was the flourishing era when the four Meiklejohn children and their mother Jane Stanton arrived again, on a Saturday in the summer of 1985.

Five years after that blurry, rainy first day in the mud, Angie was surprised again, but this time not by any naked bodies.

For the teenage rebel from the streets of central Auckland, the Centrepoint site near the quiet township of Albany now looked like an unexpectedly neat and proper place: 'So set up, very middle-class.'

They drove in over a little bridge; Jane, Angie, her brother Karl and her younger sisters Bonnie and Renee. The sun was shining, and the camellia bushes were in full bloom. A man met them at the main door: Henry Stonex, a therapy group leader and counsellor and the same man who would pick up Andreas at the airport on his visit from Berlin, years later. Stonex wore jeans, a handmade belt with a big buckle, a red striped jersey, and an earring in one ear. To Angie, he looked wild, like a pirate – 'the most interesting character I'd ever seen'. The older man's piercing blue eyes had a twinkle. He was intense and attentive.

'I felt instantly attracted to him, like, "woah, what a cool dude".'

Henry Stonex showed them around the grounds and gave them a tour of the community. Centrepoint seemed huge to the fifteen-year-old, and so different from her mum's small rental place. Here, they had a big kitchen and dining room, and benches with stainless-steel appliances. Henry took her up to the longhouses, which had rooms with lots of double beds, sometimes a single bed in between for a child, and no walls between them. Angie thought that was a cool idea: you just lean over to talk to someone, and they are right there. It looked warm and cosy to her. Welcoming and inviting. Not weird at all this time.

Outside, a working bee was underway. People in dungarees were building the swimming pool, gluing blue tiles to the walls, laughing and chatting. Some of the bronzed women were topless. Wandering around the grounds, Angie took in the carcasses of old buses with funky curtains, the rusty little sheds, A-frame houses, and hideaways in the bush. She walked past craft rooms, pottery barns and up towards the huge nursery. All the colours and the pots and the plants – it was like a magical land, so dinky and bohemian. Her heart sang.

The next weekend the five Meiklejohns moved in. Anyone was allowed to join Centrepoint; no one was ever turned down.

For $170 a week, visitors could stay and work for free. But to become a member, they first had to write a letter to Bert Potter. Only he could decide who joined. And what Bert wanted was referred to as 'Bert says', a thought-terminating doctrine to be followed by everyone.

Once you'd received Bert's approval, you had to sign over all your assets, income and belongings to the trust. If you decided to leave, you would be given $100 per person plus the clothes on your back. Some people, especially the first generation of affluent teachers, doctors, nurses and psychiatrists, had sold up their houses or liquidated their inheritances to help build Centrepoint. They were taking a huge financial risk, based on what they saw not only as a lifelong commitment but also an investment in their children's future.

Jane Stanton, who was single with four kids, was more typical of those who joined in the later years. She didn't have much, not even a car, and never bought the children anything because there was no money. Now Jane bought all four of them new duvets. It was her last spend before they moved in, a real luxury. Angie kept her duvet for years. It was bright, flowery, and always on her bed.

The teenagers' rooms were in the annex of the old Salvation Army hostel. Apart from double beds and dressers, the rooms were sparse, with white concrete walls and ranch sliders facing outwards. One boy had painted the prism from

Pink Floyd's *Dark Side of the Moon* on his wall. Beads hung down from the loft. Angie learned from her roommate to only use the visitors' toilets, which had a door that could be locked. In the adults' toilets, four bowls faced each other, in open sight; it was part of the Centrepoint philosophy to overcome shame around bodies. But Angie found it horrendous. To get to the teenagers' area, you had to walk past the loos while people were sitting on them reading books. The teenagers only used these toilets when it was night-time, and no one was around. Some kids kept pee buckets outside their rooms instead.

When they first arrived, one of the teenagers took Angie up to the kitchen and showed her where the bread and cheese was stored, to make toasted sandwiches late at night. It all felt like a holiday camp to her – exciting times. They secretly hung out in the kitchen when all the adults were asleep and they had the munchies from smoking pot.

Some girls didn't like living there, though. They seemed prudish to Angie and got up at six o'clock in the morning to have showers when no one could see them. They called Bert a filthy old man. The children of the parents who had founded Centrepoint seemed incredibly reserved, in fact, and shy in comparison to Angie. They were good scholars and popular hockey players, or nerdy gamers who played Dungeons and Dragons. Some teenagers from broken homes without any parents at the community also drifted through.

The place had its perks for all of them: absolute freedom. The teenagers could eat whenever they wanted, they could swim in the pool and roam around in the bush, and they had their own rooms – something Angie hadn't had since her brother was born. She didn't have much to do with the younger children, who slept in rooms of four or six in bunk beds.

Outside, there were always so many people walking around everywhere. Angie didn't know any of them, and since her wild life out on the streets, she was cautious of others. Some adults looked her up and down with real suspicion. The newcomer must have looked radical to them, with her mohawk, short spiky hair and a bleached rat's tail. Angie just put her head down, sensing their strong judgement of her.

Everything was such a mixed bag at Centrepoint. She loved waiting in the meal queue where all the gossip was happening. But when she received her food, the panic set in about where to sit. She ate with her family at dinner, feeling quite lonely and isolated in the beginning. The teenagers seemed like a tight-knit group, so she often sat with Henry.

Angie's initial connection with Bert Potter happened in the first days. She remembers that when he came over to her in the lounge to say hello, he 'had' her there and then, instantly. Something was transmitted when he looked into her eyes, like 'I see you'. She felt he could look right inside her, and she was afraid and exposed. Bert was always friendly, but provocative and intimidating. He called himself 'God', but that was for the adults; Angie never accorded him that respect. She and her brother Karl thought he was talking 'absolute bullshit'. Yet when he looked at her with those eyes, something happened; Angie wanted to please him and be in his favour. And not be left out.

Bert became bigger and more important to her, although the grown-ups who were following him still seemed like weird freaks, their arms wrapped around each other while listening to his talks and lining up afterwards to receive his blessing or a hug. It was the adults who had given up their possessions and decided to follow a spiritual leader; the children were only there because their parents were. All the youngsters, despite their different backgrounds, had similar opinions of what was happening: the parents had changed once they'd moved to Centrepoint.

'Actually, I don't think Mum was there because she believed in Bert,' Angie tells me now. 'She just couldn't cope with the four of us and could somehow survive there.'

Meanwhile, Jane Stanton was doing courses and had new boyfriends. She was with different men a lot; for her, it was all about where the love was. She was like a little girl: happy when she met someone new, putting on a pretty dress, skipping around. Occasionally her daughter spotted her at dinner or cuddling someone.

Angie and her new friends hardly ever saw their own parents. Interactions with other adults were in counselling or in groups, in meetings and at mealtimes. She probably had more conversations with adults there than just about anywhere else in life, Angie thinks. And that was great. She and her brother picked up different ways of being and learned how to look an adult straight in the eye. Even the younger children were mature for their age because there was no mummy to wake or dress them in the mornings. They selected clothes to wear for primary school from a shared clothing supply, known as the Kids Com, while an adult kept track of all the shoe sizes and the mending and washing as a full-time job. The adults who worked on the property clothed themselves from the Old Com, including underwear. Good Com was for when they occasionally went out. The teenagers had school uniforms bought for them and a clothing allowance.

In the beginning, Angie kept her old friends. Her whole life was still on the outside. She went to school with the Centrepoint teenagers but partied with her old mates on the weekends. Only reluctantly did she go to the teenage workshops that the senior therapists ran and where you had to reveal your deepest feelings or learn more about sex.

The weeks were structured. Adults had their jobs, therapy sessions and chores, and they had morning and afternoon tea breaks where people would 'go off' with each other for a quickie in the bushes or in the longhouses. It was part of the Centrepoint philosophy. Sex wasn't dirty and shouldn't be hidden and suppressed, but be out in the open, and not just for couples. Twice a day was what Bert recommended; three times on a Sunday when you could lie in. The humming aeroplane sounds of someone being 'blown off' or the shouts and moans from an orgasm could be heard all around the place.

There was a rule at Centrepoint that when one of your parents wasn't there, you had to choose someone to be your surrogate parent, to check with about things like homework. It was normal to not see your own parents for days. Henry Stonex was an immensely popular guy, and Angie asked him early on if he could be her Centrepoint dad. She felt quite special asking him, and him saying yes.

They started doing more things together. Henry was a beekeeper and took her for trips to the honey house, which was located at the top of the property behind the nursery, half an hour's walk away. It was a rustic wooden cottage with a few cluttered rooms, a little kitchen and a worn sofa – a beautiful place where you could look out but not be seen. Angie liked it. She thought Henry must really love her because he was showing her his favourite spot. When they walked up there, he'd offer her a joint on the way. She got paranoid on pot but could never say no.

Out the back, the honey house had an old bathtub with a tap. The first time Henry suggested a bath, Angie felt quite scared. She didn't want to be naked with him, especially when she was stoned.

'It was a slow graduation, his grooming. Being away from the community on our own, first just smoking a joint, then the bath …' Her voice trails off.

Henry lit homemade candles around the bathtub. They could hear the cicadas in the lush bush. The air smelled of summer nights and beeswax. Angie was intoxicated by the dope and Henry's charms while he turned on music. When the tub was filled with steaming water, she hopped in first, so he didn't see her body. It felt so lovely and warm. At some point Henry must have slipped in as well. It all happened so slowly, step by step. She remembers seeing him naked and being horrified by his big penis, but only for a moment. Once he sat in the bath and she only saw his shoulders and his face, it was okay.

The next time they went to the honey house, Henry asked if he could massage her foot. Angie kept telling herself that it was natural. She had only gone out with boys so far. He felt so potent and manly. Her foot knocked on his genitals when she stretched it towards him. She found it gross, scary and exciting all at once.

They talked about everything in her life. Henry was the first person who really wanted to know anything about her. She felt loved, wanted, heard and accepted. Sometimes she would cry.

Angie takes a break to have another raw juice.

'What you have to understand,' she says when she joins me again in my office, 'is that me and my brother, we were angry little fuckers. We had quite some life experience from the streets.'

The siblings got the Centrepoint teenagers all drugged up, popping car sickness pills, taking cactus and acid, drinking in the bush. Angie spent half of her sixth-form year in the sick bay. She pulls a face. 'I was lucky I didn't end up in an emergency room.'

Half of the vanload of teenagers she once took to a gig vomited in the car on the way home, and on top of that she had a drunk-driving accident. After that night, the adults finally realised that things had become out of control. It was because of the older Meiklejohn siblings that the community imposed a complete drug and alcohol ban for a year.

'Which was actually fantastic. Best thing that happened to me.'

Centrepoint had what they called 'feedback'. At any time, you could walk up to somebody and give them a straight talking-to, like: 'I really don't like the way you dress, I wouldn't let my children be dressed like that.' Or: 'I really don't like you and think you shouldn't be here.' Things like that came out of the blue.

'You get the feeling that the whole community thinks that of you,' Angie recalls.

It made her paranoid and anxious. As the recipient, you had to listen and weren't allowed a response in that moment, even if someone shouted at you. The feedback was often followed by the cynical catchphrase to 'treat it like a gift' – another Centrepointism just like the request to 'drop it'. It was always 'your stuff'. You were responsible for your own reaction, not the person who did or said something hostile to you. If you couldn't just drop it or work through your stuff, you needed to 'clear' with the giver of the gift. And if you had any doubts about Centrepoint, you needed to clear with Bert himself, or at least his top therapists, Barbara Kingsbury and Susanne Brighouse.

When Angie went up to the kitchen or the shower, she would dread who she would bump into and what they would say. One day, while she was singing away in the kitchen – which she loved to do all the time – an older woman walked up to her and said straight to her: 'I think your singing is an avoidance of what's really going on.' It was like being slapped in the face. Angie stopped singing from that moment until she entered drama school three years later.

I browse through old copies of the faded *Centrepoint* magazine that Angie brought along. It came out quarterly. Like Rajneesh in Pune who had all his talks published and distributed, Bert Potter believed in presenting his teachings to the outside world. In pre-internet times, it was a marketing tool for courses, with order sheets for his cassette tapes. One of the promotional blurbs said: 'Experience the qualities of a man whose revolutionary skill, simplicity, love and acceptance have made him New Zealand's foremost therapist and facilitator of human potential.'

In each issue, Potter elaborates on spiritual questions, relationships, and what's wrong with society. He criticises feminists, people who have left Centrepoint, and family homes that are cluttered with chairs. 'There is nowhere to get alongside each other,' he wrote, six months before his arrest in 1989. 'This is emotionally sick. The ability to reach out and touch is one of the best indications of mental health. But they don't do it out there. We've learnt here at Centrepoint to do things differently. We've learnt to open up more. We've learnt to take the barriers down.'

The barriers are down in many of the candid testimonials and personal stories that members contributed to the magazine. I pull out a special issue about the teenagers, titled 'Beyond the Wall' – referring to their own world, out of sight of the community's adults, where they forged their own kind of family. A smiling, attractive man with dark hair is called 'The teenagers' friend, Henry'.

Three pages further on, I find Angie. She is sixteen, in track pants and sweatshirt, her thick hair bleached blonde, with her brother's arm around her shoulders. Her testimonial is titled 'Trying the system'. Angie glances over it.

'That was when Mum left us all there and I started wagging school.'

She reads out the last part of her story without a trace of facetiousness.

'"I started taking counselling sessions and I still can't believe how much I've got out of them. I feel a lot lighter and my ideas and goals are a lot clearer now. I am happy and content and am going to continue to live here at least to the end of this year. I feel really good about Centrepoint and this way of life. It's different but it's enlightening."'

She puts it down and looks at me. Her voice is flat now.

'Well, this was clearly written after the shift happened.'

It all changed on a weekend teenage workshop. None of the top women were leading the course this time. Bert ran it. He was the only adult. Everyone was lying around cuddling while he was coaching the youngsters individually to release their emotions. He had a knack for finding the soft spot in them. Angie was in the hot seat to get her anger and rage about her parents out. She had to symbolically put her dad on a cushion, smash the living daylights out of him and scream. After that, she felt happy and relieved – and had Bert's full attention.

At some point in the session, he turned to Angie and pointed at her little rat's tail. 'When are you going to give up?' he confronted her. 'When are you going to give up the fight? Just allow yourself to be seen and stop being this angry fuck-you act.' *Oh my God*, she thought. *What if he just said the truth?* She had been in a fight with everything and everyone, unhappy and rebelling right from the start, and here she was, just vulnerable and broken. He saw her, how she really was underneath. It was alluring, and she wanted to please him. Now she sees it as his grooming.

'He wanted to make us girls softer, more attractive and willing. It was purely selfish.'

Next thing, she went out into the bathroom to cut off her rat's tail. For Bert and for the sake of the community.

'For me, that was it. That was the moment I gave up.'

When she found a pair of scissors and cut the tiny, plaited tail, it felt like cutting her umbilical cord to her past, the connection to her old friends. Angie held up the rat's tail and dramatically proclaimed to the next person who walked into the bathroom: 'I'm over that now! That was me, but that's not me anymore!'

For years she kept the tail in a little box by her dressing table. It still had the white bleach in it, from the time when she had moved to Centrepoint. Her hair had been light then. But she had been in the darkness, bitter and lonely.

Once she made the shift it felt like the lights came on. Now she was going to be a good community member and give up her rebellion. Bert believed in her, and she wanted to prove him right. Rather than hating what she saw around her, she now liked what she saw. There were a lot of good people who really cared, there was a lot of love and laughter. All those babies – and the food was amazing!

The shift occurred in one moment, but the indoctrination happened slowly. Angie got a job in the glass house, where she got to know people. She took part in a working bee and received lots of good feedback, and she put her name down on the noticeboard to help out in the kitchen. The more accepted she felt, the more she started to express herself like the others. She even went to business meetings and would sometimes cuddle up with an adult. Before the shift, she wouldn't be seen dead doing that.

Cuddling was a central part of the Centrepoint culture. Once Angie was spending more time in the community and felt like a real member, she would do the done thing and lie close with someone on the cushions in the lounge. It was quite a set format, during a meeting or after a meal. One person would be giver, the other receiver. As the receiver, she would scoop herself in there and rest her head on them and be stroked. When she was cuddling Henry, she loved the feel and smell of him and the attention he gave her. He was always so interested, not like a boyfriend but a father figure. Her own father was very stiff and cold with his children. Henry's embrace was not erotic but nurturing for her. She was lapping it up, from everyone she melted into. And then, suddenly, she would feel the other person's arousal.

'You can tell. They squeeze your thighs, for instance. I felt hard-ons coming on, how they turned to me to have more wedge space there. My alarm bells would go off.'

At first, she felt fear. And then guilt for turning men on. The situation on the cushions was typical of everything that went wrong at Centrepoint from the start and led to the sexual abuse, in Angie's view.

'The guys weren't conscious of what they were doing, how they weren't respecting my boundaries. There was no clear communication or set container [guidelines], nothing like it.'

'What could they have expressed, ideally?' I ask.

'Something like "I'm experiencing this desire – do you want to go further?"'

It's what she teaches in her workshops. Back at Centrepoint, she didn't have the awareness and the words she has today. Instead, she would extricate herself from the embrace and find an excuse like 'I need to go to the toilet'. The next night, she would find herself in a similar situation again, and again. Until what had seemed strange, weird and wrong at first became the norm she needed to ease into.

In the beginning, she didn't have boyfriends at Centrepoint. She only started to approach boys after she cut off the rat's tail, broke with her old punk friends and became part of the group. Then it was 'all on'.

When you fancied somebody, for instance after a workshop, you didn't go for a walk or on a date. It was more straightforward than that. You asked someone to 'come off' with you. It meant having a sexual encounter, there and then. No wooing, no romance. You didn't care if there were other people in the bed next to you. The change from being a resistant teenager to a seductress at sixteen was quite dramatic, especially in comparison to the youngsters who had been raised at Centrepoint. They kept their attitudes about their bodies and privacy, says Angie. 'Whereas I went from "Fuck you" to "Fuck me"!'

She's laughing, half bitter, half amused. 'Look … I do whatever I need to do to survive.'

Despite her burgeoning sexual interactions within the community, she hadn't yet crossed that line with Henry. He was, after all, her dad there, and 29 years older. The bathing didn't seem to be out of the ordinary at Centrepoint, where people were often naked together in outdoor bathtubs. But she knew it was their secret thing. Only later did she find out that Henry was also taking other girls up to the honey house.

During the year, Henry went on beekeeping trips. There was always someone with him, usually a woman, and Angie was jealous of them. He finally asked her to come along on a three-day trip. Feeling special, she packed food and got in his truck. They checked the hives in the morning and later arrived at the farm where they were staying. There was just a double bed in the little shed. She wondered if there was any other sleeping place, but there wasn't. The situation frightened her, and from that point on she finds that night hard to remember.

'I can see him in the bed; I can see myself not knowing what to do ...'

She wanted to leave her clothes on and keep some distance between them. But the small double bed dipped in the middle, and they rolled together. It felt too close, too intimate. Their kissing changed from a fatherly kiss to romantic pashing. She tried to justify that it was like being in the lounge at Centrepoint, so she cuddled into him and eventually pretended to go to sleep.

Angie is searching for images in her brain to tell me more, but there's only a memory of feeling absolutely guilty and disgusting the next day. 'Which makes me think something must have happened. I was in shock.'

When they got home, she couldn't get out of his truck fast enough. People asked her, 'How was your trip?' and she answered, 'Yeah, it was nice, the bees are so amazing.' But she felt like a liar. She had gone into another dimension, like she did after the rape when she was ten.

Before the trip, she hadn't had sex with an adult, only with inexperienced boys. But after the night in Henry's arms, she became sexually involved with not just teenagers in the community, but older men, too.

'That's what I thought I should be doing. Do the rounds.'

Angie became openly promiscuous, especially with young guys who came to visit the community. As soon as they arrived, she had her eyes on them and ended up having sex with them, within hours. It was exciting. She loved hearing that she was beautiful and smelled like nectar. Sex was now what she used in order to get what she needed: attention and affection. She had sex with people in the longhouses, one after the other, with women too, and couldn't get enough. She would have her showers quite out in the open, rubbing her body alluringly and giggling with a friend. The older women reacted with jealousy to the frisky, provocative young girls. Angie developed a lot of enemies.

'Imagine that competition all day, every day, because you were all living together!' She sighs.

The sexual liaisons created a lot of drama. If Angie slept with someone's husband and the wife came up to her in the kitchen and attacked her, then Bert would set one of his tasks that went as far as having people eat off the floor. In this case, he would make the complaining woman serve Angie dinner for a week, because it was not okay for her to approach Angie at all, in his view; the problem was with the husband and wife, so that's where the work should be done. Sometimes it got intense; people were throwing tantrums on the floor, screaming 'You slapped me!', even pulling other people's clothes off or throwing piss buckets at each other.

Then she had a bath with Henry again. When they sat in the warm water, Angie told him that she wanted all of him. He dried her with the towel, and they went inside the honey house.

'It wasn't that easy because of his size. It really, really hurt,' she says, struggling to explain what happened. 'I was trying to allow him in my body because I wanted him to love and adore me.'

He was gentle, there was no force on his part. She felt she was totally in control all the time – 'making him make love to me'.

I'm confused. This is not what I expected after the short brief she gave me a few months ago about her traumatic experiences at Centrepoint. 'You told me that a leading therapist raped you,' I say.

The scenario at the honey house seems to contradict the picture I had of her as a sexual-abuse victim. She was sixteen, she asked Henry to sleep with her, he didn't force himself on her. Didn't that make it consensual and legal?

Angie pauses, reflects, and then starts again.

'I actually didn't want to have sex with him, and it hurt, and it was horrible. I had no real desire for him. I forced myself to do it.'

She looks strained, as if torn between sides, holding on to her own truth while pushing out other voices in her head. I feel uneasy about my interrogation.

'I never wanted to be his girlfriend,' she carries on. 'He was my father figure. I wasn't equal to him. I was scared and overwhelmed. I was in so much pain physically and didn't enjoy it, but I did all that for him. Because I thought that's what he wanted.'

She presses the words out, sounding clearer with each one.

'I was manipulated.'

What Angie was hoping for, to be loved and adored – it never happened with Henry. He didn't treat her like a girlfriend because this affair was their secret.

Then Cordula, a new woman from Germany, arrived at Centrepoint, and she and Henry started a relationship. They were very much in love, walking around holding hands. Angie wanted to scratch Cordula's eyes out. She felt a kind of ownership and only wanted Henry to have sex with her.

Cordula, who came with a husband, seemed to know what went on at the honey house, but was still nice to Angie. Angie's sexual contact with Henry went on for years after he married Cordula. When Angie moved out of Centrepoint at eighteen and was flatting, feeling lonely and lost, she still invited Henry over for the night when he ran encounter groups in Parnell.

'It was like the abuse victim inviting the perpetrator in again so that she could remain the victim. So twisted.'

Only years later, through counselling, did Angie become angry. 'Fucking angry,' she repeats. 'The word "rape" is really harsh. But at the time, I had to leave my body mentally in order to stay physically there. Then it's against your will.'

We haven't even talked about her and Bert Potter yet.

Chapter 3

As Angie adapted and began to change within the community, her views and beliefs changed as well. She joined the teenage meetings and therapy groups. All her physical needs were taken care of by Centrepoint, from food to tampons and visits to the doctor. She had by now contracted STIs like gonorrhoea and chlamydia.

In 1988, Bert Potter distanced himself from the community and moved with his wife, son and twin babies to a house at the other end of the property.

The drug-taking phase started. Ecstasy and MDMA were made in a secret lab on the Centrepoint property that was never found by the police. LSD was manufactured off property, and ketamine came in from a goat-breeding project. The idea was to use psychedelic substances to open people up so they could get emotionally closer. MDMA, the main active ingredient in ecstasy pills, was first used for couples' counselling in the United States before it was discovered as a party drug by the techno scene. It has since been widely researched as a therapeutic cure for depression, post-traumatic stress disorder and anxiety.

The day arrived when ecstasy was given out to the whole group. There was a build-up to the first trip. Everybody knew it was happening. A note on the noticeboard said:

'Don't eat anything after 10 pm the night before.' The cut-off age was twelve.

It was early in the morning when Angie and her friends wandered up to the Glade, an enclosed field of grass on the right side of the track that led up the hill. The Glade was a magical spot, especially at this time. It was bright and sunny, the grass was still dewy, and they were all excited about what was going to happen. Over a hundred people stood around, waiting. The pills were handed out on plates, clear capsules with pure MDMA. Everyone came up on their drugs at the same time. It was a rush, like orgasmic bliss running through the whole body. Angie has a sharp memory imprint of all the colours and sounds. Her eyes were flickering. Everything suddenly looked wonderful. She thought what she was feeling was love. The other girls went hyper – dancing maniacally, showing off, seeking attention. Some of them threw off their clothes and started kissing the older guys, gushing 'Oh my God, you are so beautiful!' It was a hot day, so people got naked quickly. Everyone seemed totally out of control.

After this group initiation, ecstasy was on offer for everyone who wanted it, but in a structured way, as a therapy session: on your own, as a couple or a family, or with Bert. He was controlling it.

Like other gurus of his ilk, Bert Potter not only had a long queue of desperate women wanting his love and sexual favours, but he surrounded himself with strong women who implemented his philosophy and his control within the group. The two main therapists of his inner circle, Susanne Brighouse and Barbara Kingsbury, were known as the 'thought police'. I ask Angie what that meant.

'When you had counselling, your resistances and thoughts would come up,' she explains. 'You would share all your inner deepest thoughts with them – for instance "I don't want to be here at all and Bert's a sick old man". You're telling the women all these things, and then later Bert would know them as well. Because they'd tell him all about you. And then he is using all your fears against you.'

'Blowing off' was used as a healing modality in therapy sessions or between community members. You could make a booking in the massage room with one of the men who were listed in a book. The therapists suggested it especially when someone had tension or trauma in their body. Angie remembers it as painful because it intensely stimulates the clitoris. She would cry and scream through the pain. When Angie suffered from cystitis, she asked men to blow her off for half an hour because the therapists told her it would help. Some of the 'blowers' would expect to have sex with her afterwards.

An older girl who Angie looked up to had had a drug therapy session with Bert. Angie was in therapy with Susanne Brighouse, who recommended the same, so she booked a one-on-one ecstasy trip with him. Also, she just felt like getting wasted.

She walked up to the Potters' house in the morning. A platter with fresh grapes was sitting on the bench, which Bert's wife, Margie Potter, had put there. Margie was just leaving; she wished them a good time, and then Angie took her MDMA pill from a drawer. When the gentle rush came on, a melting and exhilaration at the same time, she wanted to be outside, near the birds and the trees. But Bert was suddenly there. He insisted: 'No, you can't go. You've got to spend time with me.' Angie thought, *But I don't want to be with you*. It was like blackmail. She had a realisation then, just as she was coming up on her drug. She knew with utter clarity that if she left now, if she stepped away from this room, this house, and this unscrupulous man, then that would be it for her. She would have to leave the community, her mum, her sisters, her only home. The thought of that was so intense that it almost sent her into shock.

So she sat with Bert in his room, where they talked. He was very calm, cross-legged on his cushion, guiding her through her resistance, intensely engaging. She tried to look into his eyes and moved into him. He was touching her, massaging her, asking her to do the same. It was the first time she was ever naked with Bert, although he had been nude around the community before. For her, there was absolutely nothing attractive about him, neither his face nor his body. She remembers the rest as only a series of different images: sitting on his face, looking out the window, tears rolling down her cheeks. She wanted to be outside by the trees, wanted to smell them, to be anywhere else. But it just kept going on and on. She was watching her own body, like she wasn't in it. Angie believed she had to do what Bert steered her to, 'because I had said I wanted to, because I signed up for it, because of what would happen when I would leave'.

Afterwards she locked herself in the bathroom and stayed there for ages. Bert was so creepy, but the water on her hands was so lovely. She wanted to stay in there forever and enjoy that sensation before going back into his room again. This time, she tried to avoid an intimate situation by suggesting a walk. It ended up in just more sex. It wasn't therapy and there was nothing spiritual.

When she left his house in the afternoon, Bert gave her an acid tablet – LSD. She was still wandering around the community at night, high on psychedelics after a day of drug rape. Desperate for someone, she climbed over sleeping people in a house bus and woke up one of the men. But he was like a cold fish, so she wandered on.

—

Like the encounters with Henry, the sex with Bert was another negative turning point. Angie's illusions about men were broken. Bert: just a horny old man, not a spiritual leader. Henry: just into sex, not a father figure. She could see through it and use it. Whenever she wanted, she walked up to whomever she wanted.

'I became the commune concubine, trying to fill that hole.'

Her little sisters had no idea that she was sleeping with her surrogate dad. Renee, the youngest, was a stroppy fighter who saw what happened to the good girls and didn't want that kind of attention. Whenever Bert passed her, she gave him the finger. When Renee's period started at twelve, he took her up to his house and told her it was time to lose her virginity. He gave her a week to report back to him. She did.

Despite how revolting the first ecstasy trip with Bert was, Angie signed up for a couple of therapy sessions over a month, but without drugs. She thought she was special because she was one of the youngest ones doing that. Margie was often in the room next door with their twins. After talking for a bit at the beginning, Bert blew Angie off straight away while she screamed out her anger. Then he would penetrate her with half an erection. She was lying there, disgusted, while he was puffing and heaving on top of her. It didn't bring her in touch with her 'loving'. Bert did the opposite of what he proclaimed he'd do.

'And that happened to me every week,' she recalls in a matter-of-fact voice.

Again, it sounds like a contradiction. Didn't she sign up for it, knowing how it would be?

She nods.

'No one made me do it. I put myself in these horrendous situations because that was on offer.' She pauses. 'I left that community feeling like I chose everything. I had a part and have to take responsibility for it. I can't just blame the men.'

In 1987, Barbara Kingsbury travelled overseas to bring back different exercises, or 'living ideas', from experimental communities in Europe. In Austria, the Friedrichshof commune operated on similar principles, and with the same disastrous consequences, under a despotic leader called Otto Mühl – not a therapist, but an avant-garde artist. They were a more radical bunch, with a uniform look of shaved heads and a daily sex roster to prevent coupledom. Barbara wanted to introduce the roster at Centrepoint, but the idea wasn't popular enough; there was already enough pressure on couples to break up and be promiscuous.

However, one souvenir from Otto Mühl's fiefdom that survived the trip to New Zealand was the 'hierarchy', which was a more accurate name than the Friedrichshof euphemism 'Struktur' (structure). It was meant to enhance group dynamics. Like anything edgy prescribed by the Centrepoint elite, it became 'the thing' and was done weekly. People lined up and would give themselves a place in terms of where they thought they belonged. They could then be moved up and down by others. This public ranking was also an opportunity to take revenge. It was merciless, humiliating and soul-destroying. There was no compassion, no resolution. Promiscuity got you to the top.

Former members of Friedrichshof have compared this Darwinist exercise to show trials of fascist dictatorships. For many people at Centrepoint, the psychological brutalisation was horrendous. The hierarchy broke their resistance to Bert and disempowered them.

Angie would usually move people up the line, unless to make a point. Jane Stanton was always at the bottom of the hierarchy. She didn't have money to contribute, and she had those unruly kids. Angie would pass the lounge and see her mum crying in a crumpled heap. Jane looked crushed. Angie felt partly disgusted, partly sorry for her. She hated her being a victim, and she hated that Jane let the others get to her. She didn't want to be anywhere near her. The group dynamics were beginning to work on Angie: don't associate with someone of a lower rank, not even your own mother – who had started sleeping with teenage boys, which put Angie off even more. Only at Christmas were they all together, outside the community at their grandmother's. There, they played happy family.

Because Angie did well in school productions, Centrepoint paid for her to go to drama school. It was hard for her when she left the community to study in Wellington. She was still in concubine land. Sometimes she would ask men in a bar to spend the night with her. At Centrepoint, most had said yes. Now it was different. There was no physical touch on tap, no more constant hugging. Angie asked her flatmate if she could have a cuddle, trying to get her in the Centrepoint cuddling position, but it didn't feel the same and was awkward. Being out of the community was like being in another country and not speaking the same language. The beliefs Angie had formed over the last year didn't just vanish overnight. In her holidays, she flew back to Auckland and went straight to Centrepoint. She took ecstasy there and felt happy.

On one of these visits, her family signed up for an ecstasy trip. Her two sisters were thirteen and fifteen, Angie eighteen. The session took place up at Bert's house again. She only has a blurry memory from that time.

'Something bad happened,' she says. 'It came out later.'

She didn't tell others in Wellington about these drug weekends.

Then everything fell over. In 1989, Bert Potter was arrested on five charges relating to possession and supply of LSD and MDMA. He was sentenced to three and a half years' imprisonment. Despite this shock, the community carried on. Angie didn't go back to Albany after the drug raid. It was her second year at drama school, and she got wasted on her weekends in Wellington instead. It was all about getting some Centrepoint 'loving'.

On 22 May 1991, the police conducted a dawn raid involving 140 officers, dogs and helicopters. Six men and two women, as well as Bert Potter and four ex-members, were charged with sexual offences ranging from indecent assault to rape of minors. Five young women laid charges. The next year, three more members were arrested in another raid.

When the court cases started, Angie was still studying in Wellington, detached from it all. Her family had moved out and the connection to the community was dwindling. But her thinking was still in line with her former home's philosophy. For years she could not see what these girls were accusing Henry and the other men of. Now she spits out what she thought of them, mimicking her old furious self: '"You fucking bitches, how can you say yes and then years later actually say no!"'

She sighs. 'I thought it's not fair to agree first and then put them through the courts later.'

When her auntie asked her about the accusations in the media, Angie told her that it wasn't true, that they were all lying. 'I just could not understand it. I was so aligned with my cult identity. And I actually think it's still in me somewhere.' She looks at me. 'And sometimes that scares me.'

Henry Stonex pleaded guilty to assaulting an eight-year-old girl and was sentenced to nine months in jail. Bert Potter was sentenced to seven and a half years. A group of Centrepointians wanted to visit him at Ohura Prison. Angie came along, out of some kind of duty. She will never forget that day. When she saw Bert in jail, it felt so weird. He was just a little old man, the mesmerising twinkle of his eyes gone. Angie didn't know what to say to him. The others were crying, 'Bert, we love you and miss you!', but she couldn't. How could she have been so gullible and given this shrivelled-up charlatan all this power over her?

The spell was broken. It was all a lie. She didn't care for Bert and had no respect for him. She couldn't understand the things she had done and believed in. That she had given him her reverence and her body and her will. It was over for her in that instant.

Angie stayed with Margie Potter that day but felt like a traitor, disconnected from those women who still adored their incarcerated leader. After the jail visit, she never looked back – never returned to Centrepoint, and never spoke to any adults from there. Her mother had left long before her and left all her kids behind. It was strange when she saw someone from the community on the streets in Wellington or at university – as if they were all survivors of some kind of extreme crash setting where you have to do certain acts to stay alive, like eat someone's arm. There's no way you would talk about that. Because you can't even find the words.

In 1999, Angie went to a court hearing for the Centrepoint trust. Leavers from the community were fighting for the 'Old Believers' to leave the land and put the assets into a new, transformed trust. When the registrar asked the court to rise, she saw Bert Potter. He was standing on the other side of the room with about a dozen of his supporters, staring at her as if looks could kill. His whole expression said that she had crossed over and was now an enemy.

Once Angie graduated from drama school in 2000, Centrepoint dropped off her radar. She was an alcoholic by then. Her life became a new disaster zone; one drunken night, she passed out while working on a musical. She became unemployable, then fell pregnant after a one-night stand with a bouncer. After marrying him and having the baby, she fell into a deep depression. She never bonded with her son and had desperate binge nights when she ended up vomiting all over herself. Another child to fix the marriage only brought more unhappiness.

One day she left the marriage and started working at Bill Crow's, a 'gentlemen's club' in Oriental Bay. There, she served men as if they were her lovers, the way she knew from Centrepoint. She got into harder drugs like speed, and lost custody of her kids. At the brothel she met a sugar daddy, left the club, and started working on *The Lord of the Rings* as a runner and later an assistant director, though she was still drinking heavily. After one bad panic attack she ended up in hospital, where she was diagnosed with post-traumatic stress disorder (PTSD) from living at Centrepoint.

While Angie was sliding deeper into her addictions, her mother's mental health was deteriorating rapidly, until in 2002, while in Angie's care, Jane Stanton killed herself by jumping off a balcony during one of her manic episodes, on Waiheke Island. Angie found her body in the bush. The night before, Jane had walked into the sea.

Angie started overdosing in clubs; people took toilet doors off their hinges to get her to emergency rooms. After a night of drunken oblivion, in 2004, Angie dragged the bar owner home with her, demanding sex. He held her instead and said: 'You are worth so much more than that.' She said, 'I'm fucking not!', went to the kitchen and got a big knife. She was going to throw herself on it, right through her heart. The man wouldn't leave until she called Alcoholics Anonymous. Since that night, she hasn't touched another drink.

She knew she had to get her act together. While trying desperately to stay sober, Angie sought refuge with her sister Renee, who had been struggling with her own addiction, in Whangamatā. Angie had been like a mother to the three younger ones, especially since their mother's funeral.

It was at Renee's house in 2007 that a comment about a banana was disclosed over dinner. A banana that was eaten out of one of their vulvas while they were all drugged up on ecstasy as a family, twenty years earlier. Renee made it sound like a bad joke, but there was disgust and anger underneath. 'I'm really messed up by this!' she threw at her sister.

Angie was in shock. She had only a patchy memory of the incident – how the girls had to strip off and stand in front of the big floor-to-ceiling mirror in Bert's house. How he was beating off in the corner, and then a flash of her sister's genitals. Once Renee brought it up, the shame stayed. What else had Angie done with Bert while on drugs that she could not recall? The banana was never mentioned again, but the gross secret made their sibling relationship awkward.

After Angie became sober she regained custody of her sons. But she still had her demons. Often, when she closed her eyes, she would see Bert. Someone at the AA meetings told her to make a 'God box' where you put the things that are too big to deal with right now. She wrote 'Bert' and 'Henry' on two pieces of paper and put them in the box.

A friend gave her books about cults to read. They were instrumental in terms of her deprogramming. It wasn't until her late thirties that she realised how dysfunctional and different she was. Then when she saw the movie *The Experiment*, based on the psychological study in which a group is divided into prison guards and inmates, the penny fully dropped. Perpetrator or victim – anyone could become either. Afterwards she sat in the cinema, sobbing. She had been in a human lab, too.

We're done for today. Angie gets up and looks out the window. 'Always remember,' she says, tucking her curls back, 'Centrepoint was a selection of average, normal people. Not monsters or freaks.'

Chapter 4

The people from Centrepoint had a utopian dream that turned into a collective nightmare. What were they thinking, the gullible lovers who competed for their turn in Bert Potter's bed, and the idealistic parents who placed their daughters at the mercy of the 60-year-old guru? And how did their children move on?

A prominent Aucklander had her name suppression lifted so she could speak on TV and in news articles about the sexual abuse she suffered in the early years of the community. She was seen as a role model and leader of the pack, laying charges against the guru and two of his cronies, but later she regretted the publicity. She now uses a lawyer to protect herself from being linked in the media to the C-word.

The only woman who wrote a book about her ordeal at Centrepoint first published it under a pseudonym, Ella James. There is only one other outspoken critic: Barri Leslie, who became an avid – and effective – activist against the Centrepoint old guard. Together with 50 of the adults and 40 former children, she spearheaded the court case that after six years saw the community restructured and renamed in 2000, with the Old Believers given $49,500 each to relinquish all claims on the Centrepoint trust and never return.

Bert and his loyalists had to leave. In other words, Barri's and the children's teams shut the place down. The trust's assets are now used to help former struggling cult members like Angie and her siblings with counselling, medical bills and other financial support.

Barri has kept a low profile since then, but she has turned into the nemesis of former Centrepoint GP Felicity Goodyear-Smith, the wife of Bert's son John Potter. When Barri and I meet near the Auckland ferry building, I'm greeted by a petite, neatly dressed 73-year-old with a frail voice but a sharp mind. Nothing about this twice-divorced passionate gardener would indicate any affiliation with a 'sex cult'.

'Well, Bert often called me mousy and blocked off,' she says with an ironic smile.

The former schoolteacher, then a psychologist and now retired, had been one of the community's founding members and edited the *Centrepoint* magazine. After thirteen years, Barri left Centrepoint with her family and not much more than the clothes on her back. By then, she had done a complete turnaround, from fanatical follower to angry disbeliever.

'Nobody joined Centrepoint because they were happy,' she tells me over our first coffee. 'And all of us are victims to some degree. We all lost those precious family years.'

She chooses to keep her own story private for the sake of her daughters. Many meetings follow at her clutter-free house in suburban Browns Bay, which I leave with stacks of photocopies and pages of notes, my head brimming with information. I work my way through Centrepoint magazines, websites and social media profiles, drawing diagrams to understand the who's who of interwoven family structures. Most couples broke up at the community and found new partners there. It's confusing for an outsider. Angie is helping me with her peers' names, some of which have changed, and she gives me hints like 'she was behind the court cases' or 'he had a big change of heart later'.

I also send a request to the High Court to release the Centrepoint court files to me. It will be a long wait.

When I send my first text messages reaching out to those who had been involved in Centrepoint, I get very few replies. 'Don't bother, not interested'; 'was 20 years ago, past is the past, let it go'. One woman replies to my email, expressing 'considerable concern' that I disclosed my interest: 'DO NOT send any such emails to me at any organisation.' Another warns me that her adult daughter would 'freak out' if I mention Centrepoint. The son of a founding member spills out in his emails what a 'hellhole' and 'mind-warp institution' Centrepoint was. He still hates the words 'loving' and 'cuddles'. After a week, the correspondence with him suddenly stops. 'I just feel that RAGE again and can't do this again for a while, sorry.'

The first phone call I have with a man who grew up in the community is short and he sounds agitated. He's a Centrepoint success story, with a scholarship and international career. His father had been found guilty of sexually assaulting young girls. I have no right to drag things up, he tells me. What happened at Centrepoint happens everywhere, the media is evil, and I'm just doing it all for the money.

My next phone conversation is longer and the person who picks up even more emotional. The Aucklander, a highly respected professional in his field, faced charges in civil court for an affair at Centrepoint, which was outside the age of consent. He had just started a family there; Bert Potter apparently set up this scenario to get back at the wife who wasn't interested in the 'modern guru'. The charges were eventually dropped.

He speaks to me in compressed, staccato sentences, as if holding back an avalanche of pain. He explains that he has been damaged, demonised and financially ruined from a short period of his life that was 25 years ago, which he deeply regrets and is ashamed of, but which doesn't define him. He has done everything he can since then to redeem himself. When he talks about his family, he almost sobs. We agree to maybe meet in person one day, when this is easier. I know it won't happen.

The gap between Angie's incredible openness and the fear and suspicion behind all the closed doors is growing wider every day. 'For God's sake, I want some of the good stuff reported!!!' a woman from the North Shore responds. She says she was one of Bert's favourite lovers and doesn't want to see another exposé that 'sensationalises something that was dear to my heart'. She writes that both her kids had a wonderful childhood at the community, the older one saying he felt really lucky – until he left Centrepoint and was met with strong judgements. He is now ashamed of being brought up there.

The Centrepoint children are split into factions as well. I soon learn that they don't seek the limelight even if they only have positive things to say about their former home. Or especially so. They are protective of their families and their childhood, fearing that mainstream society will reject or pathologise them. Some of them have seen their parents in court, endured police raids and walked past damning headlines on their way to school, where they were ostracised as 'dirty commie kids'. In my eyes, they are innocent victims, too, but of a different kind. Which leaves me with a moral dilemma: when does someone's truth that needs to be heard add to another person's trauma and pain?

One woman who was born at Centrepoint as the daughter of a leading therapist made a formal complaint to Television New Zealand in 2008. She claimed that a programme about Centrepoint was insensitive because all the children at Centrepoint were 'unfairly identified as abused children'. This had resulted in humiliation for many. She turns down my interview request.

The last child to be born at Centrepoint has taken one step out of that defensive silence. Polly is the daughter of Henry Stonex. Now in her twenties, the young woman is making a personal short documentary as an act of reclaiming a story that was only told by others. The idea came about when, as a film student, she was asked by her tutor to write down a secret she would never tell anyone. She put 'Centrepoint' on her piece of paper. Polly mentions her project on the members-only, still-active Centrepoint community website that is run by Bert's son John Potter. It's part discussion forum, part museum and archive for Bert Potter's teachings, with the majority of members still enamoured with their Centrepoint experience. On there, Polly writes about 'the deep bonds that still exist between former community children' and how she hopes to bring 'a more accurate understanding' to her place of upbringing she feels has often been misrepresented. 'I know I wouldn't be who I am today without having had that first home.'

Her mindset, born from a happy childhood in a community under threat and suspicion from the outside, deserves a voice as well. But after I meet up with her mother who pulls back her interview the next day, Polly sends me an email: 'You are just coming across as a journalist looking for their next hit and we've had enough of that already.' Access is permanently blocked – not just to her family, but to everyone from her wider group of pro-Centrepoint friends. It will be another year before Polly reads my first article about Angie and writes to us both, saying that it broke her heart to hear of the pain and horror experienced in the same place that gave her so much love and friendship. 'We grew up in two different communities.'

I turn to the other faction. It also seems impenetrable and fraught. Asking someone to talk about their most disturbing experience or deepest sexual shame will never be an instant 'yes'. It can be retraumatising.

Tania is one of the teenage survivors who laid charges. After an introduction by email, she reluctantly agrees to meet for lunch. I'm nervous when I enter the small café off Queen Street. I spot her: attractive, with greyish cropped hair and stylish glasses. She doesn't order food, just an orange juice. Soon, emotion and anger bubble up in sharp bursts. Tania wants to get one thing straight: by coming forward, she paved the way for other girls at a huge personal cost. Then she starts crying. I tell her that she's a champion and hand her tissues. I feel like an intruder. At one point her eyes light up. She looks straight at me.

'Don't let them off the hook. Blow the lid! Let it backfire for them.'

By the time she leaves, after an hour and a half, Tania seems worked up. I worry about her. The next day, I receive an email. She has come to a very clear resolution, she writes. She is not ready for this in her life. She might well be at some time, and it will be then and only then that she will tell her story.

Many are not ready for this process. There are victims as well as perpetrators in most Centrepoint families.

'After the court cases, everyone just shut down,' a young woman from a patchwork family tells me. Her parents were high up in the hierarchy and some of her siblings are survivors of sexual abuse. Nobody wanted to talk about it at family gatherings. 'They were so in shock.'

It was all swept under the carpet. When any of the older adults mentioned anything positive about Centrepoint, those who had suffered there felt dishonoured. It became taboo. They had their 'Friday-night clearings', but never mentioned the elephant in the room: their shared past in a cult.

'There is no one I can ask about what affected my family so strongly,' says the woman, who has hardly any memories of Centrepoint herself because she was too young. 'How can I get an answer? I don't know where to start.'

I hear about the justifications and outright lies from a generation in denial. Some of the adults who were demonstrating brutally honest feedback and self-expression, who screamed it all out in workshops and propagated boundless intimacy, are now spinning a web of obfuscation and silence. The ripple effect is causing ongoing damage. When I do manage to speak to a few, the questions are turned at me in true Centrepoint style: 'Have you been sexually abused?' they ask. 'Why are you doing this work?'

By chance I come across the unpublished memoir of one of the former whistle-blowers. It's on MiniDiscs from the '90s, in a stack of materials someone handed over to me without knowing what was on there. I get the discs converted and transcribed. The manuscript, which was never meant to end up in my hands, is a revelation as well as a relief: here is a parent and Centrepoint therapist who was accountable, who did the right thing. I learn from others that he became aware of the signs of sexual abuse in children through HELP in Auckland. Bert Potter had sent him there to infiltrate and take over the feminist organisation, but instead the Centrepoint man and his wife gained a better understanding of the harm happening at his community. When he addressed this in two meetings at Centrepoint, Bert and his acolytes shut him down each time. He then collected many of the victims' accounts and collaborated with the police. In the eyes of the community, that made him a traitor and their archenemy.

In my eyes, he's an unsung hero. *'How glad he'll be*, I think, *to finally tell his side of the story after all these years, and after all the words he's put down.'* When I track him down and express my respect and admiration in an email, he is not happy to hear from me at all. Worse than that, it triggers his PTSD. He panics and threatens me with legal recourse if I don't destroy his manuscript on the spot.

I have stepped into 'Bertland', a minefield of conflict and contradiction.

A famous quote in one of the old *Centrepoint* magazines says: 'You give us everything you've got – and we give you feedback.' It came from Brian, a psychotherapist at Centrepoint. In 1987 and 1989, Brian organised the two meetings with the whistle-blower whom I contacted. But Brian was also accused of sexual abuse by two women. One of his alleged victims was six at the time and claimed he had used a vibrator on her. The charges were dropped. She later became a heroin addict and a prostitute and still suffers from anxiety attacks.

When I call him one night, Brian is outside his house and smacking at something. 'Bloody cockroaches!' he swears while I hear a thump.

He's equally blunt with me and appalled that my introductory email had the words 'sex crimes' in it. 'That's just a load of bollocks for starters!' he barks.

I take a deep breath and try to find some common ground. Brian cuts in.

'I can hear your judgement dripping down the line and it's sitting there like a big slimy turd.'

I'm taken aback by this animosity, but back-pedal to get him on side.

'Listen, stop!' he shouts down the line, then tells me in clear and cutting terms that he isn't interested in what I have to say. 'I want you to know that I can bite your kneecaps off, you know? I have teeth!'

I'm swallowing hard. I've dealt with some intimidating men in my years as a reporter, but never with such an openly aggressive bully. In the end, Brian's sense of self-importance seems to override his distrust of me. Once he calms down, we arrange to meet for an interview when I'm back in the North Island again.

My pulse is racing for minutes after I put down the phone. It feels as if I've just been assaulted. I'm furious and humiliated that I couldn't put Brian in his place. What arena have I entered for the sake of a story that is not even my own?

My husband urges me to not meet this person alone. But Brian might be the only male Centrepoint insider and apologist who will ever speak to me on the record. When I tell Barri Leslie about the unpleasant phone call, she sounds almost triumphant.

'That is exactly what they would do in the groups to make you feel wrong and stupid, strip you naked until you're shaking and everything's upside down,' she says. 'Putting fear into people – now you know how it works.'

She, too, warns me to be careful. 'You're going into the lion's den.'

It's more like a sea lion's cave. I've mentally prepared myself on the drive for a frosty reception, but not for the physicality. Brian is twice the size I imagined, barefoot and in track pants when he opens the door. I interpret his casual look as meaning 'I don't have to impress you'. His protruding hairy belly, with one shirt button accidentally undone, is somewhat at odds with the steely look in his eyes.

He wastes no time with small talk. I've hardly sat down when he makes it very clear how he will come after me.

'I'm a litigious bastard!' he growls, dropping into the sofa opposite me.

He spent years fighting to clear his name and hasn't left a stone unturned. In 1990, Brian woke up with a policeman standing beside his bed. It was the start of the worst time in his life. Eighteen months later, when the accusations of sexual abuse by the two women were finally dealt with and his criminal record cleared, he was faced with the police summary sheet from his trial at his new workplace. He felt targeted. It was all downhill from there. His contract was terminated, and he had to submit to police vetting and face rumours that he was a paedophile, although he had in fact no convictions.

'At the age of sixty I found myself still under threat from allegations that were sorted out fifteen years ago for something that allegedly happened ten years before that.'

He shakes his head in anger. In the end, the Human Rights Commission ruled that the police had breached his privacy and granted him $12,500 in compensation. ACC gave him a payout on top.

Apart from this aftermath, Centrepoint was 'the most creative, exciting, satisfying, wonderful time' of Brian's life.

'It was fun. Here was a place where I could do shitloads of therapy, and a place where you get laid three times a day.' He chuckles.

Bert Potter's personality as a superb seducer made the guru enormously successful as a therapist in Brian's view. He encouraged people to take responsibility for themselves and push their own edges while he steadfastly refused to rescue them. Brian claims Bert saved an enormous number of people from suicide and helped them turn their lives around. The overwhelming majority found 'growth' or a life-affirming and liberating experience.

'Some people didn't,' says Brian with a sigh. 'And of course, those voices get heard more these days.'

He admits that Bert Potter was at times 'incredibly insensitive'. On one particular occasion, when a girl was going to a formal at her intermediate school, the community leader publicly grabbed her top and pulled it down, exposing her breasts.

'I mean, that was awful. That was absolutely totally abusive, and I should have jumped up and down and let him know, "Hey, I'm angry". I didn't and I will remain ashamed of it.'

Brian says he made 'very strenuous attempts' to reform the community, but Bert would resist them.

'The girls felt harassed and threatened. And instead, he kept insisting that they should hear that their bodies were beautiful and that they were really lovely natural creatures.'

Half an hour in, we've come to the controversy around the teenagers. In Brian's view, they were exercising their freedom and their control over their bodies. He recalls a girl coming home from school and announcing, 'Jesus, what a day, I need a fuck!', then looking around to see who might be available. He did not see that this might be a symptom of her abuse and of her compliance with the dominant culture around her.

Or the twelve-year-old who, together with her mother, once did a dance and song for Bert Potter in the kitchen dining room. 'I don't remember the song, but it was about how wonderful he was. Her display was overtly sexual. And on one level, God, that was gorgeous.'

He's unashamed about admitting that. Just like a girl from the Cook Islands he recently saw on stage at a cultural festival, 'she was turned on, she was lit up like a Christmas tree and really enjoying it'. I mentally recoil while Brian sounds excited and slaps his big thighs, equally lit up. Basically, he says, Centrepoint operated within a different paradigm, just like other countries where the age of consent is lower and sexual initiation by elders accepted. The goalposts for their norms had shifted. Where Bert got it wrong, in Brian's view, was his lack of judgement about the society around him, and lack of understanding that there would be a clash at some point, especially when the drug-taking started. Bert wasn't worried about the Health and Disability Commissioner because there wasn't one; he wasn't worried about professional bodies because he didn't belong to any. 'He wasn't worried about anything much.'

Brian says he holds everyone responsible for believing and buying into the idea that they could make their own separate society, and that they didn't consider what would happen when their kids went into the wider society. The founders had all experienced an incredibly sexually repressive childhood in the '50s in New Zealand, which they wanted to counter.

'Let's simply say, it was the Wild West.' He smirks. 'There were lots and lots of things which would horrify the good people at St Joseph's Catholic Church.'

His father, a secondary school teacher, once visited the community and said to him upon leaving: 'There's something not right here. The teenagers here won't look at me, won't talk to me. Interesting.'

It's a segue for me to tell him that Angie said she had a 'yuck feeling' around men like him. That feedback doesn't go down well. Brian tells me to stop my recording immediately, jumps up and threatens to throw me out on the spot. He points to the door. I apologise. We have a tense back-and-forth before he lets me sit down again to clear things up.

'There was actually a really strong buzz between us,' he says about Angie.

I've hurt his feelings. He also doesn't like that I use the term 'thought police' for the two top women. Another bad move. For the next hour, while I'm on tenterhooks, we debate what he calls the 'moral panic about paedophilia which has been running since 1980'. He gets up to pull out a photocopied book from the shelf behind us. It's by Larry Constantine, an American writer, computer scientist and family therapist who published *Children and Sex: New Findings, New Perspectives* in 1981. The academic proclaimed that children have the right to have sexual contact with older people, and after reviewing 130 sources concluded that negative impacts on minors who had had 'intergenerational sex' were rare. His findings became a cornerstone for paedophile apologists and were popular with Centrepoint. The author even once visited the community.

Brian and I theorise for a while about this 'discourse', with which I'm familiar. It also crept into the left-wing alternative faction in Germany in the '80s, where 'man/boy love' sailed under the umbrella of sexual liberation.

'It's so complex. There's no doubt that children were inappropriately sexualised,' Brian concludes. 'We didn't get that right.'

He takes me to his office and rifles through boxes to show me the letters he sent to Bert Potter in prison, in which he challenged him. He is more chilled now and makes me a cup of tea before I leave. As I go, I get a joke for the road, one of the many that circulated at Centrepoint.

'What's the only tool you don't have to spend two hours looking for, ask another member if you can borrow it, and then repair it before you can use it?' He laughs. 'A penis.'

The lady at the guest house where I'm staying that night is curious what brings me up north. I mention Centrepoint. She flinches and lowers her voice. Her brother, who was suffering from psychosis, committed suicide after a weekend workshop at Centrepoint. I don't know what to tell her, other than what Brian had mentioned – that some ten thousand people had gone through the groups and a huge number of them had psychiatric histories.

What I don't tell her is what Bert Potter's radical approach, according to Brian, actually looked like. This is what he told me: 'So you want to kill yourself? If you'd like to drown yourself, I'll drive you over to the lake. But I'd strongly suggest that you try a high building. And I think that it would be really good to land head-first if you can, because if you do, it won't hurt. But if you land feet-first, it'll hurt for a couple of minutes before you die. So you want to go to the lake or you want to go to a building? If you want to have a go at it yourself and cut your wrists, do it in a place down by the swimming pool so we can clean up.'

Chapter 5

The dirt road near Whangārei Heads is steep and goes on forever, with dense bush on both sides. It ends at an impressive 81-hectare property with a sprawling olive grove. I'm in Northland to meet Ulrich Schmid. The Swiss, known as Ueli, was the popular paper-maker but also the drug chemist at Centrepoint and one of the Old Believers. Although considered a 'safe adult' by many kids, in 1991 he was found guilty of sexually assaulting two girls at Centrepoint, one of them seven years old, and sentenced to one year in jail. He was also sentenced to four years for supplying and manufacturing ecstasy.

His land was bought with the payout from the commune; part of it has been sold off to the Department of Conservation. There are a few more Centrepoint families in the area, but some who were not paid out by the trust refuse to come up here.

Two electric cars are parked in the driveway. The main building looks like a wooden castle and is the communal home of Ulrich Schmid's and Richard Parker's families. The latter was convicted of the rape of a fourteen-year-old Centrepoint girl. The two men shared a cell in jail.

'Ex-Centrepoint members move onto Northland property' was the headline of an article in the *New Zealand Herald* on 26 April 2001, stating that two convicted paedophiles had moved into the area. It talked about neighbours' worries that the men planned to start another commune. But it also quoted a local saying the newcomers hadn't caused any problems and it's 'a total redneck reaction'.

Ulrich has nine children from three marriages, and numerous stepchildren, which earned him the nickname 'Papi' (German for 'Daddy') at the community. There's a prominent chef among his children and others with promising careers and artistic ambitions. They don't want to talk to me.

I only announced my visit a few hours before. Ulrich doesn't act hostile or surprised when I turn up, but he doesn't want to be formally interviewed. After the tense encounter with Brian, arriving at his place feels like a holiday. He's a slight man with a beard and smiling eyes, looking eco-bohemian in a worn-out blue cotton shirt with rolled-up sleeves. His red suspenders are imprinted with the white crosses of the Swiss flag. He opens his arms for an instant hug.

'Please, come inside!' he says.

There's an old-fashioned gentlemanly charm about him.

'Are you hungry, do you want something to eat? And you can sleep here, no problem.'

I tell him that I can only stay for a short while because I'm passing through.

Ulrich takes me up the stairs into the tower. His welcoming hospitality is especially unusual given that I'm a reporter and he is one of the main offenders in the biggest drug and paedophilia case that has ever rocked this country. He tells me he has never read any of the articles or seen TV reports about Centrepoint.

A little girl in short pink boxers traipses around in women's high heels, giggling. Green frog socks peep out from the rims of the shoes.

'They're playing dress-up. Her friends love coming up here,' says Ulrich.

I try to block out the fact that he believed in the active sexualisation of the 'free' children and supported Bert Potter inside and after prison. He spoons mushrooms into a bowl for me in his spacious kitchen. I feel like I'm befriending the enemy. He chooses his words carefully, glancing sideways at me from behind his specs while I eat. Centrepoint was a very interesting experience in his life, but he doesn't want to reflect on it now, he says.

'I'm looking ahead, not back, and I see how wonderful all my children have turned out.'

I don't bring up the fact that in 2000, one of his sons, then 30, was sentenced for having pornographic pictures of young girls on his computer at Centrepoint.

Ulrich goes on. 'I look at my children, they are so happy, they never fight, they are not into violence or drugs.'

That's ironic – or a glimpse into a distorted reality – coming from the man who was the biggest manufacturer of drugs in the '80s in New Zealand. The illegal substances were also sold, and the money is still unaccounted for. I carefully mention the children that didn't turn out quite so well after Centrepoint.

'That was the family's fault before they arrived,' he says quickly. 'That's why they had problems later.'

Since this is not an interview, I can't probe any further, but he seems to have an urge to get something out. His tone is sly. 'You could ask the mothers of those girls who declared that they had been abused at CP why they didn't do anything against that …?'

He said a Centrepoint girl once assured him that nothing that had happened there had been bad for her. 'It was only afterwards, when she spoke to social workers about it.'

He smiles at me with glee, as if this must be a new revelation for me, or a big help with my research. His version of the truth has been perpetuated by the pro-Bert camp for decades: the adults at Centrepoint did nothing wrong, only the counsellors who turned a beautiful experience into an ugly one later; harm to the children wasn't done by the community but by the outside society; and all the girls lied in court because they wanted the ACC payout.

Ulrich's teenage son comes into the kitchen, a long-haired boy with a friendly face. Through an open door, I see Ulrich's wife playing a keyboard. She looks up and gives me a warm smile, then carries on with her music. I find this scene of cosy family life, of 'Gemütlichkeit', hard to reconcile with this man's blame of victims, mothers and society. It's all one big conspiracy, according to Ulrich.

'Free groups are being destroyed all over the world, you know.' There is fervour in his voice. 'Communities are not allowed to thrive and survive because we are all seen as a threat.'

On the way out to the car he comes closer again, puts his arm around my shoulders and lowers his head to my ear, whispering, 'See, I have given you some good points to think about!'

I utter a friendly goodbye and quickly drive away. I wish I had asked Ulrich Schmid some hard questions after all, but I'm too conflicted. I wonder whether I'm helping or hurting the children at his remote castle by confronting their Papi.

Angie has stopped all her intimate session work. She tells me on the phone that she felt more and more like a 'sacred prostitute' and kept breaking her agreements with her boyfriend. She thinks she has a sex addiction and wants to start the 12 Steps programme again. But first she wants to close another chapter too.

She writes an email to Henry Stonex: 'I have often thought of you over the years. There are so many questions I have about your feelings for me at that time, as I realise I have never loved anyone the way I loved you.' She asks him for an opportunity to reconnect, and also to get more clarity for my book. Henry's name has finally come out of the 'God box'.

One evening a few weeks later, while preparing dinner, her phone rings. She goes into the lounge, where her sons are, to answer it.

'Hi, it's Henry,' the caller says.

Angie stops in her tracks.

'Hi,' she says. She walks back into the kitchen.

His voice is overjoyed and emotional, then he starts crying. 'I saw a photo of you on the Snuggle Party website. You were looking straight at me.'

After Angie hangs up, she stands in the kitchen, completely disassociated from herself. Two worlds just collided. After dinner, she disappears into her room to look at the email that Henry just sent her, titled 'Love and us'. It says how sad he felt thinking they would never meet again.

'My memories of us are so special to me and it is only to you that I can ever hope to talk over old times. As for this kind of stuff to be put into a book is even a more scary option for me to even contemplate, as I don't find ordinary people can even comprehend what you and I know is possible.' He drops her name into his sentences like a lure – 'you write well Angie' – and warns her of me, a 'stalwart of the sexual abuse industry' who is 'grooming' her – as if she's still an ignorant teenager and he knows her intimately. 'However Angie,' it goes on, 'this will not stop me from meeting with you alone some quiet place where we can chat and share like of old.'

The email deeply disturbs her. Her old cult identity suddenly resurfaces, the 'us' versus 'them'. Maybe Henry is right about the sex abuse sensationalism, and that no one can ever understand, who didn't live at Centrepoint? She is afraid she might be attracted to him again. Her whole world could come tumbling down. But she still books a flight to Auckland to meet him several weeks later. In the meantime, she moves into a community in Christchurch with her boyfriend, while her sons, who have finished school, stay in her council flat up north.

Henry arranges to use a friend's home in Mt Eden. It's around the corner from where Angie used to live with her mum and siblings. She first drives past Henry to check him out from her car. He looks like old gentry in a cap, coat and scarf, smaller and older than she remembers him – 73 years by now. She could fight him if she had to.

They hug awkwardly on the street. After climbing three flights of stairs to get to a room, Henry sits on one side of the table surrounded by chairs.

'It's wonderful to see you after all these years,' he begins nervously.

Angie is cautious and controlled, but anxious underneath. Henry confesses that he was completely and utterly in love with her. Angie explains that she loved him as a father who truly saw her. She wanted to be special but wasn't his equal. When she tells him that the sex hurt and she endured it, Henry starts crying. If he had known, he says, he would have never gone on with it. A lot of girls wanted to join him at the honey house for a bath or a joint, but he never made a move on them.

'I swear,' he says.

After a while he talks about Bert Potter, what a gifted therapist he was, and then they watch films about Centrepoint on Henry's laptop. Hours pass. Before they part, Henry stares into her eyes and asks, 'Do you love yourself, Angie?'

'No,' she replies, her voice shaky and her heart tearing. She can't get the words out that she had prepared to say: *You've ruined my life!*

From there, everything spirals out of control. Instead of returning to her boyfriend, she goes to see her former sugar daddy from her prostitution days in Wellington. He suggests she should start sex work again. After ten years of sobriety, just three days with him has her coming close to picking up a drink.

The sugar daddy pays for a trip to Bali, where she wants to go on a retreat to heal herself. When she finally returns to her new home and tells her boyfriend all this, he gets volatile and throws her out on the street. She feels like the whore of Babylon when she packs her yellow station wagon and moves out, with no place to go. It's straight downhill from there.

On the second day of her course in Bali, Angie pops her knee out and ends up in hospital in Denpasar in need of surgery, with no money for the bill. Her sugar daddy, her father and her friends all refuse to pay for it. 'It's one big fucking mess,' she messages me. A friend of a friend finally helps her out. Back in Wellington, she is on crutches for weeks, broken and broke. This is the lowest she has been since she wanted to ram a knife into her chest. One morning, she looks at the full container of diazepam pills on the kitchen counter and wants to swallow the lot.

Angie puts bedding in her car and goes bush at Waikanae Beach. That night, she sits on a park bench overlooking the sea and thinks of her mother, who walked into the water in an attempt to kill herself. There are only the stars, the moon and her. She feels a peace she has not felt in many years. The next day she awakes to a beautiful sunrise and drives up the Kāpiti Coast to see friends who live off the land. Earthy folk, they have chickens, a pig and a dog. It's like coming home. She can stay as long as she wants.

Slowly, she recovers. In the little cottage by the beach, she questions how she viewed Centrepoint all her adult life: how she chose everything that happened to her because she would never be a victim like her own mother was. At their meeting in Mt Eden, she readily accepted Henry's testimony and never once challenged him. It was a step back into Bertland, with her as the concubine.

Over the following days, Angie starts writing it all down, then sends it to me. What happened to her is clear now, like never before.

'What if I was groomed and manipulated, abused and raped over and over at Centrepoint? Until I can reclaim that feisty self-assured teenager that I buried deep down in order to survive, I will never be free.'

I need to cast a wider net to find more people from Centrepoint. But I never know which can of worms or heavily locked door I might inadvertently open. When I now carefully craft my introduction emails, I never assume a particular standpoint at the recipient's end.

When someone finally agrees to talk to me, it still gets complicated. People spill their guts for hours, then later regret how much they've let out. They impose strict limits on what I can write: I am not to use certain words like 'condoning mother' or 'cult'. Or say anything positive about the place. Or focus on the sexual abuse. Or believe what the newspapers reported. Or make anyone look bad, including Bert Potter.

It's a juggle between accuracy and accommodating the wishes of those who have put their trust in me. I have to change names, blur identities, and work out confidentiality agreements that don't restrict someone's freedom of expression and my own perceptions. Soon I'm overwhelmed by contradicting information that I can only partially use and hardly verify – and that could also be slanderous or incriminating. It's like a growing depot of toxic waste, too much for one person alone to handle.

By now, the initial enthusiasm I had when I dived into the project the year before has turned into exhaustion. A barbecue in the countryside outside of Auckland offers a much-welcomed break from the research marathon – a social distraction before I'm meeting a source called Fred the next day. The older man who lived at Centrepoint for a while was helpful on the phone and offered to liaise between me and someone who was upset about my research. Fred had some unorthodox views which I was curious to hear more about. We had a good chat, and I liked his sense of humour.

After dinner at my friends' place, I talk to a couple who live in Fred's suburb. I ask them if they know him. What are the chances, with two million people in Auckland? They do.

'Fred?' The man slams his beer on the counter, almost spitting out the name with disgust. 'Just don't mention him again, okay?!'

He turns away. I don't quite understand. His wife backs off by about a metre.

'We know quite a few people from Centrepoint, actually,' she says, slowly. Her face shows a mix of emotions that I cannot read. What is going on here? I'm confused.

'Is there some kind of problem with Fred?' I ask her husband.

He looks angry and walks away from me, shouting: 'I told you I don't want to talk about it!'

My head starts spinning, my throat feels tight, and tears shoot into my eyes. It's not just his reaction. Out of the blue, this has turned into another unexpected Centrepoint drama. Did something happen there to this couple, or someone from their family?

An irrational panic creeps up in me that I cannot control. It's like a big black ugly monster that sinks its claws into me, pulling me down. What is it about this place, its lasting shadows? I lose it at that moment; it's already late at night, I've had a few glasses of wine, and my defences are down, in this place where I least expected to have another confrontation. The couple retreats to the other end of the garden while I collapse on the sofa. I can hardly breathe. This is all too heavy, too complicated, too awful. I feel like throwing up to get it all out of my system and then never ever mentioning Centrepoint again. But I know I can't. I have to finish what I started.

When the couple is about to leave, the woman comes up to me. 'I'm sorry,' she whispers in my ear. 'It's got nothing to do with you. But this man, Fred – he has been stalking our teenage daughter. He has tried to take inappropriate pictures of her. It's really ... sick.'

This time I can read her face. It's full of pain.

I still go and see Fred the next day. 'Face the demon' is my new mantra. I need to park what I heard and stay as impartial as possible. Fred brews me a strong cup of coffee in his spacious wooden kitchen. He looks a bit worn out and is older than I thought. There is no way I could address his alleged stalking around the neighbourhood in a way that wouldn't potentially get me in trouble. It's stressful enough as it is.

When I mention the media-shy former Centrepoint kids, he tells me that they are the best children in the world.

'Light years ahead of everyone, with enough love and touch in their lives. And all supporting each other.' Tears fill his eyes. 'It's just so sad that they have been made to think by this society that something's wrong with them.'

He shakes his head and gets up abruptly, clearly upset, and reluctant to say more. Again, I have to defend myself for doing my job, while wondering what he might have to defend himself for. He holds his coffee mug tight with both hands.

'In the end,' Fred says, swallowing hard and staring into his cup, 'guys will just be wanking over these stories.'

I am taken aback. This has never crossed my mind, but obviously it has crossed his. I leave as soon as I can.

I wish I had never met Fred or the couple at the barbecue. Too much information. How can I trust anybody? Nothing is black and white anymore. The grey zone keeps getting darker with every apologist who tries to whitewash his actions. Maybe they're right, and it wasn't as bad overall as some of the survivors made it out to be? I'm lost in Bert's labyrinth.

Larry Constantine writes back to me from Boston. It was his tattered photocopied book that Brian the bully pulled off the shelf to show me as proof that Centrepoint's warped philosophy towards paedophilia was based on solid research.

'I do have serious doubts about any influence I might have had on the philosophy of Centrepoint, which was rather deeply at odds with my own thinking and direction,' the septuagenarian author admits. He was interested in group marriage, which he also researched. Since his visit to the Albany commune in the mid-1980s, he's stayed in touch with Len Oakes, the therapist and Centrepoint historian I visited in Melbourne.

'Of course, along the way I published some rather ill-thought and wrong-headed things myself, some of which others used to justify their own agendas,' Larry says. 'Metaphorically, I now hit myself upside the head and say, "What *was* I thinking?"'

His confession doesn't help me any further. It's 2014 and I'm still unravelling the aftermath of Centrepoint, with a deadline looming. By now I've checked out every lead, knocked at every door, looking for people who will talk to me. I'm ready to stop searching. There is only one more woman I haven't found, a girl mentioned in an old *Listener* article who lived by herself in a caravan at Centrepoint. She's not named. I give it a last try, but no one knows where she is or what she does now. 'She's probably quite lost,' I hear. 'She has changed her name.'

She was Louise Winn when she was a child. Hilary Elvidge, her mother, was one of Bert Potter's favourite women, and her website is still online: the Atlantean Connection. But my email to the address on the website bounces back, and the fax number is out of order. I look up all 21 people with Elvidge as a last name and finally get given a number for her second husband. He is not fazed at all when I call him. He tells me in a serious tone that I can only talk to his wife if I'm a medium: 'You can contact her through channelling.'

Hilary passed away eight years ago. The widower can't help me with finding his stepdaughter, Louise.

I reach her brother, who only sees her at Christmas, if at all, and he gives me a cell phone number. There is no reply when I send a first text message, and then a second one. When I finally make a phone call, my heart scudding, the number has been temporarily disconnected. I call the place where she last worked, in a mall. But she has quit, and no one knows anything about where she is. I'm about to give up.

When I take a deep breath one day and dial her phone number once again, she answers straight away. Unlike everyone else from Centrepoint I've spoken to, she sounds excited – as if she has been waiting for this call.

'How did you manage to find me?' she is curious to know. 'I've changed my name so many times.' 'Louise' is still her legal name though.

She tells me that she just lost her job and her house, everything. Her mother often speaks to her from above. The deceased Hilary, who can only be contacted in the ethereal world, apparently paved the way for me to her elusive daughter. Yesterday, when Louise stood outside on the deck, she heard her mum say: 'Take every opportunity.' And then I called. Otherwise, she would have never answered the phone. She laughs drily. 'You could have been a debt collector.'

She is easy to talk to, real and direct. Not chatty, but not evasive either. I'm unable to form a mental picture of the 'girl in the caravan' who must be a middle-aged woman now, slightly younger than me. But a few minutes into our conversation, her voice starts shaking.

'I have never told anyone my story, apart from the police, and even that I typed up. No one would have found me anyway.'

'Are you sure you want to do this?' I ask her.

'Are *you* sure you want to do this?' Louise replies with a warm and slightly sarcastic laugh.

I like her instantly. She's a light at the end of the tunnel of name suppressions, stonewalling, legal hurdles, secrets and paranoia.

Chapter 6

The houses on the West Auckland street are small and old. Kids kick a ball around. I park near a playground and walk up the drive. Flowers grow along the base of the old weatherboards; the door is open. A cat wanders through the crammed hallway. I have never seen a photo of Louise and am completely taken by surprise when I meet her. She is 45 but looks older than I expected. Her complexion is washed out and she wears no make-up, but her nicotine-tinged smile is genuine and shy, almost vulnerable. Her grey-blonde hair is held back with a scrunchie in a long ponytail. She wears simple metal glasses and baggy clothes – she pays no obvious attention to style. Her long purple jersey is covered in cat hair.

There's a man in the lounge, with a dirty bandage on his foot. He offered Louise a room when she got evicted from her rental place. Effectively, she's homeless. We cross the deck where she received the psychic message from her mother.

'I'm pretty good at hiding,' she tells me on her way down the steps. She never looks at her mail, skipped the last census and isn't on the electoral roll or in the phone book.

We walk to the deserted playground and sit down on a bench. It's dinnertime soon, and the children have left the street. Cicadas growl in the bushes, which give off a flowery scent. I can tell that she's nervous despite the anti-anxiety pills she says she took earlier, so I ask about counselling, hoping it might be a safe start to check if she ever received professional support after Centrepoint.

'I once went into a women's help centre,' she begins. 'It was my first and only visit, after I gave my statement in court. When I told the woman why I was there, she threw up. Into the waste basket. End of time. So I didn't go back.'

Louise pulls up her shoulders, a laconic half-smile on her face. Hang on – the therapist threw up?

'Nothing is a safe topic,' Louise warns me. 'Nothing.'

Louise Winn was ten years old, a small, skinny child with auburn hair and kidney problems when she arrived at Centrepoint with her older brother and her parents. Her mother had been suicidal, and the community was her last resort, a chance for permanent psychological care.

'I used to read the poems she wrote. I knew that she was in a really bad way and that the place could help her. I wanted a mum,' Louise tells me.

There was a trampoline at Centrepoint, so she was eager to stay. 'I wish we'd gotten a trampoline ourselves. Then I wouldn't have wanted to move there.'

Then things would be very different now.

In the beginning, the family lived in one big caravan. After they were moved into the longhouses, Louise shared a bunk room with three other girls. From then on, she was separated from her parents. She didn't trust her assigned female guardian, and the male guardians soon turned out to be sexually interested in her.

About a month after her arrival, she was upstairs in the lounge when Bert's wife Margie emerged from the kitchen, came over to the pillows where Louise and some others were sitting, and asked Louise to go to Bert's car crate with her.

Louise has no memory of that first time. She is glad about that. 'But I imagine it was the same thing because it was the same routine, every single time.'

It was Margie who would bring her to Bert. When Louise was trapped in his hut, she would sit on the bed and Margie would masturbate him to climax. Louise had to touch him too. He would perform oral sex on Margie first, then on Louise. It would hurt. Hurt like hell. He said that's what an orgasm is. His face would smell of the last woman he had been with.

In those first weeks, a note appeared on the noticeboard, next to the lists announcing the 'clean club' and 'dirty club' – those who had STIs. Louise found her name written there. They had voted the ten-year-old 'best bum'.

It wasn't just Bert. John Potter, Bert's son, did exactly the same as his father. And Dave Mendelssohn, Bert's right-hand man, was one of the worst. Louise found him revolting. He was big and messy, and wore a smelly kaftan – she called him 'Jabba the Hutt'. Once, she was in the bath when Dave hopped in on one side and his wife on the other. He touched her between the legs and said: 'You better get out now or I'll just keep playing.' Another day, Louise walked through the lounge where Dave was fondling a three-year-old girl while talking to someone else, not even paying attention to what he was doing. It wasn't shocking to Louise at all; just the sort of thing that happened. Girls got played with. When they changed the babies' nappies, some adults were blowing them off. It wasn't all done behind closed doors. So how would Louise know that what happened to her wasn't supposed to happen, wasn't okay, wasn't normal?

Once, when her mother was making school lunches in the kitchen, Dave Mendelssohn came up to her and asked her if he could have sex with Louise. Hilary took the bread knife, pointed it at him and said: 'If you go anywhere with my daughter, I will slit you from arsehole to breakfast!' They made Hilary do more therapy courses after that.

Dave's wife was Susanne Brighouse, and she held sex-education courses for the teenage girls where she and Margie masturbated in front of the group. Their private parts were brown and looked like wilted flowers. In the break, Louise called them 'dying orchids', and the kids all laughed. It took the sting off the embarrassment.

The showers were all open plan, no curtains, and Louise was terrified of them. She didn't even have pubic hair. The guys would come past and look at the girls, so she stopped taking showers. She moved into one of the single caravans on the property, first with another girl, then by herself. There was no lock on it. The door started opening at night, sometimes as late as two in the morning. She would wake up and find men behind her, in the bed, touching her. From then on, she avoided sleeping there, but would curl up in a ball under the car crates or the honey house, half a kilometre away. No one missed her.

She didn't wash any more so that they'd think she was too disgusting to be with. Then she'd 'forget' to get on the school bus so it would take her ages to get back from school.

Louise became known as a hoarder. She lived in squalor, with rats under her caravan. It was her trick, building a maze of junk in the caravan so that predators couldn't get in. She broke into the storeroom and dragged out any old stuff she could find, barricading herself in. She built a labyrinth out of kaftan material, with a cord winding through the jungle of fabric so she could turn on the light. You had to climb over things like clunky old typewriters to get to the bed. Only she knew the exact way through the mess. If the door opened in the middle of the night and she was asleep, the intruders would trip over the obstacles on the floor. She would then wake up and could escape through the window.

'I tried everything,' she says.

They kept her away from her parents, Louise had no friends, no one she could tell, and she didn't know she could ask for help anyway. This was just what happened to you; there was no option to say 'no'. If you did something that someone didn't like, people would come up and yell in your face, for as long as they wanted. It was 'feedback', and you had to take it. If you complained about anything, it was your fault. If you didn't cooperate, you'd end up in a week-long group or you'd be given a horrendous task. She saw one boy who tried to run out of the room during one of the teenage therapy workshops they had to attend, grabbed and held down by the therapists.

Her mum seemed happy there; she was popular, as one of Bert's favourite women. The men who approached Louise were hoping to get more status through the daughter. Hilary had been raped as a kid and went to one of Bert's first groups to get over it. He made her have sex with every one of the men. They had to blow her off until she stopped screaming.

Bert soon found that during sex he couldn't put a finger in Louise's vagina. He convinced her mother that the girl's hymen was too thick, an unhealthy medical condition, and asked for the community doctor to surgically remove it. Hilary taught her daughter exercises to tear her hymen instead. The prospect of an operation terrified Louise. There was no way they were going to do that. She couldn't trust the doctor anymore and was hiding from him, too. When she was sick in bed with a kidney problem, the GP had to hide the injection needle in her mother's pocket because Louise checked the doctor's coat first. She didn't trust anybody.

The library, the music room or the pottery was where she spent her time, creating things. The man who ran the pottery was her friend. When she had a migraine, which she often suffered from since the talk about her hymen operation, he would give her a head massage. Then he offered her back massages. 'Turn over,' he said, and she wasn't sure about this, but since she didn't have any breasts yet, she turned. He started fingering her. It went on forever. It only happened once, so she hoped it was just a stupid mistake.

Louise tried to keep frogs, but they didn't last very long in her care. No one looked after her, so how would she know how to look after them? She also had rabbits that she took for walks on little harnesses. Sometimes she slept inside the tiny rabbit hutch.

Once, when she walked past a window, she saw a mother giving oral sex to her son. He was maybe nine or ten years old. The curtains were not drawn – they never were at Centrepoint – and both the parent and the boy looked ashamed. Maybe it was a task they had to perform for Bert, but Louise crossed the woman off her 'safe adults list'. It wasn't the last time she saw mothers and sons together like that.

The only time she recalls being shocked was when the kids tried to raise kittens and Dave Mendelssohn came and killed them with a hammer, right in front of them, just bashed them all in the head – that shocked her.

At eleven years old, Louise tried to kill herself. A school ball was coming up. She wanted to wear a blouse of her mum's, white with pearl buttons, that had been put into the community coffer. It had been part of her life before, but no one had their own clothes. Hilary said her daughter wasn't allowed to wear it. Things escalated. Louise ran away and found a knife. She was so upset that she started cutting her wrists. She just desperately wanted something that wasn't Centrepoint, that was clean and nice.

Hilary caught her, bandaged her up and talked to Bert. The next day, he found Louise in the dining room. He sat her on his knee. 'Your mother is very upset,' he said. 'You tried to do this because you're not receiving enough love.' He told the girl she would have to see him every day for a week after school.

She knew exactly what that meant. Louise went twice, then deliberately missed the school bus. Every time she saw Bert or Margie she just ran away. She even had the keys to the tractor so that she could drive off. She got used to being bad. It was the worst time of her life, and the last time Bert ever touched her.

Louise was twelve when she first changed her name – desperate to be someone other than that dirty, disgusting girl. A new identity; not a slut. She found a key to the moneybox in the office, went into the bush with a Swiss army knife and a hacksaw blade, and forged a copy. The kids were all good at lock picking – for instance, for getting into the medicine cabinet. Every morning Louise would take some money and get a bus into town, then return late. For about a whole year no one noticed that she was mostly gone.

She started developing breasts, but she didn't know she was supposed to ask for a bra, so she made one for herself. The other girls knew how the system worked, but she didn't; she'd been alone for so long, trying to hide. When she managed to make friends at school, their parents wouldn't let them play with her because she was a horrible little Centrepoint kid. A teacher called her a 'commune bummer'.

Her parents had separated, like most couples at Centrepoint. Louise thought that if only she'd been allowed to be with them, her mum would have known about the abuse, for sure. Louise was waiting for someone to notice. For her mum to notice. Trying to kill herself hadn't worked. But no one came to rescue her.

Her time at Centrepoint came to an end in 1983, when she was fourteen. During an argument, Hilary had roared at Louise's dad when he was having a shower. In her fury, she'd slipped and cracked her head open. Louise saw her lying in the lounge injured and thought: *She can't stay here. I've got to get her out.* She grabbed a nappy bucket and filled it with clothes, arranged for one of the cars, and got her mum in there. They drove off to a friend on the outside. It was a middle-of-the-night escape because leaving usually wasn't an option. You had to apply; you only got a hundred dollars and the clothes on your back; and they'd send people out to try and drag you back. She helped her mum leave, but no one had helped her.

Louise was seventeen and three years out of Centrepoint when she finally told her mother what had happened to her. They were all in Kauri House in Auckland, flatting in an urban community. Every Friday night, a group of about 30 people took ecstasy together there. Back then, it was not a Class A drug, it was clean and not cut up with speed. It always felt great and made Louise babble.

That night, it all poured out of her, as if a valve had been opened. The whole room listened. Then one person after the other started crying. Her mum was completely silent, maybe in shock, because she really did not know what had been happening. Afterwards, when they all came down from the ecstasy, Louise was hideously embarrassed that all this had happened to her. She hoped no one would ever mention it again. It was all disgusting – and every time she disclosed it, she had to live it again.

One of the men in the room was a Centrepoint father and workshop facilitator. He was so affected by Louise's story that he went to the police. They contacted her; other girls had made statements, and they were gathering evidence. The officer who was sending her updates and contacting her was the first one who ever cared about the horror she'd suffered at the commune that preached 'loving'.

One day, Louise received a letter saying there was a court date, and she was needed to give evidence. She was 22 years old by now and had tried to leave it all behind. For the victim impact statement, she needed to go to a therapist. She went in there but ended up a blubbering mess and walked out again. Louise wrote a statement for the police and for ACC, and that was it. She didn't know what to expect; no one had told her.

One of the older Centrepoint girls, whose dad Louise was taking to court, was sent down to Louise's new home in Wellington to talk her out of laying charges. The girl had been abused herself but was still under Bert's spell. They also sent Louise's father down, who hadn't talked to her for ten years. He told her that a lot of innocent people were going to get hurt. *Well, tough shit*, she thought. It made her even more determined to go ahead.

On the day of the court case, the courtroom was cleared of media, but she still had to walk through a sea of reporters. She felt awful, exposed and paraded, like a show dog. When she heard that Bert Potter was going to be in the same courtroom, she was horrified. Thankfully, he sat behind her, so she didn't have to see him. The court case was so confusing. There were things that she hadn't put in the statement, and now she wasn't allowed to say them. She was nervous and felt used, like a puppet – as if *she* were on trial, not Bert and Margie. They were visible from out of the corner of her eye; she had to point them out. Since she had left Centrepoint, she had developed facial aphasia, an inability to recognise faces. It can be the result of severe trauma. Although Louise can't even remember what her mother looks like anymore, Bert's and Margie's faces are seared into her memory. They still come up in her mind on occasion, causing her migraines.

Because her mum was giving evidence as well, Louise wasn't allowed to talk to her. Again, she was separated from the woman whose support she needed the most and who had been missing from her life for over ten years.

After the case, she was back on the plane to Wellington, deeply frustrated and lonely. Four of the five people she had laid charges against were convicted, but it had been excruciating.

ACC assessed her level of injury at 7 per cent. The payment amounted to $1170 – a tenth of what the self-appointed therapist Brian later received for the damage to his name and income. Louise didn't know how to appeal.

The sun is setting behind the houses next to the playground. It's getting chilly, and Louise is desperate for a cigarette. Telling me her story took almost two hours. She stands up, looking frail and exhausted, while she smokes her rollie carefully so the wind won't carry the sparks to the dry shrubs behind our bench. Now I notice her long saggy skirt made of a velvety material and the practical shoes – black synthetic sneakers with socks, like a kid would wear to school.

'Not the ideal childhood,' she says. She half-smiles, coughs and takes another puff. 'So I tend to skip it all. I tell people my normal life until I was ten and then I say I lived on a farm. And then the twenties start.'

She turns to me with a self-deprecating grin, a warm glow in her eyes. 'How the hell are you going to write that book?'

I honestly don't know. 'It's hard to be sympathetic towards those adults who apparently didn't know ...' I start saying.

'How could you *not*?' she interrupts me, exasperated, and stamps out the cigarette butt. 'I know all their excuses – it was the place, it was the time, but – no. It wasn't the place or time. Because normal people wouldn't dream of doing that. It doesn't enter their heads.'

I tell her that some of the older Centrepoint adults think I'm too focused on the sexual abuse. I've heard that so often in the past months and have started to question myself and my search for the truth.

Louise blows her nose on a tissue and looks at me with pure bewilderment behind her spectacles. Her voice changes to sarcasm.

'Oh yes, sometimes we hunted frogs! And made paper.'

I mention that Margie Potter had undergone a change of mind during her husband's trial and turned to Christianity after her release from prison. She lost her job after the 2010 documentary *Beyond the Darklands*.

Louise's face hardens. 'Lost her job! Big fucking deal.' She spits the words out, then takes a long breath. 'She may have been brainwashed but she wasn't stupid to begin with. Margie was like a pimp.'

Emotion is welling up in her. 'It was four years of my life. It's ruined every relationship I've had. I haven't had any children. It's ruined my family.'

Trying to control her anger, she says that she has no compassion for Margie at all. None. 'She smiled through the whole thing. She held me down on the bed. When I was crying, "Stop, stop, stop!", she didn't do a fucking thing. I never want to see that smile again. It's burned into my brain.'

Louise is crying now, silently. I gently touch her arm, then wipe her cheek. My spontaneous gesture suddenly feels inappropriate. I pull my hand back, embarrassed and confused. I get up to fetch a jacket from my car, wondering if I have taken the questions too far. I'm not a therapist, just a reporter feeling out of my depth. It's not my role to become Louise's rescuer. Is this cathartic for her, useful at all – for anyone? Or am I just jabbing knives into 30-year-old wounds?

Louise has never had counselling as an adult because she might have to face a Centrepoint person across the room, and she does not trust therapy and hates the jargon since it was forced down her throat at the community. She has no idea that she is entitled to receive counselling sessions paid for by the New Zealand Communities Growth Trust, which was established by the High Court to reform Centrepoint; I am the first one to tell her. She has never heard any of the other children's stories or been in touch with them. It would have made such a difference to her, she says.

We get into my car to go into Henderson and find something to eat. Louise's car has no warrant anymore; she is currently broke but hopes to get back on her feet again as a computer programmer. In her last job, she was working in every mall in Auckland and even Hamilton, but she refused to work in the one in Albany, just in case one of 'them' walked in. It would give her migraines for months if they did.

She has never had Thai food before, so that's what we choose. The menu is ten pages long and Louise is a bit lost with it. She orders a glass of riesling and we relax. She laughs. Her face starts to change. It might be the effect of the wine, but under the faded, pale exterior another woman emerges, with a youthful glow. It's like a moment of shapeshifting, a glimpse into the person she could have been, comfortable in her own skin – if she hadn't been abandoned in a caravan where she was open prey for men who nearly destroyed her.

'Were you involved with any of the boys at Centrepoint?' I ask.

'No. Oh, God no.' She puts her fork aside. 'There was no way. No, I couldn't be looked at.'

I don't quite understand.

She repeats: 'I couldn't have someone look at my face.'

The abuser who fingered her prepubescent body after the massage in the pottery had said to her right afterwards: 'Your face has a funny expression when you're receiving pleasure.' It has messed her up ever since. He was the most damaging, she says.

'It's just ...' Her knuckles on the wine glass go almost white. 'There is no way to describe how that has affected me. Lights out, no one can see me.'

All her relationships end because she won't show her face. She can't look at herself in the mirror or have her photo taken. Even when she is alone in the house, she locks the bathroom door.

'I just lived like a statue. Like having a lobster shell around me, not showing any pleasure or anything.'

She always avoided sex. No boyfriend understood. She was married once; it only lasted a year. 'That's about how long it would take someone to be sick of me.'

If she could be with a 90-year-old man who was totally impotent, it would be perfect. She half-smiles at me now.

'I got cats instead.'

And when it gets too much? She smiles again.

'I hug a tree. I'm not kidding.'

—

We get her leftover curry to go. I tell Louise that she doesn't seem broken to me, but gutsy. A fighter. She says one of the best things she ever did was to learn boxing, fifteen years ago. She picked it up really fast and got herself a slam man (a boxing dummy). His name has changed a few times. She used to have dreams before, in which she would try to hit her attackers and they'd just laugh at her. When she started boxing, her dreams changed. She'd smack, and down they'd go.

On 6 May 2012, she was driving home from work in Hamilton when Radio New Zealand brought the news that Bert Potter had died. He had been living in a rest home, suffering from Alzheimer's. The man who had advocated sharing everything with hundreds of his people for over twenty years – work, childbirth, meals, beds, clothes, ablutions, sex partners – died alone, with no one by his side.

Louise couldn't believe it. It was so wonderful. She grinned the entire way back to Auckland for an hour and a half, feeling elated. A cloak of shame and disgust lifted from her and disappeared. As soon as she was home, Louise posted on Facebook, 'Ding, dong, the witch is dead'. She thought about going to Potter's funeral. To find out where he was buried. 'And then piss on his grave.'

We buy menthol cigarettes at a petrol station before I drop Louise off at her temporary home. It has started to rain, and we stand under the deck for one last smoke. It's dark, the raindrops making a clunking sound on her neighbour's old car beside us. I can't help thinking of the little girl who had her hiding holes for the night somewhere in the bush, under the longhouses, in any weather, alone and terrified.

It's getting late. Louise says she will try and read a science-fiction book tonight if her mind starts racing again. She loves to escape into fantasy stories, especially those with time machines.

'Imagine if I could go back in time! But then …'

She puts out her cigarette on the wet ground and sighs. 'I think we'd still have to go to Centrepoint. To save my mum.'

I sit in the dark car for almost half an hour. On my lap is the thick folder with Louise's letters, legal statements, diary entries and press clippings that she handed me earlier. I turn on the inside light and flick through the file. There is an affidavit from the psychiatrist who assessed her for ACC, saying: 'I have no doubt that the abuse occurred substantively as she described it, even if details can be challenged.'

I find a handwritten note on a statement that Hilary Elvidge sent to the New Zealand Police from England. It's a brief message for her daughter.

'Hope you's ok as we's is. xx Hils oo'

At the end of the pile of paperwork are Louise's poems, six or more, that she wrote in her teenage years. Some are scribbled in fountain pen on a notepad with the heading 'Things to do'. Others are typed out in capital letters. I can only get myself to read the first one. It runs diagonally down the page and starts:

CORNERED (THE ULTIMATE AGONY)

MOMMY
    I'M AFRAID
      MOMMY
        I'M HURTING

I breathe deeply in and out, still unable to turn the key in the ignition. Then I call my sons who are home alone. The younger one has accidentally set a cutting board on fire while cooking pasta for dinner. He is upset and still a bit in shock. My heart aches for him and his little domestic disaster. I'm grateful for everything that never happened to my loved ones or me.

Chapter 7

When I come back home with renewed motivation for a last round of Centrepoint interviews, Angie mentions Marianne to me. I've spoken to women who were teenage victims, I've spoken to male apologists, but not to any older women apart from Barri Leslie. The little I know about Marianne doesn't sound too controversial: a wife and mother at Centrepoint, without any obvious agenda or in any camp.

'I might not have a lot to tell you,' she announces over the phone, sounding friendly but a bit evasive.

Before I leave for my trip, I give Louise a call and tell her who I'm meeting next. Her voice is dry with sarcasm and contempt. 'Just watch her face go white when you say my name.'

Marianne lives in a quiet street in a small town. She is in her sixties, but her beautiful flowing dress and soft curls give her a youthful glow. We walk straight outside into the garden. She is welcoming and happy to talk, sprinkling New Age vernacular into the conversation.

'My soul guided me there,' is her answer to what brought her to Centrepoint.

She's a spiritual person, she says.

'You were a member of a cult,' I offer.

She nods and smiles. 'I was a member of a cult. And it was an amazing experience.'

There was the feeling of tribe, of being one big family, and the support the women gave each other when they had babies. I remember seeing Marianne as a pregnant mother, naked and radiant, in one of the old Centrepoint photos. She felt special when Bert first swept in on her and they had a threesome with another woman. She was 28, but still naive. Marianne, who was married then and is divorced now, became one of Bert's regular lovers.

'The sex wasn't that important,' she admits while she plays with her hair. 'It was about being close. He was very warm and nurturing, he could see right into me. Very present.'

In the early days, Marianne was running the kitchen, working from early morning until night. Bert once tasked her with doing all the community's dishes on her own, on top of her work – hundreds of dishes from hundreds of people. For her, that was 'honing the diamond'. Any negative feelings would become personal growth.

'Did you ever hate him?' I ask.

'Oh yes,' she admits. 'But I was compliant.'

Her then-husband connected with many other women at the time.

'We lived so openly, children were sleeping around their parents and other adults, they saw this was going on and they saw this is how you ... well, there was a lot of cuddling, then sexual things happening.'

We've come to the sensitive topic faster than I thought, where people have shut down discussion so many times before, but Marianne doesn't seem too fazed. She mentions women who were just going for what they wanted, also seeking out teenage boys. It was competitive. Even the teenage girls and children seemed predatory to her.

I'm startled.

'You're saying some of the children got more sexual attention than you?'

'Yes, which is quite hard to admit.'

'It's quite complex, isn't it?'

She nods, wiping her hair away from her forehead, not looking at me. 'It is.'

Her partner of later years, who has been hovering around in the back of the house since we sat down outside, pops his head out of the sliding door and looks at Marianne with concern. He must be sensing her growing distress, while I sense his disapproval of my questioning. She gives him a quick tense smile and carries on.

'I didn't think they were being abused because everything seemed to be done in a very loving environment. It was often the children initiating it, that's what blew me away. I thought, "Well, yes, because they see that this is the culture, this is how you get the strokes."'

Back then, she believed there could be sexual consent between adults and children. She was confused because these children were so sexualised and acting like adult women around the community with men.

When Marianne had a baby, her husband fell in love with another woman. The two would go off at lunchtime together. She felt abandoned and didn't handle the jealousy well. It was a painful time for her, full of drama and fights, and she wanted to leave the community but didn't know where to go. She felt trapped.

I ask her about parents who actively pushed their daughters into Bert Potter's arms. She confirms it's true.

'If they were going to be sexualised, it was better to be done in a loving context with someone who knew what he was doing.' It also guaranteed Bert's gratitude to the mother, 'but unspoken'.

'But the girls found Bert utterly disgusting and did not want to be near him,' I say. 'They had to endure him.'

'Did they … wow.' She looks at me. 'That's very interesting.' She pauses. 'I didn't see it from the point of view that they didn't enjoy being with him at all. I didn't know a lot of what went on.'

Marianne's face is tense now, her eyes wide open, staring beyond her garden. From inside the house, we hear her partner making noises, closing doors. It sounds like a warning.

I ask her how she's doing.

'It's bringing back the murky side and the emotional side for me, which was obviously a little bit conflicted back then. I was in quite a child state.'

I have to get closer to the question I don't dare to ask. But then I do.

'According to one of the survivors, you had the same role in the sexual abuse that Margie had for Bert. As a "go-getter".'

'Yes and no.' She seems calm. 'I mean, I was there with my husband and went along with it until the point where he was going to penetrate her. I stopped him. I said, "No, this isn't right."'

I didn't expect such a candid confession. And I need to double-check. 'Are we talking about Louise?'

Marianne's face does not turn white by the mentioning of her name. She shakes her head.

'I have no memory of that with Louise, absolutely no memory. I was talking about [Tania],' she says.

Tania, who was among the first girls to lay charges. Who met me but refused to share her story. Who told me that women were 'half of the problem'. Now I'm sitting here with one of them. Marianne goes on.

106

'I don't know about that with Louise, unless I have blocked it out totally. The only memory I have of being with a younger one was [Tania].'

It was meant to be a present for her husband. Sometimes when it was somebody's birthday, their partner would set them up with someone else. It was just what people did. Marianne thought it was a nice thing to do for him at the time. Tania was barely in her teens, but Marianne says she didn't actually participate.

'I was lying there, but I was just watching.' She cannot remember the details. 'But I'll tell you what, he was going to do the deed with her, and then I saw her face and I said, "No, you're not doing it!" And he didn't.'

A tear rolls down Marianne's cheek.

'She looked scared.'

I apologise for this being so awful. She sniffles.

'I just thought at the time, 'she's too young.' Her voice breaks up. 'I ... I saw she was a little girl. And I said, "No." The protective mother came out really strongly.'

I tell her about Louise – about her fear, her trauma, her poems. Her labyrinth in the caravan.

'I hear what you're saying,' says Marianne. 'I do feel a bit shocked that she had that experience.'

It's visible in her expression.

We go back and forth over why Louise thought Marianne had brought her into a threesome. We speculate that she might have confused her with another partner of Marianne's husband at the time.

'I feel very upset and sorry about that. Some of the things like that, that happened, I take responsibility for it.'

She was damaged too because she was quite vulnerable. 'My younger self did some things that I'm not proud of.'

It's getting dark; her partner seems restless. It must be dinnertime soon, so I leave. The next morning, before I drive back to Auckland, Marianne calls and asks me to pick up a letter for Louise on the way. I swing by her house again. She reads the letter out to me first, which I find strange. It reminds me of what Angie said about breaking down boundaries. Nothing was ever private.

'Anything that helps,' Louise texts me back when I suggest taking her to Barri Leslie. I would like to get her in touch with the anti-Centrepoint activist. Maybe I'm too optimistic, but a meeting with Barri might bring a lost daughter and a lost mother together, in a roundabout way. I just want her to be with another person who cares.

When we meet on the street in Browns Bay, Louise looks ten years younger. Her hair colour has changed to a dark red. It suits her. She wears a floral skirt.

'I had a make-over!' she exclaims.

There's a spring in her step, as if a weight has lifted. We sit inside her car. It's black and quirky, the tobacco smell strong. I hand her the letter from Marianne. Louise reads it, puts it down and looks straight out of the window, swallowing hard.

'I should feel something … but I don't. It reads as superficial. And it doesn't change anything.'

She lets out a sharp, exasperated breath. There is a fresh pain in her voice that I haven't heard before.

'What about the other one hundred and forty people?' she asks. 'Where were they? I feel like I was in an accident, and everyone just walked over me. Like I meant nothing to them.'

Louise has received a letter before. It was from Keith McKenzie, the old Centrepoint doctor. Before his death in

2005, he wrote to all the Centrepoint girls who had laid charges. I found the two pages with his small handwriting among the stack of papers that Louise gave me.

'I have recently climbed out of the pit of shame and depression that was my reward for my life at C.P.,' the convicted doctor wrote. 'I know I didn't see what I didn't want to see and avoided the indications that all was not well. I am sorry for my part in developing a C.P. in which you were not safe or heard, and the long time it took for me to accept how bad it had been.'

Now she has another letter. But it hasn't made any difference.

It's a warm welcome at Barri's place. She and Louise hug briefly, curious about what the other looks like after all these years. The house is as tidy and uncluttered as last time. Louise and I sit on the beige sofas, Barri opposite us. There's a box of tissues on the table, a writing pad and pen, glasses of water on pretty coasters. A lawn mower is blazing away outside, cutting through the tranquillity of Barri's lounge. The two women exchange some friendly news about their families. It feels like a reunion, just without the photo albums.

'I'm so sorry you lost your mother,' says Barri. 'The last time I heard from your dad was when I got the invite to his wedding some years ago.'

Louise looks startled.

'A wedding?' She shakes her head in disbelief. 'Weird. I mean, that's really ... I didn't know he married again. What the hell?!'

It's an awkward start.

Barri talks about how she remembers Louise.

'You were quirky and whimsical. And so creative too.'

Louise smiles and mentions the piano jewellery boxes and the little mice she made in the pottery.

'And you had rabbits. Oh, I let them out, remember?' Barri claps her hand on her mouth. 'I am sorry about that!'

The two women laugh, bonding over their memories. Then Barri leans forward a bit and fixes Louise with a more serious look.

'What do you want out of this?' she asks, sounding like the earnest counsellor she is.

Louise's lips quiver slightly. She shrugs her shoulders.

'I might be crying through the whole thing. You're copping it all because you're the first person I met.'

Barri doesn't flinch. She doesn't ask any more either. Instead, she goes into an explanation about the sexual repression of the '60s and '70s, the era she came from. How women who had been raped were treated like sluts at the police station. How no one had a clue about sexual abuse and the signs to look for in children. It never came up in her training as a schoolteacher. Louise listens patiently.

'It doesn't apply to how I feel,' she finally says when there is a break in the monologue. I can see her getting slightly restless.

'I mean – how many signs did I have to give out? I even slashed my wrists there ... and nothing.'

'I didn't know that.' Barri looks uncomfortable. 'It's a long story, but what I am trying to say ...'

She goes on defending her ignorance back then, explaining how the disempowerment worked, the hierarchy, the control and coercion. How she saw Tania's mother crying in the shower while the teenage princess was with Bert.

'I didn't know what was going on,' says Barri. 'I knew the Centrepoint children weren't happy, but I couldn't ... I just ...' She catches herself and gets back on track.

'Human beings can't deal with anything unless there is a language and a concept. A good Centrepoint mother had to let her child be sexually free. Now we go back and have the evidence and know it was very bad for children. But we didn't have it then.'

I look at Louise, trying to read her face and body language. I can sense a deep frustration but am not sure if Barri is aware of it.

'I just felt so alone,' Louise finally says. 'Like four years. No one came to my aid.'

'It was terrible,' Barri admits, not looking at her. 'It was terrible.'

'Four years! Everyone knew it was wrong because they were told not to talk to outsiders. Everyone cleaned up their act when visitors were around. I must have given a thousand fucking signals and no one tried to help me.'

'Yes, everyone knew it was illegal, but the pressure coming in on us was that the law is wrong.'

Barri's small body is tensing up. She presses her hands together in her lap, not looking at either of us. I feel for them both, locked in their pains of a shared past.

'There were hundreds of people there,' says Louise. Her lips are quivering again. She takes a tissue from the box. Barri shrinks into the sofa and nods.

'I know. Everyone was on their own. We had no voice in the situation.'

Louise wipes her eyes with a tissue. Barri's eyes are turning towards the kitchen.

'Right ... who would like a cup of tea, or some water?'

While Barri potters in the kitchen, Louise steps outside and rolls herself a cigarette, hunched over. She looks tense. It reminds me of our first interview, when I spontaneously wiped her cheek and feared I'd crossed a line. Months later, she told me that I could have cried with her a bit more.

I ask her if she's okay. She moves uncomfortably.

'I'm actually getting quite peed off. And at the same time, I feel I need to apologise to her.'

When we're back inside, she finally spits it out. 'I put your husband in prison. I mean – how horrible is that!'

Louise cringes and recoils. But Barri doesn't flinch. Her voice is calm and kind. She says that he wasn't her husband at that time anymore. There is nothing in her that excuses his behaviour. She would like to think that he did those things under Bert's influence and that he wouldn't have done them otherwise. Barri is back on track. She tells us how some of the adults who never abused children were put in the category of 'You're so blocked off, you've got no sexual freedom'. She had no way of arguing against those leading therapists like Bert, Barbara and Susanne. So her coping strategy was to think that maybe it was freedom. That she just had to get through her own fear.

Louise looks confused, as if she is rearranging something in her head. She asks Barri why the abusers were paid out.

'When I read that they all got almost $50,000, it was a kick in the teeth. Rewarded for staying at a place and abusing children!'

I wonder how often Barri has been through this, explaining what she did in court and why. She gets up and goes to her office, returning with therapists' addresses. She looks exhausted when she returns. One of the reasons for Louise coming here was to get financial help from the trust and then counselling. In the end she leaves with a list of information – and an experienced person at her side who will help her.

'I'm in your team,' says Barri.

After Louise has left, I don't quite know how to bring up the glaring omission I noticed throughout the conversation. I think Barri missed an opportunity for a heartfelt apology, and not just regarding Louise's rabbits. 'Sorry' is such a powerful word. Louise seemed to be pleading for someone to acknowledge that what happened to her was wrong, not for someone to explain the twisted rationale behind why she was abused.

But I'm only an observer, not a mediator. Instead, I ask Barri if she has been confronted with this anger before, maybe from her own children. She rearranges the tissue box and looks so unhappy that I feel guilty.

'Of course I have been confronted with it,' she replies. 'People like you come in and go, "This is what happened, oh my God!" Look, it's horrifying, absolutely horrifying. I know that.'

She turns to me, her eyes slightly squinting, as if she is pulling herself further inside to feel safe. She speaks about how she was lying awake night after night, how she apologised to her daughters a thousand times.

'I have been there, wanting to kill myself. But all that doesn't help, not me and not others. It doesn't inform people.'

She doesn't need more guilt, but she needs to get the message out about why it happened.

'Because it's happening right here in New Zealand in other religious communities, like Gloriavale. Have we learned nothing in those twenty years?'

Barri wants to go into her garden and pull some weeds now. It stops her from going crazy.

—

I call Louise repeatedly but get no answer. What if she has disappeared again? I worry what Barri – or I – might have unleashed.

The months I have spent mired in the damage wrought by Centrepoint have taken their toll. The weight of all the unresolved trauma of others creeps under my skin and into my body. My neck goes into painful tension. Every morning I wake up too early, thinking of the loose ends of all the stories I have dug up, how to do everyone justice and tell their truth without hurting others – or getting sued.

My correspondence with *Inside Centrepoint* author Len Oakes changes. I'm losing him as a supportive source. The cult historian is getting wary of me as I bang at his inner door, wanting to hear remorse instead of analysis. I ask him why he is not apologising to the victims of Centrepoint since he only wrote about the good side.

The High Court has released hundreds of pages of court files to me. They sit on the shelf behind my desk, burning a hole in my back and pulling me further into the labyrinth of an unresolved past. The material I've unearthed after almost two dozen interviews is overwhelming, yet I'm still missing some links. I'm holding information that could help others – or destroy them. It feels like I'm climbing Mt Everest but am stuck at Base Camp, without a Sherpa in sight. Too late to just return and go home.

When I try Louise again the next day, she picks up straight away.

'I'm so angry,' she says. I can hear the force in her voice. 'But I don't know anymore who to be angry at.'

She has just finished reading *Surviving Centrepoint* by Ella James (Rachel C. King), an account of the author's life there as a teenager, detailing her own sexual abuse, the drugs, the poisonous hierarchy. The book has stirred Louise up. She never knew how others felt and what they went through. She thought it was only her, and that no one cared.

'I always thought I wouldn't live that long anyhow, so that I wouldn't have to deal with it.'

She loudly exhales cigarette smoke. The simmering lid has come off. How many letters, how many apologies, how many well-intentioned reconciliations or tears of a compassionate listener will it take before the pain that has been percolating for decades eventually subsides? I don't know how anyone can ever undo the wrong that was done to her. I feel helpless.

'You know what I want?' she says, her voice suddenly raw and almost breaking. 'I want every Centrepoint adult in a room together and I want to scream in each of their faces "HOW COULD YOU?" And have them understand it. And feel it.'

I feel raw and shaky too. I want to put these adults in a room as well and scream at them: 'How can you not get it yet?!'

My reaction to Louise's pain is another sign that I've come too close. My research feels like it's turning into a moral crusade. I'm on a slippery slope, and not just professionally. Instead of talking to Louise, I should be seeing a therapist.

I tell her that she is not broken, that she didn't end up on drugs, in prostitution or a psychiatric ward. She pauses and takes a long breath.

'I haven't told you everything,' she says, very calmly. 'I haven't even told the police. The words don't come over my lips because I don't let them into my head. If I told this part of my story, I would totally disintegrate. It would kill me.'

I don't know what to say. My stomach is starting to churn again.

Please stop. Enough.

'For me,' she says before she hangs up, 'Centrepoint was a prison camp without an escape. An ongoing living hell. I'm still in it.'

Chapter 8

In the years I've researched Centrepoint, I've always imagined the former site to be hard to find, tucked away somewhere deep in the bush. Back when it was founded, the outskirts of Albany, one of the northernmost suburbs of Auckland, was the back of beyond. But over the last 30 years the city has mercilessly spread out, enveloping the once-rural area.

A hardware store sits like a white-and-orange temple in all its gigantic ghastliness in the heart of the Oteha Valley, where I leave the Northern Motorway. Supermarkets, malls and a stadium dominate the suburb – the normal world. Mills Lane is a small turnoff to the right, the sign 'Kawai Purapura' easy to miss. Passing the little bridge into a green colonnade of tall natives and lush flowering bushes is an antidote to the soulless concrete-slab architecture just across the road.

A spiral made from pebbles greets visitors as they come down the driveway. Pretty signs point to the Wellpark College of Natural Therapies, and other facilities. A low sun drenches the wooden buildings in soft light, making stained-glass windows glow. A tepee sits further down on the lawn behind the swimming pool. I can hear birdsong.

Kawai Purapura Retreat Centre, owned by the same trust as Wellpark, is a venue for yoga, meditation, naturopathy and other alternative healing modalities. The name Kawai Purapura was gifted by the local iwi (tribe) Ngāti Whatua and reflects the past – a tentacle – and the present – a new seed. A noticeboard next to the reception offers everything from reiki to hypnobirthing. While I'm checking in, a bearded guy with a blue turban carries his guitar into a room where a kundalini yoga class is about to start. Laughter drifts from a group of women chatting on rattan sofas in a corner. Someone in a large straw hat potters in the garden outside next to the arts and crafts studios. A pizza night is advertised on a blackboard.

The old wooden longhouses of Centrepoint are further up the hill, renovated and separated into little units with names like 'Shanti' or 'Lotus', rented out to residents. My room is down by the streamside in the former teenagers' annex where Angie and her siblings lived. It is tiny. The walls are cell-like, made of painted concrete blocks. A staff member shows me a shelf space in the self-catering vegetarian kitchen and I sense her reservations about me staying. A resident has already told me that my research is bringing 'bad energy' and 'all that stuff from the past' back.

Most people who now live at Kawai Purapura wouldn't even know this place was once built and run by a cult. Two communities lived there post-Centrepoint: Anahata and Kahikatea. But the site is so powerful that tendrils of its past continue to nudge into the present day.

Some former Centrepoint children who are attached to their old home still come here and join gatherings or hold picnics. At the opening ceremony for 'KP', as Kawai Purapura is called, a woman stepped forward and spoke emotionally about the place where her babies were born. A medical doctor who lived at Centrepoint as a child took a sentimental walk around the community some years ago.

It was recommended by her therapist, supposed to be cathartic, but staff found her on the grounds, passed out from an overdose, surrounded by empty bottles. She'd been trying to kill herself. An ambulance took her away.

This incident has made Jenny Cottingham, the manager of Kawai Purapura, wary about letting former Centrepoint people into the community. I see the long-haired woman rushing around the place, but she makes time for me.

In 2005, Jenny and her husband were newly returned from India, nursing a dream of running a free natural-therapy hospital when they saw the site in Albany up for tender. Although it was run-down then and full of squatters, they saw the original beauty of the place.

'Centrepoint did all the hard work with town planning and the council, getting the permission to have so many people live together,' Jenny tells me as we sit alone in the former lounge. 'That's a unique opportunity for New Zealand. So we are very grateful for the work that went into the infrastructure here.'

Her team spent over three months clearing the site. When they cut back the overgrowth, they found beautiful paths and garden edges. Jenny points outside the window at a scented camellia.

'There, that's very rare. Someone lovingly chose this plant back then. People focus on the bad side of Centrepoint, but a lot of positive intent created this incredible environment.' But there were still echoes of an unresolved past. Every time Jenny's workers went into a new area to start clearing, they would get sick or became 'extremely emotionally vulnerable'.

'It was like taking poison,' Jenny says.

She would go home and still feel grubby, no matter how hard she scrubbed.

'I recognised something very terrible had happened here.'

Ngāti Whātua conducted blessings on the site that former Centrepoint members attended. A day after Bert Potter died in 2012, Kawai Purapura held its first Voices of the Sacred Earth festival. It was perfect timing, says Jenny.

'The energy shifted. The land was freed.'

In the morning I put on my walking shoes and head out for a stroll. I have arranged to meet John Potter, Bert's son, on the property today. But first, I want to look around a little and see what vestiges of Centrepoint remain.

Outside the main building, an early riser is practising tai chi in the autumn sun. When I walk up the hill from the annex, I pass a sign from the past. Literally; it's an old white plank of wood lying in the grass with the words 'Centrepoint Nursery' on it in green – possibly the only piece of memorabilia still around that has the infamous name on it.

Soon I reach the rougher edge of the shiny, upmarket retreat – a conglomeration of old shacks and caravans. Some of the green and beige dwellings have tarpaulins stretched over them and look like relics from a bygone era, musky and worn. Louise's caravan was here somewhere.

Up another path at the very top is Gustav's hut. I have been warned by the KP residents that he doesn't like visitors. Gustav, originally from Sweden, is the only original Centrepointian still living in this place. He always kept a low profile, on the fringe, doing maintenance work and driving. His hut is an A-frame that he built himself. The door is open, and Gustav, a scruffy man with long grey hair and beard, quickly shuffles past me with a grunt, unwilling to talk. The last survivor disappears between some trees.

A sign leads me to the Glade, and to John Potter. He gave a public apology at his father's funeral and is the only convicted Centrepoint sex abuser willing to be interviewed.

But the voices missing in the public domain are the ones that dominate a large faction of the community behind the scenes. Parents from prominent Centrepoint families have been telling their adult children to get over it or to only cherish the good memories, and this narrative has become entrenched in parts of the second generation. I've heard first-hand about the silencing, subtle coercion, and blame-laying on others. So it was a surprise that I didn't get a frosty reception from John.

'Yes, I'm happy to talk on the record,' he wrote back to me. 'My connection with Centrepoint is not exactly secret!'

In 1992, John Potter pleaded guilty to the assault of underage girls and spent four months in jail. He is the webmaster for MENZ, an anti-feminist support group for men fighting Family Court cases. It is dedicated to 'masculinist evolution' and has posts that refer to sexual abuse counselling as an 'extremist religious cult'.

His wife, Felicity Goodyear-Smith, is a professor at Auckland University's Medical School, the author of the controversial book *First Do No Harm: The Sexual Abuse Industry*, and founding president of COSA (Casualties of Sexual Allegations). From 1988 until 1990, while living on the outskirts of Centrepoint with her husband and next door to Bert, she was also the GP at Centrepoint for a time. She has always denied that she lived at Centrepoint. Since her loyalty to the Potter family was obvious, the former girls I spoke to didn't confide in her about the sexual abuse.

After the Centrepoint trust was reformed into the New Zealand Community Growth Trust, Felicity attempted to mobilise opposition to selling the multi-million-dollar property, instead wanting it gifted to the North Shore City Council for use as a park. Her attempts failed. If they hadn't, the trust would not have had funds to help Centrepoint survivors.

John is a father of three and still lives in Albany with Felicity, together with David Mendelssohn's former wife Susanne Brighouse.

I step into the Glade, the large enclosed grassy patch where hundreds of people once took ecstasy together for the first time, and where placentas and stillborn babies are buried. Each year, a group of women gather here to commemorate them. A marquee is set up for an upcoming yoga festival. John Potter, an avid cyclist, arrives by bike via a back track – he still knows the property well. He got married in the Glade twice.

John looks sporty, with a shaved head and an earring in one lobe. We sit down in the grass with birdsong around us. The former 'prince of the commune' is guarded but friendly, like a tour guide happy to fill any knowledge gaps.

'I was never really a Bert devotee,' he says. 'He certainly had a huge influence on me, and a lot of his values I still hold. I came here because he was my dad. And it was a neat place to live.'

Bert controlled every aspect of everyone's life, once giving a talk about how to wipe your bum on the toilet. But the fact that there were all these wonderful available women around kind of made it worthwhile for young John. He points behind him with a half-smile.

'If you walked up the track, chances are you'd stumble across a couple in a little clearing. Sex was everywhere.' But sexual abuse, he says, was 'such a tiny part of the Centrepoint story'. He's willing to talk to me about it; after all, he apologised at his father's funeral.

'I wanted to send a message to the people who feel like they were damaged by this place,' he explains.

'"Feel" that they were damaged?' I want to know, 'or *were* they damaged?'

He sounds confident. 'I'm sure they feel they're damaged.'

Children just copied what they saw adults doing, he says. 'There was the belief that young kids … well, basically you went along with their energy and encouraged them.'

They all thought they were overcoming hang-ups from Christian conservatism and were at the forefront of the sexual revolution, that it was just a matter of time before everybody else caught up. The idea of a division between adults and children just didn't exist in the first few years. It sounds similar to what Marianne and Brian told me; teenagers were treated as adults. John's wife brought one of them to him for a threesome to celebrate his birthday. Those kinds of arrangements were not uncommon. He looks uncomfortable when I bring this up.

'Obviously it was a gift horse that I should have looked in the mouth, and … I mean, at the time, I couldn't believe my luck. In a lot of ways, she would have been higher up the hierarchy than me.'

He says she was 'kind of a leader and a wonderful sexy teenager'. Going with a woman like her was like a reward for him.

I ask him whether he realised that the 'woman' was actually a child.

'I think to be honest I did,' he says, not acting so confident anymore. 'I mean, we're talking about half an hour, it's not like it was …'

He explains that she was beautiful and there under his nose, naked a lot of the time around the community.

'When I look back now, I think, how did I get in that situation? That's the stupid thing; it wasn't an important thing for me to have done. It would have been so easy just to say, "No, forget it, go away." And that would have been such a good decision for the rest of my life.'

I ask him about his other victim, Louise Winn. Just like Marianne, he claims he can't remember anything either.

'I'm not saying that at some point I might not have done something inappropriate with her, but it certainly wasn't enough that it registered in my memory.'

I'm stunned.

'She remembers,' I say. 'She took you to court.'

'Yeah, that was surprising. Because I'd seen her a few times before I was charged, and she seemed friendly and stuff, and I've racked my brain ... But having said that, there's lots of times I did inappropriate things with people under the age of consent.'

John pleaded guilty to both of his charges. There was no trial, only two lines on the charge sheet, and that was the end of it. He looks down. 'I feel unhappy that she's out there thinking that I'm some kind of monster. That seems really weird to me.'

I tell him that he didn't just break the law, but he broke some girls' souls. John is speechless for a moment, then chokes on his words.

'That is a little bit hard for me to accept. I mean, if they feel like that, then I guess I am responsible, and I feel bad about it, because my intention was exactly the opposite. I believed that we were doing something in their interests.'

He says Louise was not a happy girl at Centrepoint.

'You were one of the reasons,' I say. 'She tried to kill herself when she was eleven.'

He doesn't look at me but pulls at the grass. 'Yeah, and I guess I am sorry if I contributed to that.'

I tell him that Louise is still scared of coming to Albany because she could bump into him. Now he looks at me.

'I find that pretty surprising that I would be such an important part of her life, when I can barely remember. When we were charged, it was quite difficult feeling guilty for something that I didn't remember doing.'

My mind goes back to my conversations with Louise. She can still remember where the bed was, the candles, how high the shelves were. It's stuck in her head, forever.

I ask John if he wants to add anything, regarding Louise. His pause is long this time.

'No, not really. I'm surprised actually, by what you've told me, that I figure so importantly. And I feel bad that I did. There wasn't anything in it for me.'

He says he's not sexually attracted to young girls, never has been. 'It's not something that is part of my reality.'

After the conviction, John was in the protection wing at Mt Eden with all the other men from Centrepoint. He never encountered any hatred in prison. Within an hour of getting there, he saw his dad. John laughs a bit while he tells me that Bert managed to get the guards to open a few gates.

'He could come and give me a hug and catch up, which was really nice and reassuring.'

Bert Potter worked in the prison sewing shop and arranged for John to join him.

'He was very popular. That was the kind of guy he was – actually interested in people.'

There was only one incident at Mt Eden when the guards left Bert in a yard and a prisoner punched out his two front teeth. Louise had told me about this too. Something about it made me wonder whether it wasn't accidental on the part of the guards and one of his victims had a hand in it. Bert had a gap in his teeth for the rest of his life.

John was transferred to Ōhura, an old coal-mining camp. There wasn't even a fence around it, and he found it 'actually quite pleasant'.

'I look back on it as a bit of an adventure, really. We spent our days in the outdoors chopping down trees and cutting up firewood.'

It sounds like a holiday camp, or a working bee at Centrepoint. Not a lifelong prison like the one Louise still lives in. Would he like to live in a community again? John shakes his head and gets up from the grass.

'No. The idea of having to go to a meeting and get a unanimous decision before you can buy a two-dollar watch battery – I just don't ever want to go there again.'

Never wanting to go there again: how different that can look. After John has mounted his bike and left, I pull out one of Louise's poems I brought with me.

Disappearing into the night
Seen then unseen.
No one to answer to.
No one to tie myself to.
Just blissful loneliness.

You are not my life.
No one owns me – no one touches me.
I touch myself – do you hear me!

No one hurts me.
There's only me.
Only myself.
Only me.

That night, indigenous elders from Canada and New Mexico have arrived at the retreat centre to hold a sweat lodge. A Mohawk woman asks me what brings me here. She has never heard of Centrepoint. Through the night, I can hear their chanting from across the lawn, where they are holding their ceremony. At lunchtime the next day, the Mohawk woman approaches me again.

'I had a dream after our sweat lodge,' she says.

She saw an adolescent boy and girl behind a window, both in need of help. 'Their souls are stuck; they can't move on.'

She asks me if suicides have happened here. I confirm it. The Canadian takes my hands, holds my eyes with a firm gaze and invites me to come along to a sacred women's ceremony. 'The ancestors are calling us. This land needs healing.'

I don't have the heart to tell her that she is not the first one on that mission.

Later that afternoon I join the cohort on their 'walk of healing'. They smudge me first with a smouldering piece of wood and two eagle feathers. We each put a pinch of tobacco into the Native American pipe. The medicine woman who had the dream hands me a tiny piece of a root to leave in my mouth, 'for protection'. One woman carries a candle, another a massive crystal, and others take gemstones and incense sticks with them.

They are humming while our procession sets off across a little bridge into the forest. I'm right in the middle and feel out of place. When we pass the massive kahikatea tree that towers at the edge of Kawai Purapura, I stop and step closer. On impulse, I kick my jandals off and stretch my arms around the trunk of the solid giant. When I press my face into the bark, my feet on the forest floor, something inside me breaks. Lumps that have been sitting in my chest move up through my throat and come out as a wail.

When I let go of the tree, arms hold me from behind. A hand is gently stroking my spinning head. The medicine woman takes a drag from her pipe and puffs the smoke on my chest as a blessing for my heart. The other women watch in silence. Words pour out of me. I tell them about a girl who once lived here in a caravan, lonely and scared. When she needed to hide, she went into the bush right behind us. It protected her. She still goes and hugs trees. Or sways with them in the wind to stop her fear.

We all thank the tree, then break into a song. A clumsy kererū (wood pigeon) lands in the branches above us with a crash and everyone laughs.

The women invite me back with them for fresh cake. In the dining room, where volunteers are wiping off the wooden tables and watering pot plants, I sit down to check my email.

While I was out by the trees, Len Oakes wrote to me from Melbourne.

'Dear Anke,' he says. 'I am prepared to seriously consider your wish that I "stand in front of those victims and say what needs to finally be said".'

I give Louise a call to tell her about the email and the ceremony. But she is not moved at all.

'There's no way you can heal that place when there are actual people like me who have a memory.' She almost snorts. 'It's like a toilet, you know? You can flush it, but there's still shit going in.'

On my last morning, I climb up a hill to an elevated clearing with a wooden bench. Below me is the big blue swimming pool and faded green roofs of the retreat centre, an oasis of tranquillity to which so many people have dedicated their lives. Louise often sat up here on this lookout. She read books and fantasised about being a sniper. Someone who could take the men out down there, one by one. Or send a flaming arrow into the gas tank. *Boom* – the whole place gone.

When I walk back down, I pass an honesty box with free-range eggs for six dollars a dozen. The handwritten sign says: 'What goes around, comes around. The universe is always watching. Namaste.'

PART 2

Toxic Tantra

Chapter 9

My memories of Cologne, the West German city where I grew up, are dotted with the colours of sunset. In the '80s, many of the twenty-to-thirty-somethings in the hip quarters wore only red, pink and orange. They were sannyasins: followers of Bhagwan Shree Rajneesh, meaning 'Holy Glorious Lord of Darkness', the immensely influential pop-culture guru who later rebranded himself as Osho. The enigmatic Indian professor of philosophy attracted hundreds of thousands of Westerners to his ashram in Pune, including many Kiwis, but predominantly Germans. Two thirds had college degrees, good incomes and highbrow careers; more than half of them were women. Cologne was their European headquarters.

In my final school year, I often danced at the squeaky clean Zorba the Buddha discotheque. The attractive folk who ran it had an air of friendly aloofness and all seemed to vibe off each other. Their official motto was the three 'L's – love, life, and laughter – plus two unofficial 'M's: materialism and mating. The money from their hospitality businesses went straight to Pune.

To me, the sannyasins were like a cross between yogis and ravers. Seven of them flatted in the apartment above. Early in the morning, I could hear them jumping up and down doing Dynamic Meditation, a practice as essential to

Oshoism as the Holy Communion to Catholics. I admired their courage to step out of the mainstream for something that enriched their lives, but since I was into anti-nuclear protests, feminism and social justice, their apolitical self-centred hedonism didn't appeal to me much. Their teacher, born in one of the poorest countries in the world, had been very clear on not wasting time on the road to enlightenment with helping the disadvantaged. This transcendent capitalism equally fascinated and repulsed me. I also questioned how anyone from my country, which had been led into fascism and genocide by a captivating leader, could blindly follow a guru who paraded his 93 Rolls-Royces in front of his ecstatic devotees, handed them new names and made them wear a locket with his photo on a necklace (or mala). All this conformity for more fun and freedom? I didn't get it.

To his countless fans, including celebrities like Lady Gaga, Osho is still a spiritual revolutionary with a powerful message of radical awakening – both enlightened mystic and intellectual agent provocateur. His diamond watches and luxury cars were all just meant to be a big joke about consumerism by a non-white genius to provoke the West and demonstrate their obsession with wealth.

Since a massive industry continues to spread Osho's words and merchandise without a trace of critical evaluation, it's worth remembering that the godman was also a clever mass seducer and exploitative conman who made homophobic, sexist and anti-Semitic statements in his hundreds of extemporaneous talks that were translated into more than 60 languages.

He was openly against having children – not because of climate issues and overpopulation, but because in his view families hindered personal growth. Young followers were pressured to have abortions and sterilisations. The kids who grew up in his ashram or other centres that had sprung up around the world were separated from their parents as early as five years old. Non-attachment was not just the highest form of love for adults but also for parents. Many sannyasins' children later reported neglect, early sexualisation and sexual abuse. Some didn't make it through adulthood because of drugs and suicide.

In 1981, Osho – who was still Bhagwan then – left his Indian enclave for America. Over five years, coral-clad cult members transformed a desert in Oregon into a boom town, happily working up to twelve hours daily without pay. The vibrant oasis called Rajneeshpuram had its own airline, hotel, artificial lake and paramilitary forces. Rising aggression between the redneck locals in neighbouring Antelope and the equally paranoid members on the ranch climaxed in heavy armoury, a mass biological poisoning attack, drugging homeless people and plots for murder, all secretly masterminded by Osho's former secretary Ma Anand Sheela. The 'Goebbels to the guru', as some called her, went to jail while her master publicly burned her books and robes and protested his innocence. Osho was arrested for visa violations and held in prison – according to the official organ *Osho Times*, a 'US government conspiracy from the White House on down'. He was deported with a half-million-dollar fine and finally made it back to Pune after an odyssey around the world in his private jet. He died in his ashram in 1990.

Despite his former fights with Indian authorities and the trail of destruction in America, Osho has been rehabilitated, posthumously, as a religious authority in his birth country where the *Hindustan Times* regularly ran his quotes, 'Osho says'. The former ashram has since been turned into an upmarket meditation retreat. It is also popular with wealthy Indians who only pay half price to enter.

After twenty years of marriage, my husband and I renew our vows in a small ceremony with friends. Our second honeymoon is a month-long trip to India. In 2017, a year before the Netflix series *Wild Wild Country* goes to air, we book the weeklong Living In programme at the Osho International Meditation Resort (OIMR). We want to check out where the cathartic therapies and the holistic approach to sexuality in the neo-tantra field originated from.

It's also the place that inspired Bert Potter – but is the Indian guru to blame for that? Some good people who benefitted from their time with Osho or his books had become our friends in the past few years. I want to look deeper than just the sex and crime surface I've absorbed over the decades. Because I'm still recovering from the Centrepoint research, and also reeling from the fallout after another cult exposé, I'm going as a tourist rather than a journalist. Maybe I missed something back in Cologne. It's time to find out.

The motor rickshaw drops us off at a police checkpoint in a leafy, quiet street in Koregaon Park, the richest part of the noisy, busy city of Pune, three hours by car from Mumbai. We find ourselves in front of an enormous black wall with a security gate – the Iron Curtain to the OIMR. Seven years ago, there was a deadly bomb attack that killed eighteen people at the popular German bakery just around the corner. The café is still frequented by sannyasins.

While I put my bags on the conveyor belt, I feel equally apprehensive and adventurous. Am I going to dive deeper into my soul or into a reformed cult masking as a business? 'Life begins where fear ends' is one of Osho's numerous quotes, now popular on Pinterest and Instagram. I decide to follow those words for now.

Once inside the gates, shiny cool black surrounds us there too. The parklike compound is quiet, clean, empty and very Zen. Water trickles down one of the imposing marble walls, tall trees offer shadowy resting places. I cannot spot a picture of the dark-eyed bearded sage with his signature tea-cosy cap anywhere. But everyone on this side of the wall, apart from the local cleaning and service staff, is dressed in long maroon robes. We are escorted to the resort shop where we must buy similar gowns, plus a white one that looks like a nightie and is only for the evening talk. Even the day visitors are required to make these purchases.

To extract as much money as possible from the seekers is fully in tune with Osho, who once said: 'Let me look after the rich.'

The formalities, such as buying coupons for meals and getting a security ID pass, are complicated. At least we don't have to take HIV tests anymore – the Indian government now considers this discrimination. But Indian men are required to sit through a prep talk that basically tells them not to treat Western women in the resort like prey. For this, the OIMR has been called 'racist' by angry reviewers on Tripadvisor.

Our group gets a short intro to Dynamic Meditation and watches compulsory videos explaining the lay of the land. To loosen things up and get us into a more cheerful mode, we each have to dance to a song from our country. It's 'Poi E' for us from New Zealand and 'Gangnam Style' for a Korean woman, who looks uncomfortable while she dances. Most in our group are from Japan.

It takes half a day before us new arrivals have gone through all the instructions, currency exchange, compulsory shopping and paperwork. The bureaucracy is tiring and the list of restrictions impressive. If we sneeze or cough in the meditation hall, we will be thrown out. Ditto if we wear the wrong colour at the restaurant. Hygiene is super strict and taking photos or wearing perfume is not allowed. A lot of 'verboten', even for a German.

The Multiversity is the faculty for all the New Age therapy. With offerings from astrology to family constellation to rebirthing, it's like an esoteric supermarket. 'Mystic Rose' is a 21-day-long course where in the first week you only laugh, in the second you only cry, and in the third you're completely silent. I pick and click from a screen, feeling the pressure to optimise my self-exploration, while my husband is not too fazed by all the bizarreness but instead annoyed by my restless mood.

When I have my one-on-one check-in with an admin who is helping us to choose the right session from the therapy hodgepodge, I'm so irritated that I swallow back tears.

'I might need help with my anger and control issues,' I admit to her. The stressful arrival has taken me far away from the peace and serenity I'd been hoping to find.

The guest house, where we each have a single room as part of our package, looks more like a private hospital or seminar hotel, with a concierge in a white shirt and tie. All the staff apart from the office workers and facilitators are locals, but the accommodation could not feel any less Indian. While we check in, we can hear the loud drums and whistles of a wedding party parading through town outside our walls – a stark contrast to the lifeless building with its cool marble floors. Nothing hints at a sex cult anymore. According to ex-disciples, some group sessions in Pune when it was still Poona were orgies that lasted over days.

Tantra courses have become rare at the OIMR these days and are no different to those in the West. Indian guests are not welcome at any of them. Back in the day, group leaders – called the 'pussy pool' – would often pick out which woman they wanted after a group, lock the room, and get it on with her. The sexism was tremendous, even though most departments were run by women and Osho claimed he was liberating them.

Today, there are no hammocks or cuddle zones, not even sun loungers in the swimming area to chill out on. The gym has a state-of-the-art sauna with separate quarters for men and women. If the loose image of the wild old days is attracting libidinous guests, then they must be disappointed by the aseptic environment. I have not seen any long hugs or even hand-holding anywhere. To use the pool, I first have to buy overpriced maroon togs and pay another steep fee every time I want a quick dip. The robotic staff, the ridiculous regulations, the obsession with cleanliness and the overt monetising of every step has the opposite effect of relaxation for me.

'Only the laundry service is free in this cashram,' I bitch to my husband while he quickly retreats towards his monastic room. I can feel cabin fever coming on.

At 6.40 p.m., not a minute later, we must arrive dressed in white at the Osho auditorium – or we have to remain inside our rooms. A security guard reminds us that we can't wander around the grounds either.

It looks straight out of a trippy sci-fi movie or *The Handmaid's Tale* series when one nightie wearer after another floats up the black stone stairs in the dusk towards a gigantic pyramid-shaped auditorium. The building was Osho's own architectural vision.

We're patted down by security first before, in silence, we can join the devotees. The Zen temple is cool inside and dimly lit, like a monstrous UFO that has picked us earthlings up. A helper beams at me while I unroll my mat and proclaims, 'Yes, you've made it now!' It gets more surreal once we sit down. The upbeat jazzy music suddenly stops, everyone raises their arms and shouts 'Osho!' This ritual repeats a few times. The master himself appears on a large screen and speaks to us from a video recording, sharp and sophisticated but hard to understand because of his accent. Something sticks from the lecture: 'If you will it, you cannot enjoy it. If you enjoy it, you don't have to will it.' It might as well be this week's motto for me.

Osho always ends with jokes. Everyone in the hall is cackling along, apart from someone who is being sent outside because he coughed. The man escorting the rule-breaker to the door is tall and slim, with striking snow-white hair. He is unmistakably Amrito, commonly named Dr John Andrews, who was Dr George Meredith or Swami Devaraj earlier in his sannyas career. The multi-named bearded Englishman in his seventies is Osho's former personal physician, which makes him an eminence in this fiefdom. Sheela, the infamous ego-tripping lieutenant, had plotted to kill him with a buttock injection back at the ranch in Oregon to get him out of her guru's way. She claimed that Amrito got Osho addicted to drugs and planned to euthanise him. Watching him up close, elegantly exercising his power, feels like being on a film set for a cult thriller sequel where historical characters are suddenly coming to life.

Dynamic Meditation – one of the pillars of Osho's teachings – starts at 6 a.m. in the auditorium: puffing through the nose, cathartic screaming, shouting 'hoo hoo' while jumping up and down, and then freestyle dancing, all at ten-minute intervals. The mandatory maroon blindfolds for this exercise can also be bought at the shop.

Afterwards there's yoga in the morning sunshine outside, done in our long robes, no leggings allowed. I'm getting more and more rebellious and do a few clandestine laps in the pool without paying the extra fee. It helps my sanity. The 'Zennis' court – tennis combined with meditation – is empty, the large canteen closed. A tiny glass of wine costs around twelve dollars. Abstinence will come easy at this price.

My husband wants to try the jacuzzi and needs to pay for it at the spa, where they hand him a kimono, slippers and a locker key. He didn't bring the right vouchers along so has to traipse back through the gates and across the road to the guest house on the other side of the compound.

'I think I need a walk outside,' he says, sounding as frustrated as me the day before. 'No more meditation with security checks please!'

We muse whether this is all deliberate – just like the Rolls-Royces were allegedly only there to hold up a mirror to Osho's critics. Maybe these rules are meant to trigger us and bring up all our 'stuff' so that we can then spend more money to get it out of our system?

'You have to hand it to these guys,' says my husband. 'They're smart.'

A grey, shaggy-haired sannyasin with a missing tooth sits in the smokers' corner as a lone representative of a hippie past. 'The old party spirit has gone,' the Swiss man confides. 'We used to cook together, clean and plant stuff – we were a community. Now it's all commerce instead of a real commune.'

He sounds sentimental as he describes how the monkeys raced over the tin roof when they all listened to Osho's recorded talks, and how they then fell into each other's arms and beds. It was 'lively and crazy' – such a different time and place. He arrived in 1993, 'after Osho left his body', and stayed for seven years until everything was transformed to the current model in 2000 – which he blames on 'those bastards in Delhi or Mumbai who hated Osho and made him pay tax'.

The Swiss hippie still comes to the resort once a year to 'be with Osho', hoping to meet equally nostalgic friends who might show up. Meanwhile, he spends his days in the air-conditioned office of the OIMR headquarters on the compound where he looks after the online shopping website. Work without pay for a multi-million-dollar imperium? He shrugs his shoulders and rolls himself another cigarette from his tobacco pouch.

'People here don't really answer your questions,' he says with an evasive smile that means goodbye.

Chapter 10

The first therapy I get as part of my Living In programme sounds innocuous: 'Breathing'. I follow the therapist in a black Zen suit with white sash down to the catacombs where he leads me to a windowless cellar room with padded walls the colour of urine. Images from the former encounter therapy groups that took place down here during Osho's days pop into my mind. In those confrontational weeklong sessions, the participants let off steam in the most explosive ways. Some ended with broken bones; some were raped. While the therapist turns on the air-conditioner, I wonder what monstrosities these walls have seen.

The therapist sits opposite me and asks me how I feel about my parents, my partner, and my work, and where that 'manifests' in my body. I point at my throat and tell him about the pressure I feel there when I'm vulnerable, especially when trying to speak my truth.

'You will not get the love and be seen by doing the masculine things,' is his advice. 'It is your feminine side that will give you all that, without you having to achieve. If you try to get it from the outside, it will never satisfy you.'

Then the practical part starts. After jogging on the spot to activate my energy, I lie down on a yellow sheet and breathe in a specific rhythm deep into my chest. While my head starts spinning, the therapist presses forcefully on acupressure points on my body to release my emotional blockages. This is called 'de-armouring' and is viewed critically by many trauma therapists – a short-cut that can be retraumatising. For me, it's extremely painful but does the job. I scream, twitch, slap my hands on the floor and stomp my feet in a release of rage. At the height of the catharsis, while my body buckles in resistance and then collapses in surrender, it feels as if a beam of energy penetrates me from above. I shiver and sigh and then soften. The therapist pats my arm and tells me to rest. After ten minutes, he helps me to get up to take some careful steps around the room.

'Gentle, gentle,' he soothes.

I'm in an altered state, like a chrysalis that turned into a butterfly and is using its wings for the first time. I thank my torturer with a hug and then drift up the steps towards the sunlight, feeling light and joyful. For an hour I wander dreamily through the Zen garden where I brush against plants and marvel at peacocks and red dragonflies. Everything around me is so exquisite and sensual. I made the shift. The haven in Absurdistan which I had secretly dubbed *Animal Farm* has turned into a beautiful place after all. Something is working.

My blissful state of peace is over once I'm inside the UFO pyramid again. Because it's so chilly in the auditorium that evening, I have put on a light-grey silk dress under my white robe. Not quite subtle enough though. One of the guards taps me on the shoulder. He wants me to go outside and take off the dress underneath immediately.

'Wrong colour. It's distracting,' he tells me with a stern face.

At least he doesn't hit me with a Zen stick.

Osho's video talk that night is about women: how they're way ahead of men because they have more love and operate more from the heart than the intellect. Women can become enlightened quicker while men can become Alexander the Great. The audience laughs, in the hall and on the recording, but Osho the Great has lost me from there. The women's movement, he says, is led by 'stupid women'. Because what we really want, in his view, is just a nice house with a pool. I wish we could end the show with a healthy debate about Osho's anti-feminism, but there's no such thing on offer. Critical discourse is not part of the Multiversity curriculum. Love it or leave it is the only way.

The next day I meet another renegade, a young British lad with a diamond stud in his nostril. He wants to try Primal Deconditioning, a Freudian-based therapy, but is not allowed to participate because his dad is of Indian origin.

'Osho said that it takes three generations before Asians can get rid of the social conditioning around their parents,' he tells me with a shrug, repeating what he was told by the management.

I can feel his disappointment bordering on humiliation.

'I'm as British as it gets!' he insists, slightly worked up now. 'My dad was born in the UK; my mum is British. I have zero Indian conditioning. But they treat you different here with darker skin.'

Instead of staying for an extra week he now contemplates getting stoned in Goa instead. We head to the outdoor disco to shake it all off. Every day before lunch, a DJ plays in the Buddha Grove. Osho said that if you must decide between celebration and meditation, you should always go for celebration. That sounds like a good option. My husband has just finished a tai chi class and joins us. We jump and twitch around to cheesy Bollywood pop, '50s rock and '80s disco hits. A small man with a bucket hat twirls on the dance floor like a dervish. It's called Sufi Whirling and offered as a meditation class this afternoon, which I join.

Sufism is a mystical form of early Islam and the poet Rumi its most famous artist, whose words I can relate to. But I never knew what whirling has to do with it all. The instructions are simple: point your right arm up and your left one down, focus on your upper hand and start turning around on the spot against the clock. After five minutes of spinning, I feel an ecstatic high. Fantastic – I can finally let go of all my thoughts! After fifteen minutes I feel dizzy. Then nauseous. After half an hour, I almost collapse and stagger out of the hall. Because there are no places to lie down anywhere in this impeccable institution, I sink into the manicured lawn. My husband finds me there after the session; he is on an ecstatic whirling high.

'Best thing so far!' he claims, while I'm too queasy to attend the evening talk in the pyramid.

My first bout of sickness in India hasn't come from food poisoning but from meditation.

Chronic stress relief is my next therapy session, led by an empathic German woman. I learn how to make my legs shake while lying on my back, to release old trauma. The tremor leads to tears that lead to calm. I'm curled up like a foetus under a blanket while the practitioner speaks soothing words. She is one of thousands of sannyasins who offer body–mind treatments around the world. I can easily embrace this side of the Oshoverse.

Straight after my session, I find a note in my room to come to the Living In office. Which rule did I break? Did someone spot me doing my secret laps in the pool? Do I have to swap my yellow day pack for a maroon one because it upsets the monochrome colour code? Or did the torture therapist pass on to management that I'm a snooping journalist and will they kick me out?

My paranoia is unjustified. A chirpy Japanese volunteer just gives me another introduction to the many things on offer. They really don't want me to miss out.

I opt for the classic Sitting Meditation in Osho's former residence, the Lao Tzu house. It's half museum, half mausoleum, with one of the master's beige Rolls-Royces displayed at the entrance without a trace of irony. As at the Taj Mahal, everyone is required to put on white socks so as not to damage the fine marble floor inside.

I walk through the guru's former library, which is filled with thousands of books ranging from Carlos Castaneda to Carl Jung. The next room with mirror walls has Osho's dentist chair on display. The sanctuary where we're going to do a 'no mind' meditation – first speaking in gibberish, then sitting in silence – is a temple hall in gold and white marble, all pomp, magic and glory of a bygone cult era. A mirrored platform holds the guru's ashes. Osho only spent one night in his palatial sanctuary. His shrine bears the inscription: 'Never born, Never died. Only Visited this Planet Earth.'

Osho died mysteriously on 19 January 1990 at the age of 58. According to his loyalists, the cause of death was a creeping poison: thallium, fed to him secretly during his week in a US prison. The death certificate states a cardiac arrest. Osho was hastily cremated and didn't leave any last records or instructions in writing. Twenty-three years later a will appeared, likely false, that is still in the Indian courts.

A senior journalist from Pune for years investigated the contradictions and conspiracies surrounding the rapid passing of the Bhagwan and concluded that they point towards either foul play by his entourage, suicide or euthanasia. I manage to find a Wi-Fi spot and contact Abhay Vaidya, the author of *Who killed Osho*, to read his just-released book – and then feel like a traitor who secretly ordered contraband when Amrito crosses my path on my way to the café. He was with Osho at the time of his death and didn't get him any intensive medical care, supposedly to respect his master's wishes. The journalist's research puts him under suspicion, too.

I soon get to meet another figurehead. Raj – bald head, broad body, constant Buddha smile – is the tai chi teacher and belongs to the inner circle of the Osho imperium. The 64-year-old Canadian, his brother, and doctor Amrito run things in Pune, which he plays down with a laugh when we sit down for a coffee outside the Multiversity. He lets me record our conversation. In his earlier life as D'Arcy O'Byrne he was a lawyer.

'It was a very stressful existence, competitive, working with people who were not aware, not even alive at all. They built a nice prison – nice car, nice TV, nice wife, nice children,' says Raj and points around us. 'The nice thing here is that I'm living with people who want to wake up. They are living right on the edge.'

When he arrived in Rajneeshpuram in Oregon in 1984, he was 'the most unhappy person compared to all the five thousand others'. Clearly something very special was happening there. He stayed for a week, then quit his job, returned to live at the ranch and never looked back.

His team has just won a lengthy trademark case at the European Court for the OIF, the Osho International Foundation in Switzerland. Amrito is a vice-chair. Brand Osho is now protected, from every meditation on YouTube to the signature green boxes of tissues for all the snot and tears in the padded cells. This is a milestone victory after they lost a ten-year court battle with their rival OFI (Osho Friends International) in 2009. Monty Python's *Life of Brian* comes to mind where two liberation movements with almost identical names, the Judean People's Front and the People's Front of Judea, are feuding. But for Osho's devotees, it's not a joke. There are deep rifts between disgruntled sannyasin factions from Europe to Delhi who feel they have been pushed over by the management in Pune. They accuse the OIF of being money hungry and dictatorial. The keepers of the Holy Grail on the other hand see themselves as purists who hold secure Osho's teachings and estate.

'He asked us to keep it twenty-four-carat gold,' says Raj and points around us again. 'Look at this place, it's beautiful, it's stunningly clean. From the outside, it looks like a cult. But when you walk in, this is like the anti-cult.' I've heard this term before – from groups that have come under attack and claim that their work is in fact the best protection against falling into a cult.

No one spoke up against organised religion more than Osho, he claims. Had they kept the ashram going, then everyone coming here would be bowing down to the old people who had met the master 'in the body'. Not what Osho wanted.

'Totally the opposite here. Go to any ashram in India and all you're gonna see is foot touching. Doesn't exist here. Not even pictures. You walk into a church, there is Jesus on the cross everywhere. Not here.'

But why all the rules, the uni-coloured gowns then?

'This is not for everybody,' he explains. 'Osho set up some barriers. So don't come if you're not ready. If you cannot drop your street clothes for a day and wear a robe, then you're not ready.'

In his view the guests are not here to escape the world. They realise that they have everything, but they're not happy.

'So they start searching. They all have this space of divine discontent.'

We are briefly interrupted by a new arrival, an elegant older lady with a large maroon sunhat and expensive jewellery and, according to Raj, one of the richest women in Brazil. She disappears towards one of the luxury suites. Those are left over from way back and can be leased for a lifetime, with your own whirlpool in the bedroom. That leads us straight to the wild old days. Does Raj miss them?

'No, please,' he laughs, 'absolutely not! But it was a beautiful experiment.'

Osho was so deeply misunderstood as a 'sex guru' because he wrote a book titled *From Sex to Superconsciousness*.

'People went crazy on this – how can a godman talk about a vagina and a penis? – but the whole book is about consciousness.' He chuckles. 'If you're repressed, you're only gonna see sex in this book.'

For him, the real book of tantra is *The Book of Secrets* with 108 meditations, only three of which involve sex.

'It's about energy. It's about expansion. Real tantra is about meditation. Red tantra, white tantra – look, they're just making shit up as they go. It's just pure business out there.'

If tantra as it's taught at the OIMR today is not about sex, then it makes even less sense to me why supposedly repressed or predatory Indians are not allowed to participate. I mention the young British guy who was turned away from the Primal course.

'You think you're so smart,' says Raj, his voice turning colder. 'The guy is Indian. Believe me. He really thinks he knows more than Osho. And I know from direct experience that is not true. It's not prejudice. We're not here to save them. You're just a dirty-minded journalist and coming from the mind again.'

His smile switches back on, but the vibe has changed. We still have to talk about what went down in Rajneeshpuram.

'They painted Osho with that,' he says, flicking his hand. 'He was completely railroaded. These people' – he means Sheela and her crew – 'all got caught up in something really dark.'

He tells me in a scathing tone that he doesn't care about the past but is more interested in having amazing experiences through meditation, 'and not in what happened in 1984'. I ask him why there is a bookshop full of Osho's publications in the resort but nothing anywhere that explains the darkest part of the Rajneeshees' history. Raj sounds exasperated now and rolls his eyes.

'Look, most people don't care what happened – they were not even born then. The only person who has asked me this in twenty years is you!'

Three and a half million of Osho's books are sold a year, and even young Hollywood hipsters like Will Smith's children have been spotted with them – so, according to Raj, how can I not get it?

He sends me off with an Osho quote to show me where to focus: 'I'm pointing to the moon. Don't get lost on my finger.'

On day six I get caught by a security guard at last while doing my clandestine laps for free in the pool. She beckons me and shouts: 'You have to come out of the water NOW!'

I'm glad I'm not being frogmarched to the changing room.

Staff in light-blue uniforms, with stoic faces and extended mops that must be 10 metres long, are cleaning the shining black wall of the Multiversity. Friday night is for 'taking sannyas' – the induction for those who are going to live their life with Osho. These days you are allowed to choose your spiritual Indian name yourself. We can join the ceremony.

The newbies sit on cushions on the dance floor, sprinkled by colourful laser lights. The house band with flute and guitar plays cheesy tunes, Osho speaks from a recording, everyone gets emotional, and at the end of the rite the freshly baptised all dance together. A German woman who is a regular at the resort shakes her head in disbelief and whispers to me over the music that this is nothing like what they used to have in the old days. For her it's a disappointingly poor imitation. For me it's just comical.

By now I take in everything around me with amused acceptance. During Dynamic Meditation the next morning, I'm silly and giggly instead of yelling out repressed hurt. My last session for the week is a 'bliss massage' from head to toe, which leaves me almost levitating. I've even made peace with putting on an overpriced gown that I will only ever wear to a dress-up party again – much easier than choosing an outfit every morning. At midday I'm dancing happily in the sunshine. 'Go for broke!' says a middle-aged French guy who works in international finance, beaming at me while he lets loose.

I don't skip the evening talk this time, but instead of shouting 'Osho!' in a chorus when the music stops, I just shout my own name. Such fun. Either the lewd jokes of the immortalised master are improving, or my mood is. In either case, I'm laughing more.

We run into Raj at our last breakfast.

'It's a special once-in-a-lifetime experience here!' the mighty tai chi teacher declares with his Buddha smile switched on, misreading my relief that we're finally packing up. 'The work speaks for itself. It's only about freedom.'

Our ID pass expires at 9 a.m.; we need to rush off. Three minutes after checking out, I realise that I've left my yoga mat on the inside and now have difficulty retrieving it from the black fortress. Stern looks from the gatekeepers serve as a farewell when I pass them for the very last time. I'm craving a free hammock on a beach after this once-in-a-lifetime experience. But my new maroon bikini was a good spend.

Chapter 11

When I was twenty, I did a journalism internship in Los Angeles. One night, still new to the big city, I was mugged in a back alley on my way to my car. My attackers – six or seven men – strangled me, pushed me to the ground, felt me up and threatened to rape me while they stood over me. Since that didn't happen in the end, I considered myself lucky: only my tights were ripped, my purse gone, and the car tyres slashed. I didn't get any counselling back then but I took up martial arts. The gang attack became one of my LA war stories, nothing that I dwelled on, eventually forgotten.

When the #MeToo movement started, it never occurred to me to post the hashtag myself. Only in 2018, when a comedian was raped and murdered in a Melbourne park as she walked home, did the floodgates open inside me. It took me 33 years to realise that I was a survivor of sexual violence.

The #MeToo movement also kicks off a golden era of cult revelations. Like the film industry before it, the wellness and woo world finally comes under scrutiny. With celebrities and powerful moguls like Harvey Weinstein called out over their sexual assaults, #MeToo finally catches up with spiritual leaders.

The head of Shambhala International, one of the largest Western Buddhist organisations with meditation centres in over 30 countries, has to step down after a report that he had spent years sexually abusing and exploiting some of his most devoted followers.

Similar allegations about Rigpa, another Buddhist group, emerge. The famous Brazilian faith healer John of God, a favourite with Oprah Winfrey, also falls from grace as a fraud and sex pest. Women break their silence about K. Pattabhi Jois, the deceased founder of ashtanga yoga. A Czech court sentences Jaroslav Dobeš, dubbed Guru Jára, to seven years imprisonment for raping six women during seminars at his esoteric school. *The New York Times* breaks the story about Keith Raniere's cult NXIVM, where women were branded with hot irons. OneTaste, the exploitative personal development enterprise selling Orgasmic Meditation (or OM), implodes.

Cults have entered the mainstream. Millions of people who'd never before heard of any of these groups, teachers or gurus watch the six-part Netflix documentary *Wild Wild Country* about Bhagwan Shree Rajneesh. Though the documentary focuses on the crime saga instead of the psychological damage suffered by followers and gives more talking time to still-enamoured top dogs than victims' voices from the inside, it's still an incredible eye-opener for uninitiated viewers. But the stories told on Netflix are just entertainment; bringing toxic group dynamics to light can be a taxing, lonely mission.

For the last year, I've been following the work of American Be Scofield, a travelling gonzo journalist in her late thirties who churns out cult exposés, which she publishes online. She blows the cover of false prophets, around the world, unmasking abuse in spiritual disguise. Be, a trans woman, draws both the ire and admiration of many; she's loathed, feared, attacked and heralded for fighting justice in her own way. Her opponents accuse her of sensationalism, fraud, fake news. Some call her work a witch hunt.

But while Be's critics discredit her for ignoring media protocol, she has a worldwide network of sources and the support of cult experts and survivor networks who see her as a trailblazer. No one else has her reach on the internet, enabling her to shine a light into dark corners.

Some of the culprits on her radar are narcissistic modern women with huge influence. In 2018, Be went after New Age sensation Teal Swan, branding her the 'Gucci Guru' and 'a posh prophet in killer heels'. Teal Swan, claims she was satanically abused as a child, can astral travel as an alien and has x-ray vision. She has a YouTube channel with more than a million subscribers. She's dubbed her devoted followers the 'Teal Tribe', a fervent cyber-congregation where critical voices get expelled. Teal has no psychological qualifications but she claims to be able to heal repressed traumatic memories. Some of her blunt comments come across as encouraging suicide – she calls death a 'reset button'. She has been accused of inciting some of her followers' suicides. After Be revealed what she calls Teal's 'quest for global domination', the guru ended up on the front page of the *Daily Mail* and was subsequently dropped from the Hay House World Summit, a global symposium for inspirational speakers, the same year.

To say that Be is controversial is an understatement. She is also elusive. The anti-cult superhero of the digital age has never before given an interview, so I'm delighted when she grants me one. Since I started writing in-depth about Centrepoint in 2015, I've found myself in a niche. Cult reporting is under-represented in the media, and unlike other areas such as sports coverage or movie reviews, it's not usually undertaken by anyone specialised in that field. There's an instant bond between writers circling the same drain – although I'm still a novice and, unlike Be, only publish in established news outlets.

Our first meeting is online, with me in New Zealand looking at Be on the screen in a dimly lit wooden cabin, somewhere on the East Coast of the United States. She won't say where, exactly, but it looks rural and peaceful. Be is lying on the bed, wearing a singlet, with her trademark scarf wrapped around her head. She's munching on blue corn chips from a bag.

She has so far pulled a dozen people in the spiritual and self-help scene from their fake thrones. Not because she hates the world of woo, but as someone practising astrology and reiki, she understands it more than most.

'I'm into spirituality – and I'm willing to stand up and fight against those harming people,' she tells me.

The 'guru hunter' – a term Be hates because 'not all gurus are bad or do harm' – has her own cult history. In 2006, she was a cultural anthropology student at San Francisco's California Institute of Integral Studies (CIIS), a hothouse for progressive academia and the human potential movement. There, she fell under the spell of two professors who were systematically controlling and abusing their students, yelling at them, creating paranoia, telling them they were part of 'the revolution'. When Be realised the extent of her teachers' manipulation and mental abuse, all under the guise of social justice, everything unravelled. It culminated in a night of her screaming in pain from the deep betrayal. For years after, she suffered PTSD. The professors were eventually fired for creating a cult-like environment, exploiting students and causing serious dysfunction. Be's post-escape writings kept the pressure on the faculty.

Despite the disturbing experience, Be stayed on the spiritual path, attending an interfaith Unitarian Universalist seminary from 2008 where she specialised in Martin Luther King's teachings. But instead of becoming a minister, her experience in San Francisco led her to explore social issues and abuse in alternative movements. She started the website Decolonizing Yoga, which bridged social justice with spirituality and exposed oppression within yoga.

In 2017, Be spent a month undercover in Arizona chasing Bentinho Massaro. She dubbed him the 'Tech Bro Guru' thanks to his mix of cosmic appeal and a slick web presence promising self-actualisation and enlightenment – 'Steve Jobs meets Jim Jones'. It was pure chance – or mysterious intervention, according to Be, because her astrologer sent her there – that she landed in Sedona in 2017. The town was full of psychics, healers, UFO-spotters and crystal shops – the perfect place for Massaro to create a twenty-first-century cult. Once Be arrived, it didn't take long for her to hear of the spiritual hedonist with a penchant for cigars, fine whisky, exotic retreats and multiple girlfriends.

Massaro's masterstroke was using technology to attract young followers. His devotees were soon everywhere, craving a live-in community centred around him, believing he could control the weather with his mind and was sent here on a mission to save the planet – an awakened being more evolved than Jesus. Massaro was looking for land to buy.

To infiltrate his expanding emporium, Be had to use an alias, so 'Shakti Hunter' was born. With her background in web design and marketing, she made the perfect volunteer. It didn't take long before a former staff member told her she feared Massaro was setting people up for a mass suicide, calling it 'The Harvest'. A possible repeat of the 1978

Jonestown massacre – an intentional civilian mass killing with 909 dead – lent Be's undercover mission more urgency.

But it was intense spending weeks embedded under a false identity, gathering information in secret, putting it together every night. She learned about the inner workings of the organisation, which no one had outed as a cult before: all the money it made while most didn't get paid, and all the outlandish things Massaro's devotees believed about the pint-sized megalomaniac.

She published her article in December 2017 on the blog platform *Medium* where it soon gathered more than 200,000 views. The attention didn't end there. She says she's never received 'so much blind hatred from thousands of people whom I've never had a dialogue with'. Nine days after the story broke, one of the cult's followers committed suicide. Bentinho Massaro shut down his Sedona operations and went into hiding with his girlfriends. Since then, former lovers and supporters have spoken out about him on podcasts and in magazines like *Rolling Stone*, revealing a crazy reign of financial and sexual exploitation.

'His propaganda still outweighs my warning,' says Be.

She says her work to expose cult leaders doesn't rely on legal checks, police records or affidavits, but on the voices of the victims themselves. 'If I have seventeen testimonials against you, then I'm sorry. What you're getting is not going to jail,' she says.

Defamation claims usually don't bother her. She shrugs her shoulders. 'Who's going to find me to serve me papers? I move around.'

The day after our interview, Be drives up the East Coast of the United States to a neo-tantra festival. It's a new field she's curious about, and sceptical of. I know the feeling.

'No gurus here,' she reports back to me on the weekend. 'Great people.'

That night, she receives an energy healing session. Within minutes, she feels a current move through her, like a serpent. Her whole body convulses and twitches, a roller-coaster pummelling her for an hour and leaving her with burning pain afterwards. She even considers going to the hospital.

'I didn't think I'd come back,' she writes online. 'It felt like a birth. It felt like a death.'

She'd experienced a 'kundalini awakening', a well-documented phenomenon with sometimes powerful physical symptoms. It can be scary, and in Be's case, it's life-changing. She feels her 'soul coming back'. Then she starts to empty everything out. She sells and donates all her books, reducing them from four hundred to seven. Everything but her backpack, her computer and a yoga mat must go. She spends her days meditating at the community where she's staying. As a final act, the social media star shuts down her Facebook account.

'I'm burned out,' her emotional farewell post states. 'I've lost interest in spirituality, cults and all this stuff. I'm repelled by it. I'll pop up again at some point in the future.'

She starts a bodywork training in Florida. I'm not expecting to ever hear from her again.

But the future arrives sooner than expected. In July 2018, Be is back on the net with her biggest scoop so far: Agama, the largest yoga school in the world, situated on Thailand's Koh Phangan. It's been going for fifteen years, attracting thousands of students from around the world. But it's a breeding ground of sexual transgression and patriarchal misogyny – all in the name of wellbeing.

Thirty-one women have made allegations against their tantric guru, a Romanian man named Narcis Tarcau with a

Hindu title: Swami Vivekananda Saraswati. Some of the accusations go as far as rape. Four days after Be's explicit exposé, the Romanian flees Thailand, along with three accused teachers. Agama temporarily closes. Their international yoga community is in turmoil.

Unlike her undercover investigation in Sedona, Be never went to Agama. Instead, her material came from a group of Agama women pleading for her to get involved. She was their last resort.

'I didn't want to,' Be tells me when we speak briefly the week after she launched her latest rocket. 'But once I saw the severity of what had been going on, I knew I have to do this.'

She has since set up a website, Agama Justice, to support the survivors, but she's aware that in taking down the top players, she might also destroy a whole community. In her view, they are mostly innocent people exploited by the guru. To her, they're victims, controlled and manipulated, even if some have turned awful. It's a dilemma for Be.

This fierce fighter for justice won't set foot on the tropical island where the Agama drama is currently playing out.

'I would not feel safe there.'

I need to check out Agama – for myself as well as for my work. A tantric community with a guru on an island sounds like the extreme fringe of the new field I'm also curious about for personal reasons.

Since the Taste of Love festival in Byron Bay six years earlier, where I had my own blissed-out awakening, I've been on a roller-coaster of exploration, from the Balinese rainforest to the desert in Israel and into every corner of my heart. My husband and I started attending workshops, from somatic therapy to shamanism. While committed to each other, we wanted to expand our sexuality as well as our minds. This was our next big adventure since living on an atoll in the South Pacific and then immigrating to New Zealand. I craved the emotional openness and the playful vibe the new 'tribe' offered, especially after raising children and settling into a middle-class life in Christchurch where many social interactions felt more timid and shallow than the Germanic intensity of my earlier life.

The initial weeklong training I took in Australia with ISTA (International School of Temple Arts) turned out to be more cathartic than erotic. We mainly learned 'emotional release tools' where you bash cushions and scream into your hand – teachings from the human potential movement and Osho's encounter groups. In one of the role-play exercises, I channelled a younger Louise from Centrepoint. Overcome with rage, I kicked and yelled at invisible men until I collapsed.

We held rituals out in nature that were raw, tender and physical, and we sat in sharing circles to reveal our fears, wounds and desires. Men embraced their dormant femininity, women expressed their inert masculinity – all to heal parts of us that are unhealthy or repressed, and to gain self-awareness. I felt like I had found the missing pieces of me. From now on, I hoped, they were going to enrich my life on every level.

'Embodiment' was the buzzword surrounding this visceral experience. It was a moving, empowering, educational deep dive that satiated an emotional hunger. All our masks came off. We laughed, cried and bonded. I flew off the edge and wished everyone around me could experience it too. Soon I started to pull more friends in so they could get the same benefits I found.

But a few years on, more came off than just masks. The shiny new world of love, liberation and learning that enticed me and also improved my relationship revealed its first cracks. There was a covert harem culture that felt predatory.

Male pioneers of the movement surrounded themselves with young female lovers, often from their trainings, who were then accelerated to apprentices and facilitators. Some of these women later got involved in a pyramid scheme called a 'gifting circle' that masquerades as female empowerment. My disillusion grew the more I understood the insidious nature of this scam. In 2016, I exposed it in *Sunday* magazine under the headline 'Spiritually Transmitted Disease', one that is fuelled by our longing for growth and connection – which is my own Achilles heel, too. The personal fallout from my investigation was painful, and it stopped me from going to any more courses. It took until 2018 to reconcile with the former 'sisters' whose anger I had evoked, and to feel comfortable around them again.

I'm ready to look into new directions now – with more discernment, and equipped with a better understanding of cultic dynamics that are not always obvious when we join what looks like a good thing.

I'm booked for my annual trip back to Germany, but I change my flights. Instead of a few hours' stopover in Bangkok, I will spend a week on Koh Phangan.

Chapter 12

In August 2018, I'm sitting on Zen Beach while the sun sets over the Gulf of Thailand. Soft drum beats float across the warm golden sand. Dreadlocked jugglers toss fluorescent sticks and balls. Someone behind me plays a slide guitar.

On its eastern side, Koh Phangan is famous for its full-moon parties. On its western, it's a hub for alternative healing, attracting an international crowd of seekers similar to those who flock to Bali's Ubud, India's Rishikesh, or the Rainbow Region of Byron Bay. The noticeboards in the township of Srithanu are layered with flyers for shamanic workshops, sensual massage, meditation circles and ecstatic dance events. Gift shops sell jade eggs to strengthen pelvic floor muscles, and detox clinics offer colonics with organic coffee enemas.

Today, it's a ghost town. Following Be Scofield's report, the laid-back hippie island's community has dispersed, and the man at the centre of it all has not been heard from since. Narcis Tarcau has crossed the land border to Malaysia and apparently no one knows where he is hiding.

Until a month ago, Agama Yoga was Koh Phangan's business magnet. While mopeds zoom past us at a street stall, a local Thai yoga teacher tells me over a watermelon smoothie that the islanders are torn between morals and money.

Generous donations from Swami to the Buddhist temple have always kept rumours at bay. In the last weeks, his loyalists canvassed shops, restaurants and massage parlours, asking their owners to sign a petition for the school to stay open because their guru was doing Buddha's work. Many did. But they now see yoga as something evil or sexual.

The owner of the backpacker resort where I'm staying has nothing good to say either. Hearing that I'm here because of Agama makes him visibly upset and ashamed. He tells me to stay away from them, shaking his head.

'Not safe, not safe! Is bad!'

An American expat who serves as an admin of the island's most-trafficked community Facebook group tells me that the 30,000 inhabitants ignored the rumours because there was general esteem for the yoga programme. The Agamis he's met are all friendly and genuinely concerned. But online, he gets 'creepy and infuriating' messages from the radical fringe, many from overseas, who remind him of religious extremists.

'Their attitude is aggressive, entitled and irrational,' he says.

Be Scofield's revelations have rippled around the world. Yoga Alliance, an overseeing professional body, has suspended Agama Yoga's licence, and their Austrian school has closed. Agama yogis who run their own centres and workshops internationally are now either under suspicion or have to publicly denounce their affiliation. Some feel guilty for recommending it to their friends. A purging of emotional and confessional posts, ranging from redemption to attacks, erupts on social media.

'I really thought till today that you would have the balls to send a response or a resignation letter,' a former male student addresses the absent Swami. 'So with this I distance myself from you and Agama. Please disregard anything from me that was pro Agama. I have changed my mind.'

At the other end of the spectrum, a woman writes that in her eight months as a full-time student, everything was wonderful. She was alone on a few occasions with senior male teachers and praises the way they approached her: 'What a privilege to be not only seen, but celebrated confidently as divinely feminine. How liberating!' At times she fantasised about a male instructor 'lovingly ravishing' her. When she eventually had sex at Agama after a period of abstinence, it was one of the most orgasmic and transformational experiences ever. 'I was treated with respect the entire time. Not once did I feel threatened. Not once did I feel forced to believe or do something against my will.'

Her passionate testimonial sparks fury and ridicule, including speculation that she was paid for this post. It has a familiar ring to it: 'But it helped me' or 'I had a different experience' gets used to discredit victims' accounts. As with Centrepoint, some passionately defend what others denounce. As I get deeper into my research, I begin to receive angry messages accusing me of spreading hate to seek fame and attention, and that I'm out to destroy 'something beautiful that has helped so many'. I'm back on old terrain.

'First off, no one goes to yoga because they're fine,' a Canadian tells me who doesn't want to reveal which city he lives in or what he does for a living because he fears that being associated with Agama could hurt his career. 'The Zen of the teachings was incredible. And that's why it's so messed up.'

———

The first time I heard about Agama was at Taste of Love. An Israeli presenter with a cocky masculinity had spent many years on Koh Phangan and was giving private sessions for women. He has written a book about the female orgasm in which he thanks Swami Vivekananda Saraswati. When I message him, he says it's time to edit that. I wonder how hard it must be to call out a teacher when you're also grateful to him.

Melbourne's large conscious community is full of people who came from Agama. I've been at their workshops and ecstatic dance events. Before Be Scofield's revelations, those I've met who attended Agama never referred to it as a cult, but as a tantric community. It sounded intriguing. Some of them had been on a yogic or Buddhist path. They weren't looking for a counterculture around a saviour to lift them out of their misery, and they weren't that different from me. So who are the thousands who made Agama their life? And did they all keep quiet while they knew what was happening?

'Choose Evolution' is Agama's promotional tagline that their opponents on the island have turned into the war cry 'Choose Revolution'. A Facebook group called 'Boycott Agama' is rapidly growing. Their members want to hold a memorial for abuse victims across the street from the school – a prayer vigil with flowers, candles, fruit. They have started a fundraiser to help women take legal action once an international arrest warrant is underway. It must be soon, they predict.

In their first flush of outrage, the activists planned to print t-shirts with a photo of Swami that says 'Don't support rape', to hand out free to freshly arrived tourists at the ferry. Even their supporters found that too offensive. Someone sprayed 'rape cult' in red across the Agama signs. They have since been removed, but the cult accusations are nothing new. Even a few years ago, graffiti outside an Agama building declared: 'We wash brains'.

Swami's videos have disappeared from YouTube, but the school has reopened – though the website states it's 'going through some temporary restructuring'. I'm planning to go there later this week.

I meet a British trauma recovery therapist for dinner. She belongs to the boycott group that tries to clean up after the Swami, as she puts it. At the next Phangan Slam, she will perform 'Perils of the Patriarchy', an ode she wrote inspired by the tumultuous last weeks.

'Yoga is like this new religion and just as rife with distortion,' she says while we study the vegetarian menu. Agama attracts women with sexual wounding – potentially dangerous when they try and heal it with entitled predatory men because they are easily caught in a 'freeze'.

'Trauma can destroy your ability to speak up and state a boundary. And who do you trust if the person who abused you is your spiritual master?' Those scars will affect people's sex lives and relationships forever, she predicts. In her view, Agama and its staff are criminal. If the legal system won't work, then the Thai mafia might sort it out.

'Swami has nowhere to run. Agama is done.'

This weekend, the therapist offers a womb healing circle for her 'sisters' on the island who have been affected by recent events. She pokes her salad greens. Agama, she says, is like a festering boil that has finally burst.

Back at my beach bungalow, I step out onto the veranda. Listening to the soft sounds of the tropical night, the dinner conversation replays in my mind. It's ironic, or a tragedy for me, that a lot of abuse and trauma is happening in alternative spaces for sexual healing, even when they're not cults.

Looking back at another feature I wrote for *Sunday* magazine about sexual healers, to lift the taboo around this new profession, I feel now that I was not discerning enough about whom I interviewed, although a certified sex therapist supported the piece. But what I've learned from my research, and the courses I've attended over the years, is that most of us lack the language, safety and experience to develop our own sexuality healthily. If we keep it in the dark and don't celebrate it, it becomes distorted. Even without the burden of abuse trauma, physical dysfunction, gender transition, birthing damage or porn addiction, our love lives are complicated enough. Unlike learning to cook or drive a car, we can't just book a session with a licenced instructor at the community centre who shows us how to achieve greater fulfilment in the bedroom. But because the need is huge, and female arousal and desire are so complex, we now have a massive unregulated market of self-appointed experts and healers where gynaecologists and psychologists can't help. That's why institutions like Agama thrived, and tantra, once seen as an esoteric niche, has become popular. It's the new yoga.

But ask a dozen tantra teachers to define their work and you'll get a dozen different answers. There is little correct knowledge about tantra's history and meaning in either the 'sacred sexuality' industry or the colonised, commercial yoga world. Classical tantra is thousands of years old and has its roots in India, Nepal and Tibet. It stems from pre-Vedic indigenous teachings and Indian philosophy. There are over 60 different schools of tantra, some with a modern philosophical approach. They don't focus on sexual pleasure, but on freeing the mind.

Many of the Western teachers who promote tantra advertise full-body orgasms and a deeper connection with your intimate partner, their websites listing nebulous terms like 'sacred masculine', 'divine feminine' and 'circulating energy'. Slow, soulful sex and sensuality can indeed bring on bliss, and techniques like unison breathing and eye-gazing can open the body and heart. But all this is neo-tantra, which emerged through Aleister Crowley's 'Sex Magick' in the 1920s in San Francisco and Osho's ashram in Pune in the '70s.

Meanwhile, cynics and Christian conservatives think tantra is a fancy synonym for swinging, and in sex work, 'tantric massage' is just another flavour on the menu. Many people who hear the word or even practise under it wouldn't know it's rooted in tenth-century South Asian philosophy. To confuse neo-tantra with traditional tantra is, in the view of many religious scholars, cultural appropriation or even patriarchal perversion.

The spiritual practices of an ancient tantrika are thus a far cry from the hands-on treatments of a self-styled modern sexual shaman. The two have as much in common as McDonald's and macrobiotics. But at Agama Yoga, they merge.

Chapter 13

Once upon a time, nothing at Agama's training centre seemed worrying or weird. It called itself a 'yoga university'. To become a hatha yoga teacher meant advancing through three levels and assisting with teaching lower levels while studying, a production line built on a points system. Ranks were shown through a rainbow system of sashes, as in kung fu. The highest level was 24 and came with a green sash. Later, there was also blue for the most advanced teachers.

The most popular course was the month-long, full-time Yoga Intensive introduction, costing around US$400 – a bargain compared to yoga training centres in developed countries, and affordable for the thousands of backpackers who land on Koh Phangan every week. Word of mouth and posters around the island drew them in if they hadn't already seen a promotional video on the ferry ride from Koh Samui.

The Agama website advertised the centre in mouthwatering terms:

> Enjoy a fresh mango and coconut for breakfast, take a yoga
> class, relax on a hammock with an ocean view. Agama is the
> pioneer of yoga on the tropical island paradise of Koh
> Phangan. The school was founded on the island in 2003 by
> Swami Vivekananda Saraswati, a yogi for over 30 years who

has dedicated his life to teaching an authentic form of
Hatha Yoga in a modern scientific approach.

The first day was always free. Once students enrolled at the
school, a vibrant community awaited them, with meditation
classes, men's and women's circles, and gatherings at the
school-run organic café. It was an eclectic international
crowd happy to study and connect. Unlike most yoga
training centres, it also offered tantra courses – another
attraction.

For the first month, attendees underwent a strict
purification regime along with their yoga classes: a
macrobiotic diet of mainly brown rice, purging in the
morning after drinking litres of salt water (vamana dhauti),
and intestine cleanses with enemas (shanka prakshalana).
You had to be dedicated and could only miss three or four of
the 150 hours. Agama Yoga was serious and disciplined; the
name literally means 'tradition'.

There were different types of students. For most, it was
just a periodical experience when they returned every year
for a month or two. Only a small number focused strongly
on Swami and eventually lost touch with reality.

Participants' physical health was the domain of Ananda
Maha, born Mihaiela Pentiuc and known as Maha. A
homeopathic doctor, also from Romania, she is the director
of the yoga therapy programme and still runs her own clinic,
the Agama Healing Centre, next to the campus. Everyone
describes her as caring and compassionate, a sweet mother
figure for the mostly younger flock. Narcis Tarcau had
mentored Maha since she was eighteen, when she followed
him to India. It was there that Narcis acquired his Swami
title and name in Rishikesh, studying under another swami.
His new names, Vivekananda Saraswati, mean 'the bliss of

discernment' and 'goddess of wisdom', and recall a famous lineage of respected monastic teachers and yoga pioneers. He started his first school in India but left the country in 2003, after allegations of a marriage of legal convenience with an Indian woman who later turned against him.

Narcis Tarcau, or Swami, is a former electronics engineer. At six feet and more than 100 kilograms, he cut an imposing figure in his long orange gown when he held meditations or nightly satsangs (talks) twice a week on the Thai island, though he favoured shorts and Hawaiian shirts when he was out and about on his sidecar motorbike. He makes it known that he speaks five languages, and comes across as intellectual and intimidating: charismatic, sometimes charming, often rude. His blunt expression was seen as the sign of a holy man in 'crazy wisdom' teaching, a world where gurus are meant to shock your system, provoke you, wake you up. Since only the enlightened have transcended their egos, they are not to be held to the same standard as ordinary mortals. Normal rules don't apply. That means it's sometimes hard to tell whether a spiritual rogue is brilliant – or a psychopath.

Agama was listed on Tripadvisor in 2012, and a year later, bad experiences began to trickle in via reviews, like this one in early 2013:

> Yes, when you do your Level One course it all seems super-exciting, but Agama Yoga has a dark underbelly. The senior male teachers are, almost without exception, sexual predators who think nothing of using NLP (neuro-linguistic programming) techniques to seduce young (and often vulnerable) women into their rarely cold beds. Sure, you will learn a lot of interesting facts about yoga and you will be

inspired to improve your yoga practice and change your lifestyle for a healthier one, but if you are a woman (or a 'Shakti' as they like to say at Agama) expect to undergo an ongoing regime of brainwashing. You'll start your career at Agama as a feminist and end up a Stepford Wife. You'll briefly be flavour of the month with a senior teacher and you'll feel 'special' for a bit, even if you've got to share him with two others. Before you know it, you'll be volunteering to cook the head of the school his suppers, or you'll be one of the minions of his second-in-command, whose main Shakti will give you a list of 'dos and don'ts' to please your man. You think this won't happen to you? You think you are above it all. Well, I've seen many a feisty feminist turned into an adoring doormat at Agama. Be warned!

But the lure of a fresh mango breakfast and a yogified body relaxing in a hammock must have been stronger as those warnings were usually ignored. Agama encouraged new students to leave overenthusiastic five-star endorsements to drown out the critical takedowns, and they had negative reviews deleted. Tripadvisor has since faced allegations of letting businesses like Agama remove unfavourable and defamatory reviews, including allegations of sexual abuse.

Newcomers at Agama didn't know that the accusations against Swami echo the alleged crimes of Maha and Swami's own former guru, Gregorian Bivolaru. The fellow Romanian started MISA (Movement for Spiritual Integration into the Absolute), a large esoteric yoga school under the umbrella of the ATMAN Yoga Federation. It has 28 outlets around the world, like Tara Yoga Centre in the UK, Natha Yoga in Scandinavia, Maha Vidya in Austria, and Rezonance in the Czech Republic.

According to international media reports, MISA is an exploitative sex cult. It coerces women into sexual practices designed to transform them into a 'divine goddess', and ultimately to have sex with the guru. It has been reported that some women are also coerced into stripping, sex work and performing in hardcore porn films, activities the group calls 'karma yoga', meaning volunteer work. MISA survivors have alleged that Bivolaru – Grieg to his followers – handpicks women around Europe from photos, who are brought to him to be 'initiated'. The guru reportedly indoctrinates them to put on weight to please his taste before he meets them in his hide-out, where they wait for him for days, alone.

Back in 1977, Bivolaru was prosecuted in Romania by the communist Ceauşescu regime for distributing pornographic and occult material. In 2004, after allegations about prostitution and drug trading, MISA centres and ashrams were raided in Bucharest and other cities. Bivolaru was arrested and charged with sex with a minor. He fled to Sweden where he was granted asylum because he managed to present himself as having been persecuted for his religious beliefs. In 2013, he was sentenced in his absence to six years' imprisonment. Because MISA made porn films that were sold in Denmark through their online shop, the school was expelled from the European Yoga Alliance in 2008.

Bivolaru was arrested in Paris in 2016 and extradited to Romania, which he left again in 2017, the day after he was released from nearly two years in jail. A week later, Finland filed an international arrest warrant, seeking him for human trafficking and sexual assault in nine cases. As of 2022, the guru is still a criminal on the run and still on Interpol's 'Wanted' list, while the aggressively litigious Romanian cult is still going. MISA holds annual 'Miss Shakti' contests at its summer camps where participants apply by sending in photos of them in their lingerie. Sex with the septuagenarian Grieg is seen as a sacred act and the highest honour his devotees can attain. Traumatised cult survivors from MISA are currently in psychotherapy treatment in Romania, Australia, Sweden and the UK.

However, Swami from Agama claimed Bivolaru had been unfairly prosecuted in his home country because yoga was illegal there for many years. Swami – just Narcis back then – had joined the underground Romanian yoga group as a 21-year-old student, at the time known to be a mathematics geek with an unusual bent penis who wasn't popular with girls. He gathered his sexual experience through MISA and strived to become a copy-paste version of Bivolaru. Before he became a swami in India, he founded and led a MISA school in Denmark.

Agama is not affiliated with any of the MISA-derived schools in the ATMAN Yoga Federation, although Swami was featured on a cover of MISA's Romanian yoga magazine around 2000. There are various versions of why depending on whom you speak to: Swami was either excommunicated or chose to leave so he didn't have to pay fees to his former guru. But Bivolaru's deeply misogynistic views, outlandish conspiracy theories and dangerously obscure health claims, such as suppressing the flow of menstrual blood through a rigid yoga practice, shaped the Agama curriculum. Some of their course material was directly lifted from MISA booklets.

Hundreds of students who passed through Agama were from Australia and there were also a few dozen from New Zealand over the years. While I'm on the island, I find one former long-timer in the Facebook group Boycott Agama and talk to her on the phone.

It takes the acupuncturist from Auckland a while before she trusts me; I can hear the anxiety in her voice when she reaches into her memories. Tina was 32 and travelling the world on a sabbatical, wanting to deepen her yoga practice, when her best friend told her what an amazing place Agama was. In 2007, the travelling Kiwi found a room in Srithanu and enrolled for the entry course, giving the full-moon rave on the eastern side of the island a miss. Her course mates looked down on partying; they were destined for higher things, on the fast track to enlightenment.

'We were the real deal,' Tina says, sounding equally nostalgic, sarcastic and embarrassed. Those were the best years for her.

The first weeks were intense. She fell into lockstep with the others, doing what she was told to do. The results were amazing. But if her body revolted, with pain or other symptoms, it was explained away as part of the purification process or as her bad karma. So she tried harder.

When she met Swami at a satsang for the first time, she noticed his intense brown eyes behind rimless glasses, reminiscent of a university professor. He was charming, but he could be 'full-on', swearing and making people laugh. To her he seemed more like a big baby than a rebel and renegade – an unhappy, complicated person trapped in his own power structure.

'But incredibly intelligent and fascinating,' she recalls.

The month ended with a special ceremony. While beautiful music played, Tina was blessed with a red dot on the forehead, a traditional necklace made from flowers and a coloured sash to show her rank. It was ritualistic love bombing; that's how she sees it now. Back then, she was on a high. 'We all were.'

As soon as she was back in New Zealand, she felt an urge to return to the island for more. A whole new world had opened to her, one in which the next level was always just out of reach. The higher the levels in the strict Agama hierarchy, the more secret they became. Only once you paid up for the next month was that knowledge released. If you told others about the content, it would bring terrible consequences. Tina was hooked and entered a twelve-month teacher training course.

The New Zealander also received special mantras that she wasn't supposed to share with others. Most students did 'seva' or 'karma' yoga – working in the office, cooking and cleaning, for the school as well as for Swami at his house. Tina wasn't allowed to clean near a main hall one week, so that she couldn't pick up what was being taught there. That knowledge was only for the more advanced people. As she tried to climb the ranks, to work more and adapt better, she found it more difficult to relate to people outside of Agama who didn't understand how exceptional they all were on their unique and beautiful path.

At the end of Tina's year, Swami tied a white ribbon around her wrist in a final ceremony. It symbolised her eternal bond with him. By then, her whole life revolved around the school, and she even helped Swami to come to New Zealand in 2007. He had been looking for land to buy there or in South America so he could start an ashram in 2012, when a third world war would supposedly break out. To save his flock, he asked his students to give him money for this doomsday mission. Many paid up. Agama students hosted him while he held workshops around the country.

Tina says she learned a lot during her time at the school, and not just about yoga. Exploring her sexuality through tantra led to incredible realisations for her. But back then, no one mentioned consent and boundaries. Instead, the teachers emphasised the polarity between masculine and feminine. Agama had an old-school approach to these ancient tantric teachings. Women were taught from day one that they needed to become more feminine: put on a dress, be submissive, be receptive, surrender. Senior teachers ran the Complete Femininity course at the time, and later the Agama Tantra Initiation (ATI), the most advanced course. One of the senior teachers was Justine Baruch from America who had arrived at Agama in her twenties as a feminist, but had since changed. She often told Tina that she was too masculine.

'That programming was strong,' says Tina.

Women – 'shaktis' – outnumbered men – 'shivas' – but men pursued them from the beginning. The culture at Agama was promiscuous, and open relationships were the norm. Tina, who was in a monogamous liaison, mostly kept her guard up; it added protection. She found that many of the men had a creepy edge and wanted to be like Swami – 'God's gift to women,' she says. Even though there was a rule that teachers should not sexually engage with the students in the first three months, Tina still had invitations from them, Swami included. He would make suggestions to her, but she refrained.

In the beginning, she was very careful not to be alone with the guru because of past trauma; she disliked his strong, aggressive power. Swami always looked at her like he could turn her into a better shakti if only she would let him. He called her reluctance to sleep with many men – three orgasms a day was what he recommended, depending on your star sign – as a 'karma block'.

The constant pressure to have sex with him and other teachers continued the higher she progressed in the school, and the indoctrination about surrendering to male power was subtle but relentless. Women were encouraged to have threesomes with other women and a male. Gay male sex, however, was a no-go. When Tina gave in and finally slept with someone else, everyone was happy that she was 'opening her heart'. No one ever called it 'having sex', but instead 'practising tantra' or 'making love'. It was meant to be healing and transforming, and Swami's top women – Justine and Maha – recommended yoni massages and suggested seeing Swami for private consultations. Yoni is the Sanskrit word for vulva and vagina.

After a ten-month kundalini training, Tina joined the chakra programme. By then, every other female student on her level was sleeping with Swami. From what they reported, it was just basic penetration – nothing explorative, tender or romantic. Gross, but powerful. The tantric dogma for the men was to withhold their ejaculation. Because condoms were viewed as stopping the energetic flow, their use was not encouraged. That meant chlamydia and other STIs were common.

In 2008, Swami invited Tina to his house for a one-on-one healing meditation in his office, which was next to his bedroom. When their silent sitting and breathing was done and she was still in an altered state, the heavy man, then in his fifties, moved over on the sofa, and started kissing her and taking her clothes off without asking. She firmly said 'no', but he kept pushing her to sleep with him. Disgusted, she refused.

What disturbed her even more was a senior teacher's reaction afterwards. He seemed amused and asked her: 'Wow, how did you manage to leave without making love?! That *never* happens.' Tina was angry about Swami's transgression, and embarrassed that she almost fell for it –

too naive to realise that 'meditate' meant having sex. But she tried to hide it all and push it down. What had happened at Swami's house was only her problem that she needed to overcome.

If Tina and others tried to mention unwanted sexual advances to the school management, they were told that they needed to be more open in their heart chakra. It was the students' karma to work through it, especially if something happened more than once. The tipping point for Tina came when she was upset about two male teachers who had lied to her, so she complained to Justine Baruch. Instead of admonishing the men, the senior teacher told Tina it was all her fault; she'd attracted that dishonesty because of the negative energy she was putting out.

Thinking about it all still makes her so uncomfortable that she struggles to find words. Down the phone line, I can feel how hard it is for her to drag it up again, even years later. She doesn't want to be seen as a victim. Because it feels weak. Like being humilated again.

There is a term for the kind of blaming, shaming and diverting she encountered: gaslighting. It means being told by others that something bad you experienced is either in your imagination or actually your fault. Spiritual bypassing means also telling this to yourself – that those bad experiences were indeed beneficial for you or all happening for a higher reason. The tactic of forgiving perpetrators in the guise of being spiritually advanced stops them from being held to account. At Agama, as in many religious groups and yoga schools, this collective cop-out is woven into the tapestry. It partly explains why it took so long for the allegations there to finally come to light.

According to investigative yoga journalist Matthew Remski, the rationalisation and spiritualisation of abuse in neo-tantra and yoga means the threshold for revealing abuse is even higher and more difficult to overcome.

'A whole network of people surrounded Harvey Weinstein to cover up and enable him,' the soft-spoken Canadian cult expert tells me when I call him. 'But nobody regarded him as an enlightened spiritual master or thought he was healing sexual trauma. Power is still the primary currency here, misogyny is the context, and rape culture is the landscape.'

Chapter 14

The 'yoga university' is like an island on the island. The campus is green and quiet, inland by a river, a ten-minute walk from the Srithanu town centre. Agama's slogan, 'Choose Evolution', has disappeared not just online but from the white wall outside the school as well. Only three scooters are parked at the entrance where normally there would be over 50. No one sits inside the Agama restaurant when I walk past the building. The upcoming teacher training and month-long yoga course have been cancelled. Their clothes store has also shut down.

I study the noticeboard. There is no more tantra on offer on the new schedule, but regular spiritual movie nights for the public and the community are still happening. *Mother Teresa* is showing next. One of Agama's upcoming workshops is aptly called 'The Art of Dying'.

I take a wander around the one-storey buildings before my class starts. The lawns and walkways are adorned with Indian goddess statues. One dwelling is called Enlightenment Hall. A sign in the lavatory that explains how to properly dispose of toilet paper starts with the line 'You are a conscious being'. Normally the place would be buzzing with around a hundred students and staff. This morning, I'm the only one in the empty yoga hall where the free drop-in class takes place. The Brazilian teacher is gently spoken. Like everyone at Agama, she is dressed in white. She talks a lot about 'divine energy' but looks sad and subdued. Only when she mentions Maha's upcoming birthday celebration at the next half-moon does her face light up.

After the solitary class, I share an al fresco lunch with a tall, slender woman in a flowing white dress with long dark hair. It's Yogita (Vered Shikman), an Israeli, leading the Complete Femininity trainings. She's also the go-to person for yoni massage. Yogita blesses her food with a mumbled prayer before she lifts her fork and slowly takes a bite. It's an act of consecration. We have mutual acquaintances, but upon learning that I'm a visiting reporter, she only mentions that what I've heard and read isn't true.

'Just lies,' she says with a fixed smile.

What she's happy to share is that the Agama practice has helped her to heal her chronic urinary tract infection and other physical problems. On her website, she expresses her 'eternal gratitude to Swami Vivekananda Saraswati who founded this exceptional Yoga school'.

As Swami has fled, his disciple and former lover Maha is the head of the school and holds the satsangs. The Romanian doctor stops by for a quick chat with Yogita while we sit outside in the shade. Maha, an attractive, middle-aged woman with bouncy blonde coiffured curls and a warm, engaging presence, wears tight white pants, a figure-hugging top and make-up, and throws me a genuinely friendly smile.

According to some of the survivors in Boycott Agama, Maha enabled or allowed some of the alleged crimes to occur. But I've since spoken to Agama leavers who don't judge her that harshly and have compassion for her difficult role of keeping Swami at bay and students happy while genuinely believing that he can heal and help them.

'Everyone loves Maha,' they told me. Since she's like a mother for many, and also their doctor, people trust her. She's not around when I drop in to her practice later. Her secretary gives me her email.

When I leave the campus, a handful of women in their twenties venture out of an eight-day Complete Femininity workshop that usually attracts around 30. It's a course that one Norwegian woman I've contacted walked out of in 2017, disgusted by the sexist stereotyping and the claims that women secretly want to be raped. When she wrote about it on social media, she had over 500 responses.

'It's fantastic,' is all that a young, model-pretty American says before she gets on her scooter. She doesn't want to say more. When I ask her about the recent allegations, which she must have heard of by now, she says they were never discussed. Since Swami has disappeared from the scene, the freshly graduated 'shaktis' didn't have to do the required seductive dance in front of the guru. It's usually ritually performed as a special honour at the end of the workshop.

The men's equivalent to the femininity course has equally questionable content. It teaches pick-up artistry from the book *The Game*, such as 'negging' – putting a woman down emotionally and then building her up again – and ends with an excursion into local bars to practise those tricks. A German who attended the 'Vira' (hero) training in June 2018 told me that on day three they were shown techniques to enlarge their penises. He was repulsed by the overall sexist, heteronormative message that sounded like it was lifted straight from an incel (involuntary celibate) manual, not ancient texts: men are the victims in society because so many of them are in jail; women are controlling, evil, impure and intellectually inferior; and only if men ravish and take them are they truly empowered.

Another student on an earlier course has made a secret recording of Swami's opening talk. The audio has since been uploaded on the Agama Justice website. Swami can be heard boasting that around a hundred women had their first orgasm with him, which in his eyes makes him a sex therapist and a sex worker. These services require pushing himself on women because tantric men like him know what those women need. He goes on about Indian doctors 'of the third kind' who overpower resistant patients and shove the remedy into their mouths to save them. Swami says that he has given that up a long time ago, 'simply because the modern society is so democratic and so politically correct, I don't want to go there'. He tells the room that just earlier, a woman came to see him for her cervical pain.

'I can solve that in five meetings, probably from the first, you know? It's so difficult to restrain when you know I could make this woman happy in one week.' He asks himself why he should hold back. 'I know I can do it.'

Before I head back to the township, I drop in to the shop next door to the school compound. I'm the only customer there. The manager behind the counter, a tall lanky European with an Austrian accent, first denies that his business is affiliated with Agama but then defends them as 'the best yoga training in the world'. A rape cult? He scoffs. In his view, the sex abuse allegations are nothing but jealousy from competing yoga schools and revenge from fired Agama staff. He finally lets on that he belongs to Agama's inner circle and knows the full background, whereas I'm just being played by deceitful and mentally unstable women wanting attention. Swami's house, he sneers, is surrounded by Thai families.

'If girls were raped there' – he is getting worked up – 'how come no one heard them screaming or saw them running outside?' His anger sounds desperate by now.

'We're pretty much finished,' he admits before I leave. He means not just his shop, but the entire yoga school.

One of the women the Austrian shopkeeper tried to discredit is Mangala Holland, a British sex educator in her forties. She attended Agama for several months at a time over five years and was their operations manager until 2015.

'A big piece of shit in the middle of the honeypot which I was constantly trying to swim around' is how she describes Swami to me when I call her at her temporary home in Australia. I ask her why everyone turned a blind eye to him.

'You know, we were all assaulted all the time and expected to enjoy it and appreciate the attention,' she says, her voice dripping with sarcasm, 'because that's what a good shakti does.'

It's hard for an outsider like me to grasp how this could carry on for so long. Why didn't those women protest and leave? I have an inkling from something the trauma recovery therapist mentioned. She described it as fawning, which is part of the 'freeze' trauma response, similar to Stockholm syndrome. You play along in order to survive, befriending the enemy. And then you convince yourself that it's not abuse, but what you choose – so that you won't be cast out.

It's still a process to understand for Mangala, too. She tries to explain what she's only coming to terms with now: that the guru manipulated the whole school by making sure as many people in positions of power were in his bed, so he could control and dominate everything. Swami eventually raped her. We don't go into the details. Mangala tells me that at the time, she couldn't address what he had done to her.

'He knocked down my confidence so much,' she says. 'I kept hitting a wall of silence.'

In 2015, a huge scandal erupted – not the first one. Swami claimed that the school was bankrupt and couldn't pay the yoga teachers. An accountant who offered to help discovered that US$30,000 a month was ending up in Swami's Romanian bank account. On top of that, students raised concerns about sexual relations between teachers and students. A large group of staff and teachers walked out.

The financial scandal was the last straw for Mangala. When she was ready to quit, the school had a final ceremony around that time and wanted to hand her a big bouquet of flowers as a farewell. Mangala was supposed to go up to the stage and receive the white string around her wrist from Swami. She refused his blessing in front of him, in front of the whole school. He looked at her bizarrely and laughed. She just walked off. It was the last time Mangala ever faced him. But when she left the island, she also lost all her friends, her whole community.

'Nobody believed me,' she says. 'Everyone was told I'd gone crazy.'

She moved to Australia and started a new life with only $500 to her name. It took a long time before she understood what Swami had done, and only after speaking to an Agama survivor who had been through the same. Mangala started counselling to find out what her 'men and power and daddy issues' were, so that she knows what pulled her in. She's still in therapy.

Saturday night is Agama's weekly Bhajan – a devotional singing ceremony, open to everyone. I'm invited too. It will open my heart so I can let go of all my bad thoughts and really see all the love that is there, I'm told.

It's a magical setting. The campus is dark when I arrive, the yoga hall in the back lit with candles and decorated with tropical flowers. It looks soft, sensual, peaceful – a feminine space with a churchy vibe. Swami never attended these celebrations; the intellectual superior is not one for dancing and singing with a crowd.

Everyone sits in a circle, dressed in white. Yogita, who leads the event, greets me with a smile, then whispers something to the man next to her. He looks concerned, then flashes me an even bigger smile. We're handed song sheets and are encouraged to film with our phones to put it on social media later. Every bit helps in these difficult times. Yogita reads out a spiritual text that we meditate on before she starts the chanting. It's a call and response, with her as the solo singer and the rest as the choir. While deities like Krishna and Kali are evoked by her melodic voice, we sway and clap to the music, accompanied by a harmonium and guitar. Some devotees have brought hand drums; the volume intensifies. The hall is humming with rhythm and emotion. People get up to dance around me, eyes closed, raptured expressions on their faces. Any bad thoughts must have gone.

I've been to similar events called kirtan before and always enjoyed the singing that takes me out of my head. But here, I feel like a fraud. The enraptured dancers remind me of the musicians on the *Titanic*, playing on while the ship is sinking. Obedient, oblivious, doomed. It's both sad and infuriating.

Chapter 15

Very few Agama survivors are willing to talk; it's still too raw. There's suspicion of being portrayed as pitiful, a bed-hopping bliss ninny. Or worse, oblivious to sexual abuse.

Sadhana, a European in her mid-thirties, with long wavy hair and almost translucent skin, seems tormented. She repeatedly bursts into tears when we talk on a video call. She asks me to use Narcis Tarcau's real name instead of the holy title 'Swami'. Unlike Mangala Holland in Australia, she is not a rape victim. And unlike so many of her peers, she never slept with Swami. But what she put herself through in the ATI, the Agama Tantra Initiation, is also abuse in her view – spiritually and psychologically.

Sadhana was born to a narcissistic, high-achieving father and a housewife mother. She got her new name from an Indian guru who was her inspiration for years. But as much as that teacher spoke to her heart, there weren't enough intellectual answers for the passionate seeker. A 'yoga university' was perfect. Looking back, she can see how she was a target: someone who wanted to heal from her past, and who was trying to focus on the light, not the dark. People warned her about Agama's culture while they praised some of the teachings. She held on to the positive.

When she entered the school in 2016, she found 600 people wanting to connect. But it wasn't just the guru at the top who was a seducing predator. The community followed the same vision and rules. The first taste of it was sweet; overwhelming and life-changing. Sadhana thought she had found paradise: a supportive environment in which to study and become a better version of herself, so she could later guide others on their path. She committed to stay for as long as that would take.

Once she was hooked, abuse became insidious and normalised. Sadhana calls it the 'gaslight game'. Tantric women are meant to surrender, have multiple sex partners, and not be attached. The more you did that – and worked unpaid for the school – the more you were a true spiritual aspirant. If Sadhana refused to follow the doctrine, she was 'running away from truth' or 'thinking from her lower chakras'. It was made clear that only Agama understands the truth. Other teachers and schools were discredited.

The indoctrination worked. While trying to fit in, Sadhana began to doubt her entire reality, her past and her inner truth. Since she'd never even had a one-night stand, she remained reserved in the first months. Sex for her is only possible in a loving relationship; she had no desire to go to the sex parties, dubbed 'sacred rituals'. She overheard male teachers making bets about the 'fresh meat' coming in, and she would see men slap women's bottoms in the school's restaurant. If that prompted a bad reaction, the women were labelled prudes and their anger dismissed as a 'shakti storm'. The message was clear: the more flesh you revealed and the more approachable you appeared, the more people welcomed you as part of Agama. You had to be okay to be grabbed in public, or you were acting hysterical. Not worth talking to. An outsider.

Once she'd nearly finished her yoga teacher training course, the male teachers' behaviour changed. They asked flirty questions and became touchy with female students, asking them on dates. At the final ceremony, one of the most senior leaders of the school and another man came up on either side of her, touched her, made comments about her body, and joked about going to another hall for group sex.

'They totally objectified me,' Sadhana says. She pretended to laugh until she could escape. That same leader later sent her unsolicited pictures of his penis, one with a red ribbon tied around it.

The elixir that Sadhana had received in the yoga training was slowly poisoned by everything around it. It felt so twisted. But she wanted to stay and get all the benefits her new path promised. During her first interview with the head of the school, Narcis/Swami was polite and patronising, retaining his façade as a benevolent father figure. He advised her to have lots of sex with tantric men because of her star sign, which he repeatedly got wrong. In a later meeting, while she was sitting cross-legged on the couch, he told her she was causing too much drama. Instead, she should share her 'gifts' with the community.

'You have beautiful tits,' Narcis carried on. 'I wonder what is under those shorts. I'm curious. How's your pussy?'

She was speechless when she left his office – nauseated and disgusted, violated and drained. When she got to her motorbike, she was shaking and didn't know where to drive. She had been fine when she went in there. Now she didn't know who she was anymore. All she had asked for was guidance to choose between branches of the curriculum.

The signs were there early; she just didn't recognise them. Her senior yoga teacher on her first course charmed her from the start.

'I really enjoy your presence in the room,' the American texted her, 'even though your beautiful smile distracts me a little too often while I'm teaching ...' When she asked him about a good massage therapist – preferably a male because she needed some grounding energy – he replied: 'Heeeeeelllooooo! You have to be careful asking a tantric yoga teacher for some masculine energy! I certainly know a few methods, but all of them take much longer than 15 minutes.' He added a winking emoji.

Two weeks later, the teacher tried to have sex with her. They started a relationship, which he hid in public to appear available to others. As soon as one lover would leave the island, he replaced her. His phone was filled with pictures of women he was chasing or those he had been with, including sex videos. Sadhana found intercourse with him was often painful. He would enter her before she was fully ready, moving far too hard and fast. A few times, when she asked him to stop, she had to push him off her with her arms and knees because she was having a panic attack.

He tried to convince her that going through this trauma would be good for her, and that she should trust him. But if she was still crying afterwards, he would quickly shower and leave. Every time she tried to break away from him, he would once again become Prince Charming. Once she was newly confident, he would go back to ordering her around, telling her she was too young and immature on the spiritual path.

The relationship was open for him; 'take it or leave it' was his condition. But she had no desire for others. Yet she felt the pressure of the group telling her she wasn't evolved enough if she stayed monogamous, just a delusional romantic little girl. Promiscuous women were more respected. Ironically, there was still a lot of hurt when open relationship rules were broken.

She finally enrolled for the Agama Tantra Initiation, much to the surprise of those who thought of her as prudish. The six-week course is a rite of passage even for seasoned Agamis. You gain status in the community for being an 'ATI survivor'. Sadhana went because of the higher yogic teachings, to reach a more spiritual sexuality – and to please her boyfriend. The content was secret and past participants weren't allowed to speak about it. In the intake form with her booking, Sadhana mentioned that she felt scared and didn't want to be involved in any group sex.

One of the first exercises was 'Dress to Impress', where you had to remove your clothing in front of the others, while explaining which vulnerabilities and insecurities you hid under them. It was already a huge stretch for her, but she managed okay.

On many mornings they practised self-love in front of the mirror in the hall, naked. They were instructed to touch their own genitals and nipples. To Sadhana, it felt more 'like self-rape'. She was in panic and tears while she pushed through her 'blockages', as course leader Justine Baruch called it. When Sadhana decided to skip the mandatory sessions, she was treated as being wimpy and weak.

One morning, Sadhana broke her toe. One of the day's exercises saw everyone go into the middle of the room and thrash around, punching pillows and screaming to loud music. Sadhana was worried her injury would get worse if she fully released into this cathartic chaos. But when she told Justine, the instructor dismissed her worry as not valid and again described it as a 'block'. Sadhana did the physical exorcism and, as she had feared, reinjured her toe. Instead of getting sympathy, she was told not to blame others.

As the weeks went on, the students became more exposed to their deepest shames and fears. At some point during the course, they had to go through a 'transformational process': a ten-day-long silent retreat during which each one of them would have to sit in the middle of the circle and listen to the group telling them about their best and worst qualities.

'There was no possibility to talk to anyone but the team before the end of that week,' says Sadhana. Justine was keeping all their phones and computers at her house. Some people were relentlessly pushed and lost it, one to the point of being suicidal.

Half of the course curriculum was based on Jungian shadow work, the rest on sexuality. One of the lessons was an exchange of lingam (phallus) and yoni massage. Sadhana trusted the man who did hers. But 'yoni gazing' was challenging. The women sat in a circle naked, open-legged, as the men admired their genitals. When it was the men's turn to present their penises for adoration, they all used a special piece of bamboo to hold them up.

In the last week, Narcis joined them as a spectator for a group masturbation ritual, 'holding space' from his throne. Sadhana felt deeply uncomfortable about this session, but she also didn't want to disturb the circle where they all had to sit for the ritual. She was confused about the constant stream of mixed messages, like all the talk about boundaries. But once she expressed hers and wanted to pull back, the neo-tantra teacher made her feel ashamed for letting the group down.

'Either I'm with the group or I'm out,' she remembers, her voice wreathed with hurt. 'And if I'm out, it was implied that I better leave on the spot and for good.'

The ceremonial highlight of the six weeks was a group sex ritual in a private house. Mattresses were put out on the floor. Narcis was also there to 'hold space'. The students were asked: 'Are you a dog, or a cat, or a bird?' Dogs will let anyone approach them. Birds will fly away. Cats are somewhere in the middle. Four people out of their group of twenty decided last-minute not to engage because they had partners.

Sadhana felt frozen. Too frozen to fly away. She tried to stay in the bathroom for as long as she could, to get over her resistance. The school's assistants followed her to get her back into the room. Sadhana knew that this was what her boyfriend wanted, to be more open. She was fed up with being told 'you'll never know if you never try'. She wanted to prove it to everyone, especially Justine, who had so much in common with her father. If she showed them that she was able to do it, they would shut up and let her be. She was worn out from the pressure she had received for months from her boyfriend, the teachers, the whole community. After six weeks of ego death and cushion beating in the ATI, she didn't know who she was anymore. Sadhana doubted everything about herself, even down to her name. Until she embraced the dark or repressed side of her sexuality, she would never reach the depth of spirituality she desired. To overcome what she thought was wrong with her, she had to open her heart – and her legs – to the group.

The ritual started with the usual ingredients to make it 'spiritual': soft music, a heart-opening meditation, eye-gazing. Then foreplay, until the music changed, and the facilitator announced that now was the time to have intercourse. Sadhana disassociated while she tried to engage with men, her mind detached from her body. When it was all over, she stayed on for another hour, still having penetrative sex, like a puppet.

Whatever they told her she was meant to get from this, she didn't. She had betrayed herself, and the others had too;

she felt they had pushed her to do this. Justine even said 'well done!' at the final ceremony where they were given a certificate. But her heart didn't crack open, like she had been promised. She hadn't entered a new paradigm of love and light. Instead, she felt broken and dirty, and left alone to deal with it all.

Her boyfriend was no support either. He left her. Sadhana lost all respect for most of the senior teachers. They told her she was free to go, but the message was clear: if you leave the school, you're immature and you'll miss the best opportunity of your life. She wouldn't be welcomed back.

Eventually she returned, believing that anything that had gone wrong at Agama was her fault. A Melbourne therapist who was around the school at that time finally informed her about narcissism and abusive relationships. Today, Sadhana says she's still emotional, still afraid of the people who lied to her, and resentful towards those who supported them. She doesn't want to regret anything that happened. But she wants the school shut down, and everyone to know why.

Chapter 16

Like Centrepoint, Agama was full of likeable, intelligent and caring people. They just wanted to deepen their knowledge in a reputable Eastern tradition or earn their certificate as a yoga teacher in a warmer climate. Swami wasn't the drawcard – in fact, he put many of them off. Which makes it harder to unpack why so many stayed until it was too late to leave. Or too late to look away.

I'm trying to speak to those who stuck it out, and who weren't victims of sexual assault, when I finally find Jenny Hale. With her husband, Tom, she rents a house on the western side of Koh Phangan, by the lake. Jenny sits outside on the porch, which is frequented by a bat that often hangs upside down from their roof at night and feasts on beetles. Her eyes are rimmed with laugh lines, but her demeanour is calm and serious. She comes across as a solid problem-solver, not a flaky Instagram yogini.

In 2013, Jenny and her husband left their consulting business in Australia to go on a long-planned, multi-year overseas experience. They were coming out of a meditation retreat in Malaysia when they heard about a place in Thailand that was 'next level'. They enrolled at Agama in 2014. The yoga was rigorous, the students dedicated, and the teachings a mishmash of traditional tantra, neo-tantra, orthodox Christianity, Taoism, Gnostic mysticism – 'and a truckload of unexamined Eastern European communist cultural baggage', as Jenny puts it.

'Vertical' is how Agama describes its curriculum: strict, consistent, hierarchical – which is what made it so efficient. To understand what happened later, I first have to understand all the good stuff there, Jenny insists. People got genuine value from the classes. 'But even if only one per cent of the people there got hurt, that's still too many,' she says.

Jenny and Tom have a polyamorous marriage and she now works as a relationship coach. But what they encountered at Agama was 'insane', in her eyes. Swami was fundamentally opposed to relationships because they were 'bourgeois' and distracted from the spiritual path. Love between people was written off as based in ego, and the ego needed to be destroyed. Agama's doctrine – similar to Osho's – was non-attachment, and tantric partners were there to practise with, not for romance.

The Australian newbies were older than most students and started weekly relationship discussion groups to fix what they found was an unhealthy culture that didn't look after people's emotional needs properly.

Jenny returned in 2015 after a long break when the financial scandal erupted, which had made Mangala leave. As a response, Agama released Swami's 'transmission to the world' and to all those in doubt. 'Agama is not a democracy,' it said. 'You are not here to change Agama. Agama is here to change you.' The last two sentences were hung up as a sign by the reception desk.

There was now a rule in place that no teachers should have sex with new students during their first three months of a course, but it was mostly ignored. Together with Justine Baruch, Jenny started to revise and rewrite the tantra course material. She says they tried to remove the sexism, homophobia and medically suspect information from the course books but had no control over what teachers chose to say in class. In his weekly talks, Swami mixed Eastern philosophy with racist occult teachings he learned from Gregorian Bivolaru, and preached against psychotherapy and feminism. The yogic master recommended drinking your own urine and controlling menstruation with rigid postures. One of Swami's MISA-inspired false claims was that vaccines cause illness and STIs cannot be transmitted if your 'vibration' is high enough.

For women, the main healing tool besides yoga was a man's penis. Whether someone saw Swami in their grief because a family member had died, or they suffered from depression or sexual trauma, the guru would always recommend sex as a cure: an orgasm a day keeps the doctor away. Men who had only been in the organisation for a few months were instructed by Swami to do as he did and put their lingam to good use. Many women were convinced through a long grooming process to literally ask for it. Peer pressure also came from senior female teachers who insisted that orgasm problems could best be fixed by Swami.

'Look, there's actually some benefit to being initiated by someone who knows what they're doing,' a former student said to me, explaining his take on Swami as a master sexual healer of women. He said it's like pressure cleaning a car's cooling system. 'It blows you open, and you're spacey for a day or two afterwards, because it's actually too much, too fast.'

By the time Jenny had finished Level Two, she knew that something wasn't right. Because of her background in psychology, younger women started confiding in her. A 22-year-old New Zealander told her that a senior teacher pushed her for sex right after a yoni massage. Jenny raised the transgression with one of the senior tantra teachers who said he would deal with it. A week or two later, a leading teacher and a pillar of Agama allegedly raped a woman during another yoni massage. According to Be Scofield's report, the woman had her eyes closed when he stuck his penis inside her without asking, and without a condom. She was completely in shock, frozen to the spot.

The alleged rape victim went to see Justine Baruch and her partner Michael Dunn about the assault and was told to speak nothing of it. The allegations were also quashed from the top by Muktananda Mistry, the deputy head of the school. The alleged attacker hastily left the island. At this point, Jenny was ready to leave, too.

'But I thought if everyone like me keeps leaving, nothing will ever change,' she says with a sigh, tucking her long hair away from her face. It's obvious how conflicted she is. She doesn't want to paint herself as a hero, but she doesn't want to be tainted as an enabler either.

The rape rumour had a short, sobering effect on Swami, but he acted like he was the victim. Those who complained were ungrateful, impure, jealous, possessed by demons or creating 'ego-driven drama'. By now, it was an open secret that the head of the school couldn't contain himself and was sexually harassing staff and students. Swami messaged them with compliments and invited them for a tantric meditation to 'feel the chakras'. It was code for having sex with the boss and came with the job. 'Five cervical orgasms will blow your reservations to the moon,' he said in an attempt to persuade one of them.

At the start of a required business meeting, he bit one manager in the neck during the customary embrace, then slid a hand up her loose shorts and felt her thighs while he made an appreciative sound. In another meeting, he let on that he could buy underage Thai girls for sex because of his local connections. A new Brazilian operations manager was told that if she didn't want him jumping staff, she should only hire men. When she quit, burned out, Swami finally agreed to address his behaviour. He promised to not get sexually involved with students again and to only see women together with his secretary.

Swami was experienced in hypnosis and NLP (neuro-linguistic programming), a therapeutic modality that is also popular with con artists, sociopaths and narcissists. It enabled the guru to embed messages into people's brains in unethical ways. Some of his bed partners became inappropriately obsessive about him after he got them to repeat the phrase 'I'm your woman' during orgasm. They already believed he had supernatural powers. The fear of repercussions in the astral realm, or of bad karma like getting sick, stopped them from speaking up.

There were several untreated cancer cases on Swami's watch. Australian Deborah Topp, a student at Agama in 2017, suffered from breast cancer. She refused to return to Australia for treatment and instead followed Swami's health advice. He instructed her to eat only brown rice and drink her own urine and menstrual blood. When the young woman finally returned home, it was too late. The tumour had by then grown so large that a mastectomy couldn't save her life.

In the same year, a group of over twenty affected students, some of them Australians, were by now talking to the Melbourne psychotherapist who gave a 'Yoga & Psychotherapy' course at the school. As in any abusive relationship, they didn't want the connection to their abuser to stop, just the abuse. The female therapist tried to counter some of the toxic tantric stereotypes that were perpetuated in Agama's teachings, and to help women set better boundaries. Maha, the school's doctor, who was appearing to grow more distanced from her father figure Swami, supported these attempts. Not surprisingly, the Australian therapist wasn't popular with the main culprit. Swami had a robust, communist Romanian distrust of psychology. His 'spiritual protection' would be sufficient to shield participants from harm – for instance, in the ATI that had damaged Sadhana and was extremely likely to trigger trauma with its highly sexual content. He did not see a reason to have trauma-aware assistants in the room or mental health professionals on call. 'Everyone is an adult here,' was his catchphrase.

In April 2017, a woman suffered psychosis after being urged to have group sex. She had to be sedated and hospitalised when her condition deteriorated. The Melbourne therapist asked Maha to set up an emergency response team, and to better vet people with a history of trauma. Her suggestion was ignored. Later that year, Agama's listing from a booking website was removed because they had too many complaints about sexual harassment.

Swami's goal at that time was to make enough money to buy an island in Greece or somewhere where the laws around sexuality would be less strict than in Thailand, so his closest people could practise sexual tantra all day without having to work.

'We need to get as many souls as possible,' he told staff members.

—

In April 2018, Swami held an internal meeting to discuss a letter that one of the female yoga teachers had written, suggesting solutions to the growing mountain of complaints and concerns.

'Our tantra is like the motto of the French legionnaires: "Walk or die",' Swami said in response. The meeting was recorded. Muktananda, the second in command, also responded. He disagreed with the #MeToo movement, saying women are playing 'too much the victim' and men are getting squashed.

'If you don't like Agama, don't come,' he said. Swami said that Mukta, as everyone calls him, had been accused of rape in his home country of India, making it sound benign. He then defended sex between Agama students and teachers, and said that no one needed protection from anyone. He and Muktananda were 'not the big bad wolf'. If you went to a kung fu school, you would spar with the grand master. So in a tantric school, 'you bump pelvises till you turn blue'. He wanted an army of men to do his job, because so many women who came to Agama were 'frigid' in his view. 'We are famous,' he boasted. 'I want stormtroopers with lingams.'

For anyone who attempted to change the culture from within, this was the leadership they faced.

Then came the fatal month of May 2018: another rape allegation. A young student in a fragile emotional state stopped by Swami's house late at night. She was drunk and her memory later fragmented. She had slept with Swami in the past, but at that time she was in a relationship and not willing to have sex with him again. She said the guru took advantage of her and penetrated her with his fingers and his penis. When she finally regained some memory of the night, friends encouraged her to go to the police.

But the local police are notoriously reluctant to investigate such cases. Having been drunk at the time, the victim would not have made a good witness. In Thailand, if there is consensual sex before an incident of sexual coercion, it's usually considered a domestic matter rather than a crime. Like many working at Agama, the young woman didn't have a work permit and was scared to get deported and banned. On top of that, Swami's loyalists told her that if she brought trouble to a spiritual school, there would be negative karmic consequences. Muktananda suggested Swami should put his penis in her again to 'get the demons out'. She just wanted to get off the island to leave it all behind.

It became a tipping point. About 40 people got together in a private group, including Jenny and Tom. 'Agamis for Ahimsa' was born – ahimsa meaning 'no harm', one of the yogic principles. Half of the group were men, one a well-known musical artist. The cross-section of Ahimsas included loyal Swami followers who saw him as a father figure, women who said they had been abused by him, and others still frequenting his bed. Jenny says it was difficult to navigate.

'But we all wanted this stuff to stop and we also wanted to save our school.'

One of the things the Ahimsa group pushed for was mandatory consent trainings to stop the locker-room vibe at the school. The idea of people respecting a 'no' didn't land well with Swami. His response was that it would make women less willing to have sex. He found them already too reluctant, which stopped them from advancing spiritually.

Agamis for Ahimsa wrote a manifesto that sounded amicable but stated their demands: atone, apologise, learn and change. None of it happened, so they held a meeting with Swami who appeared apologetic about his wrongdoings but didn't admit any specifics. The group eventually sent an email around, asking for anonymous testimonials. They wanted to hear about anything troubling, from financial shadiness to teachers aggressively hitting on Level One students, which had made some newcomers lose all interest in yoga.

'The line has been crossed again,' the email's author wrote. 'We all said "ENOUGH, that must be the last!"'

Dozens of written statements poured in. But Agamis for Ahimsa were facing the institutional challenges of trying to push back against a megalomaniac leader ready to double down. The group set up a petition that asked the Agama Foundation for a public statement acknowledging a past history of sexual harassment, for an apology for everyone concerned, and for a mandatory anti-harassment curriculum. Thirty-eight people signed a petition in mid-July, when the whole community met in a yoga hall. There were heated discussions about the definition of rape.

'Can we still have compassion for someone as a rapist?' someone pleaded.

While solutions were sought and fought over, a group of victims decided to give their testimonials to a journalist who could strike hard and fast: Be Scofield. The horse had bolted.

Jenny was away from the campus that day. She can still remember that it was 11 p.m. when the story broke. The exposé upset her. 'It was actually really unhelpful for us.'

She says the testimonials were given in confidence and then leaked. Others involved confirm that it was an intentional move to go public. One woman tells me that she gave Be her consent to publish her account in parts, but later regretted it when other teachers treated her like a traitor and liar because they had identified her. There was suspicion and chaos. Jenny didn't know whom to trust and stopped all electronic communication with the Ahimsa WhatsApp group.

Be's exposé was the end of any cooperation from Swami. Their mission to change the school from inside had failed.

Besides the shock on the ground, the article was a turning point for the wider tantra scene. The #MeToo volcano had finally erupted in yoga land, and Canadian author Jeff Brown promptly dubbed the movement #SriToo – Sri being an honorific for a holy person. The lava stream burned some of the worst predators in the business.

Afterwards, Swami made a dramatic retirement announcement, handed the school over to Maha and left the island, together with the other accused teachers. Very few people knew he was leaving. While he was packing, Maha held a teachers' meeting where she downplayed the allegations, taking the traditional line: when you teach sexual tantra, people are going to get confused and their issues will surface – a form of 'karmic purging'. Some understood this as victim blaming, with the woman in charge seen as Swami's puppet. There's speculation that Maha was left with little power, despite pure motivations for renewal. Swami's supporters are now acting as a shadow government. I'm told he still instructs his former lover from his hide-out.

At the end of July 2018, Be Scofield followed up her bombshell with an article about the rapist guru fleeing the island. It landed another heavy blow. The school cancelled its yoga therapy training, then stopped all classes for the week. The accused teachers' bios disappeared from the website as well as videos of Swami, his biography, and the newsletter archive.

The police in Koh Phangan asked victims to come forward and did a check at the school, but only for overstayers and visa issues. Because many foreign teachers didn't have work permits, some of the higher-level classes were secretly held in private houses – which again gave Agama control over non-residents, who had to accept whatever exploitative terms the school offered.

With the help of others, Maha hired Helen Nolan, an external consultant who specialised in institutionalised sexual abuse. But because she had been recommended by a Swami loyalist who was once her client, many victims were reluctant to come forward again. Some didn't trust that their private information wouldn't be shared with Swami. The fear of karmic repercussions and his supernatural powers was too strong.

While more Agama teachers resigned, Maha posted a public statement calling the abuse scandal a 'media war'. She claimed that those who remained at Agama wanted to support the affected women in any way they could. It sounded like a desperate plea: 'We are changing. Change also takes time.' Meanwhile, Swami announced via the head of the Agama school in Colombia that he was going to make a statement to set the record straight. It hasn't yet eventuated.

Chapter 17

On 17 August 2018, after weeks of soul-searching and support meetings with the Australian psychotherapist who had also been at Agama, Mangala Holland walks into the Thai consulate in Melbourne to lay a criminal complaint against Narcis Tarcau. The lengthy statement describes how she was anally raped by him. It ends like this:

> My whole life was connected to the school and community and I didn't think anyone would believe me. He is a well-known hypnotist and many in the school are under a 'spell'. In short, I now believe Agama Yoga is a religious cult. I am still dealing with the trauma of this.

The consul at the Thai embassy is a friendly Englishman who takes Mangala's statement, stamps it and files it. Once she walks out of the embassy, the tension she has been holding for years drops out of her body. She receives an email thanking her for the information, with an offer to help her if she wants to come to Thailand to report the alleged rape there. But she tells me over the phone that the prospect of a court case scares her. The chances of success are dismal. A sex cult run by promiscuous Westerners is not a priority for Thai authorities; the country is fighting much bigger crimes against local boys and girls in the sex industry. And

Thailand has a very short statute of limitations for rape charges. A complaint must be lodged with the police within three months of the incident, otherwise there can be no investigation. Nine out of ten rapes in Thailand go unreported, and only 4 per cent of those accusations then result in an arrest warrant.

What stopped many Agama survivors from coming forward in due time is not just the process it took to untangle themselves from the school and realise fully what happened, or Swami's spell on them, but their mistrust of Koh Phangan's police, who they claim regularly receive bribes from Agama.

The Siam kingdom has a deep-rooted culture of victim blaming – and on top of that, draconian defamation laws. After the rape and murder of a British tourist in 2014, Prime Minister Prayut Chan-o-cha made a telling statement. 'There are always problems with tourist safety,' he was quoted as saying. 'They think our country is beautiful and is safe so they can do whatever they want, they can wear bikinis and walk everywhere.'

Narcis Tarcau, the alleged rapist Swami, chose his third home well.

Before I check out of my modest resort on Koh Phangan, I have lunch with an Agami for Ahimsa in the open-air restaurant out the front. Paolo is from Italy, in his early thirties, slender and muscular in cotton fisherman's pants, his long hair in a ponytail. His English is impeccable and his manner reserved. He seems conflicted about even meeting me. Everyone is lying low right now; a mutual friend had to connect us first.

After finishing his 24 levels this year, the pensive yogi left.

'It's not easy to reconcile it all,' he says, opening up slowly while we order our curries. Everything is still fresh for him. He defends the 'yoga university' that saved so many. 'Thousands of people walked in there like zombies and came out alive afterwards.'

We discuss whether Agama is a cult, which is always hard to spot from the inside. He shrugs his shoulders.

'No one had a knife under their throat, or their passports taken away so they couldn't leave.' He looks at me. 'But was there psychological pushing? For sure.'

I tell him that it makes it harder to push back when the coercion is not brutally obvious – and ingrained in teachings that demand 'complete surrender'.

Paolo sounds more and more defeated as our lunch goes on. Agama should close now and get its act together, but then again, so many of his friends have built a life around it. When Be Scofield's story came out, there was disbelief and denial – and a sense of betrayal – all at once. He stopped wearing his Agama shirt in public.

The waiters around us are clearing plates, tourists walk past with kids licking ice creams, and gentle waves lap the sand along the coastline behind us. But I feel completely disconnected from this beach setting, oblivious to the beauty around me. A despair that I know all too well slowly rises inside me. I haven't felt it since I lost myself in the darkness of Centrepoint, too empathic to people's perspectives and pain, questioning whether I've got it all wrong. It's time to stop my mission and leave.

Yet others keep going and the revelations keep coming. While I sit in a taxi to the ferry, an Australian arrives back on the island and drives to the police headquarters on Koh Phangan. She files a rape complaint against Narcis Tarcau.

211

Like Mangala, she states that Swami brutally sodomised her against her will when she was cleaning his house in 2016. He didn't stop or react when she told him it hurt. She was left in pain and later became depressed.

The three-month time window has long lapsed, but the victim still wants the violation to go on record to pave the way for further complaints. According to one activist, who comes along as the woman's support, ten military policemen walk in and out of the room taking pictures, 'just being idiots'. They don't even write Narcis Eduard Tarcau's legal name down but just refer to him as 'Swami'. The Australian is questioned why she didn't flee, fight back or complain sooner. She feels their resistance to take her claim seriously.

Hours later, police vehicles pull up outside Agama. Armed officers disappear inside. Passing locals film the raid and post the footage to social media, speculating that arrests must be finally taking place. Others claim it's just for appearances so that the officers don't look as if they're sitting on their hands. But nothing comes of it. The local police commander tells the press that the surprise visit was just another routine check for work visas.

Two days later, *Coconuts* in Bangkok is the first news outlet to launch an investigative article under the headline 'Being Broken: Years of sexual abuse alleged at Agama yoga school on Koh Phangan'. *The Guardian* follows suit with 'Under Swami's spell: 14 tourists claim sexual assault by guru at Thai yoga retreat'. International media from Asia to Europe report about the yoga scandal. I write a story for the *New Zealand Herald*, *Die Presse* in Austria and *Die Zeit* in Germany. 'Namaste, mein Vergewaltiger' ('Namaste, my rapist') is their most-read online story that day. No one from Agama agreed to be interviewed for it because, as Maha tells me via email, their 'internal independent investigation' and an official police report are still underway.

The week after the international stories break, the school shuts down again – to restructure, as they announce in their latest of a series of statements. 'We sincerely apologize once more for any harm that any Agama teacher may have caused,' one begins. It acknowledges that they failed to ensure a proper procedure to report 'discomfort or potential abuse'. They claim that they are currently processing the results of the investigation and will shortly publish them. The open letter 'to our dear community' promises a list of changes, including a critical review of the tantra curriculum. In future, any sort of sexual relationship between students and teachers would require a signed consent form.

The vocal members of Boycott Agama think this is a disingenuous attempt at whitewashing, while the reformists in Agamis for Ahimsa still hope for positive renewal. Two days after Agama's latest PR move, a video appears, posted by Layla Martin. She's a popular trauma-informed sexuality coach in the US with thousands of followers on her YouTube channel where she promotes jade yoni eggs.

'It's time for me to share my #MeToo experience in the tantra and yoga world,' Layla says, opening a twenty-minute speech about how Swami coerced her into sex.

It's a bold disclosure. The international neo-tantra celebrity that *Cosmopolitan* once touted as a 'Sexpert Extraordinaire' reaches a different demographic than *The Guardian* or *Die Zeit*. She puts a prominent name to a victim's account, which shakes the remaining doubters out of denial. The dam has burst.

The same night on Koh Phangan, the Shambhala Hall in the Agama compound goes up in flames, and a video of the fire appears online. The hall hasn't been used, so it's unlikely someone left a candle burning inside. A tropical downpour that evening stops the flames from spreading from the dry palm roof to an elementary school nearby. Luckily no one is hurt, and firefighters are able to put the blaze out.

According to authorities it was probably an electrical malfunction, not arson. But a former Agama teacher from Australia who now lives in New Zealand is an electrician. He knew the wiring in the school well and confirms there was no electrical infrastructure in the part of the hall where the flames started. He suspects that whoever took a video of the fire must have lit it.

Agama is about to collapse beneath the domestic hostility and international pressure. There are now over 50 articles published in two dozen countries. As the school's silence is broadly viewed as an admission of guilt, the cries for consequences grow louder. The next voice to speak up sends another shock wave through the torn and divided community. A former Agama operations manager writes a Facebook post based on her old diary entries. Her 2000 words start with a trigger warning.

The woman describes in disturbing detail how she became suicidal after two years of rebelling against the school's pressure to get 'shaktified'. She could not leave because of money and visa issues. As a cure for her depression and 'karma blocks', Swami told her to hand her life over to him and become his sex slave. The yoga teacher ended up in a psychiatric ward.

In late October 2018, Narcis Tarcau slips back into Srithanu. It's been exactly three months and Thailand's statute of limitations for reporting a rape has expired. A couple of nights after his return, Swami holds a well-attended party that goes on late into the night. Loud music can be heard from his house. People are cheering.

'Dear divine souls,' Agama writes in a statement to its students to announce a new beginning. 'Our beloved school has been facing the greatest spiritual test so far.' It promises to become 'safer and stronger'.

For Maha, it's the end. The doctor resigns from Agama with an emotional post expressing her 'deep sadness' that she doesn't have either the authority or the support to continue the restructuring she had in mind. The last months have taken a heavy toll on her health and wellbeing. Mihaiela Pentiuc packs up her life on Koh Phangan and leaves Thailand for good. The internal investigation which she commissioned doesn't get published. Others, like Jenny, have also left. Only Swami's loyalists remain.

Christmas comes around with a gift from Agama. To celebrate their relaunch after the three-month hiatus, the school offers its Level One Yoga Intensive for free. As flyers saying 'Beware of Agama' circulate in Srithanu, only ten people show up for the training. On the weekend it finishes, someone throws a bag of human faeces over the front of Agama's health-food store and restaurant. The stench is revolting.

The 'official shit-show', as Boycott Agama describes it the next day with unveiled excitement, is far from official. Half a year has passed, and no state authorities have stepped in – only internet communities and the media. It's a common scenario. Deconstructing a cult is an arduous process that takes its toll on reporters too. The onus to overthrow an abusive, narcissistic, controlling master falls on deeply manipulated and traumatised victims, some of whom need years to untangle themselves first and who live in fear of repercussions for coming forward. While they attempt to build their lives back up, they also try to bring a cult down. There is little support from police, government, health services – or from the public who often sees them as naive and stupid.

Centrepoint was finally toppled by court cases. Since that hasn't yet happened with Agama, I can only hope that their business on Paradise Island dies a slow death.

Chapter 18

The shell in my palm is white and ribbed. I glide my fingertips slowly over its smooth spines. I'm not sitting on a beach this time, but on a cushion in a circle. I'm back in Byron Bay to attend a 'Wheel of Consent' workshop with thirteen others. They're mainly women: body workers, therapists, a law lecturer from Sydney. Every morning, we each explore an object to 'wake up our hands', as our facilitator calls the exercise. We're meant to just enjoy the touch, as innocently as a child stroking a cat, taking in the sensory information. It's the first step to understanding consent on a somatic level.

American chiropractor Betty Martin created a model that shows how all our interactions happen in a different quadrant of a circle: serve, take, accept, allow. Someone offering you a foot massage but actually wanting to touch you to get closer is not serving, but covertly taking. The wheel concept gets more complicated – who is the 'doer', who it is for, and why that matters. We also learn about our nerves: what mixed messages we give out because of the fight, flight or freeze responses, and the confusion that creates – in our bodies, and in society. Stress activates the sympathetic nervous system. It seems to be my default setting.

The course leader draws arrows on the whiteboard. The 'wheel', as he calls it, is not so much a mental construct;

it needs to 'land in the body'. He has a wide smile and a shaved head and likes to put on dance music in the breaks. 'No one can "give" you pleasure,' is his message. 'You can only feel it yourself.' Slowing down is key. He quotes Betty Martin: 'Ninety per cent of what we need to learn about great sex, we learn before we ever get our clothes off.' Mainly, how to feel safe, and how to communicate. We practise hands-on in small increments, asking freely for what we want in each moment, like 'May I hug you?'

On our third day, I get blindfolded and then led around the room for some free taking, not from people though. I spend minutes stroking a long velvet curtain, enjoying its sensual texture. I don't need to worry whether the fabric has a good time too. There's no expectation of reciprocation, it's only for my pleasure. Maybe I have a secret velvet fetish.

Later that day, much darker secrets come to light. Be Scofield has just exposed the eccentric Australian founder of TNT (The New Tantra) – the Dutch outfit I visited the year before and found disturbing. The report is so shocking that *Medium* takes it off its website, but the Dutch national newspaper *de Volkskrant* investigates further. The ripple effect of the latest detonation in tantra land is felt in our consent workshop too. The course leader with the monkish look was deeply involved in TNT before he became one of their whistle-blowers and started a Facebook group with the same acronyms, 'Tantra Not Trauma'. The group has since become the #MeToo platform of the neo-tantra scene. Many members want to see a regulating professional organisation for tantric bodywork because they have witnessed too much retriggering of trauma, and the shutdown of those who speak up. The red flags are not always obvious and embedded in content that works for many, at least in the beginning. It's harder to recognise abuse when the majority has an amazing beneficial experience. I too found plenty of gold in a terrain that got muddier and muddier.

One man called out as an alleged rapist in another article by Be Scofield is the sexual energy healer who demonstrated the impressive de-armouring session on stage at the Taste of Love event back in 2012, where a woman twitched and moaned under his hands. He now stands accused of penetrating a woman without her consent (and without a condom) during a 'healing session' on the sidelines of a European ISTA festival, two years before I met him.

While I finish the Wheel of Consent course in Byron Bay, I also close a chapter in my life that began in the Pacific seaside town almost seven years earlier. This time I'm not feeling any bliss. I question how informed consent can exist in intimate interactions between students and teachers – even if they teach a holistic sexuality – given the inherent power differential, the projection on facilitators, and with course content shrouded in secrecy. Intense group work, often back-to-back from one level to the next without time to ground yourself, works on the nervous system like being on drugs. It's called a 'workshop high' for a reason. In a weeklong 24/7 training full of rituals, circle confessions and cathartic release, a potent cocktail of endorphins, dopamine and oxytocin floods your system and clouds your thinking. Constantly 'dropping the mind' while you're loved up or turned on can result in overriding your inner 'yes' or 'no' – assuming you're even aware of it, especially if past trauma is retriggered, which can easily happen. If you want cosmic bangs for your bucks and crave a desired outcome like the rest of the enthralled tribe, then you won't speak up when something doesn't feel right – especially if you don't want to be labelled as 'acting from your wounding' or 'stuck in victim consciousness'.

I stop recommending the ISTA trainings I once raved about. Researching Agama has revealed my own blind and soft spots as well. This new world of self-exploration had transformed me, but while I was chasing healing around the world, I blocked out its shadow. The price has since become too high – and not just the five figures I've spent on international travel and workshop fees.

I'm wary of charismatic leaders creating a residential community around them and dismissing justified criticism as 'witch hunts' or 'gossip'. I'm frustrated by faculties that are good at marketing, but don't have complaint and aftercare systems in place for participants because they feel exempt from proper codes of conduct by virtue of their evolutionary cause. I've seen too much arrogance and obfuscation among the ranks by now, with word salads of jargon like 'loving', and not enough accountability and trauma awareness from the top. A swami accused of rape is an extreme, but not the only rotten core of other yoga, neo-tantra and embodiment businesses that care more about their income and reputation than about the people they've harmed.

My innocence has gone. I suddenly wonder where I've unwittingly pushed people's boundaries as a workshop assistant, with best intentions so that everyone gets with the programme and stays in the room; and because I wanted to keep playing with the cool kids. Although I was never as involved anywhere as deeply as the Agamis for Ahimsa were, I know the conflict of integrity too well: wanting to hold on to what worked while calling out what is wrong. It's painful to realise that achieving both might not be possible. Despite my misgivings, I'm also grieving. There are many people in the 'sacred sexuality' world who I respect and will miss. Instead of rattling the cage, I quietly step out of it.

—

On a small island in the Asia Pacific, things seem to be finally changing too. One year after the Agama scandal erupted, all their signs on Koh Phangan are being replaced and the school rebrands itself as 'Phangan Yoga' – after putting out a plea for money to 'nurture our little oasis of spiritual hope and aspiration'. It almost makes me feel sorry for the last ones still standing. Are they delusional – or deceitful? While I'm shedding my skins, so are others. Justine Baruch puts out a lengthy public statement that is half atonement, half whitewashing. 'I am sorry for any pain my actions or guidance has caused anyone,' it ends. All references to Agama disappear from her Facebook timeline, but she still offers similar content in her own events, including the ATI.

Phangan Yoga never takes off. A few months later, the Agama sign goes back up. But any hopes of seeing a reformed and consent-conscious institution emerge from the rubble vanish with an interview that the school puts out in its December 2019 newsletter. Muktananda Mistry, one of the accused, explains 'what really happened in Agama Yoga in 2018 during those weeks of confusion'. Since it's not stated who the interviewer is, it feels fake.

The first question to the new Indian head of the school is whether there was ever any sexual abuse or rape at Agama. 'Absolutely not,' is the beginning of his lengthy answer that reads like a communiqué from a totalitarian political party. To sum it up: it's a 'big lie', 'preposterous lie', 'ridiculous lie', 'damned lie', 'shocking', 'fake news', 'trumped up'. Agama, he assures, has always been a very safe environment for women to 'unfold their spiritual quest' – with a success rate of 99.7 per cent if out of the 10,000 women who went through the school, only five or six 'or even 31' complained.

Muktananda repeatedly refers to trans female journalist Be Scofield as 'he', a 'dubious character'. The senior teacher then ends on a note of elitist spiritual bypassing: a tantric community might have been too much for beginners, for people coming 'from the profane world out there, full of bourgeois and selfish ideals without enough spiritual aspiration'. As soon as they are confronted with the 'emotional challenges' of their 'shadow', these people then 'project their misery' and accuse the whole world around them 'for whatever trouble befalls them'.

At the start of the pandemic, some local yoga businesses on Koh Phangan that were dependent on tourism shut down. Antithetically, Agama picks up more students worldwide by offering courses online. Parallel to its surge in business, it is lifted out of obscurity and onto the screen in 2020. A *Jezebel* documentary with the tagline 'The Predatory Guru' and an episode of the Netflix series *(Un)Well* both shine a critical light on the rape cult, with more women now speaking out on camera. One of them still hasn't watched her interview when I call her a year later. After going public, she had a nervous breakdown because of all the hateful messages she received from Agama's defenders.

The Netflix documentary should have been the final nail in Agama's coffin. But when I check the school's website a year on, it's like a déjà vu of the days before the palace revolution. Apart from a consent-based Conscious Touch workshop that is now a prerequisite for any tantra courses, nothing has visibly changed. 'Welcome, To Paradise Island' the header over a tropical beach photo beams at me. Fresh mango and coconut for breakfast is advertised again, plus the hammock and afternoon massage after a yoga class. The vibe is erotic: 'Become multi orgasmic', 'Practice sexual secrets', 'Discover true love'. The highest level is now a purple sash.

Under the link 'Founder & Vision' I stare at a portrait photo of the man himself – 'Swamiji to his students' – and absorb five glowing paragraphs. 'Although restrained by a modesty that usually prevents him from discussing it, Swamiji has reached high states of spiritual realisation', I learn. 'Swamiji inspires by personal example.' The website has a two-hour satsang video with him, but not a single statement or apology regarding the rape and sexual abuse allegations.

At the end of 2021, the start of Agama's high season, their social media is ramping up with links to Swami's 'tantric relationships' videos, full-moon gatherings and new courses. The rigid stereotypes of 'superior masculine' and 'surrendering feminine' are perpetuated in a promotional photo that shows three people, all dressed in white: Muktananda sitting in the middle like a pasha, holding his arms possessively around two sexy women in flimsy tops and long split skirts that show their thighs. One of them is Yogita, the Complete Femininity course teacher I'd shared lunch with three years ago. Their foreheads are painted with a white symbol and their hands are folded in a prayer gesture on the senior teacher's chest. 'Good times at Agama! Thank you Shiva for our wonderful spiritual family', the caption reads.

On Koh Phangan, posters of Swami's upcoming talks hang outside Agama's main entrance on a large noticeboard, with his photo. He is available for private sessions during office hours. The ATI – the tantra intensive with group sex – is on offer again. It's like 2018 never happened.

My next surprise, which slowly turns to dismay, arrives when I contact my old sources for an update. The Australian who filed the rape complaint with the police on Koh Phangan has disappeared from Facebook. The last time I messaged her, she was dealing with PTSD. Other sexual abuse survivors and whistle-blowers who spoke out three years earlier express to me how triggered they are even having to think about Agama, or hearing Swami's name, let alone revisit the place in their minds. Mental health problems flare up. They wish me luck with my book but cannot talk. It's too stressful.

Their responses are so similar that I wonder for a moment whether Agama has tried to silence these women. It's not completely far-fetched. MISA, the litigious Romanian esoteric yoga cult that is the backdrop for Agama's teachings, is known to intimidate its critics – including scholars and published authors – through cease-and-desist letters from lawyers acting for their worldwide umbrella, the ATMAN Yoga Federation.

But for the Agama victims I know, the common denominator is not the fear of defamation lawsuits but simply the fact that three years on, they are deflated or defeated. Putting themselves through all the reporting, the interviews, the public exposure, and then seeing nothing come out of this exhausting and retraumatising battle apart from media coverage, must be devastating. Unlike with Harvey Weinstein or NXIVM founder Keith Raniere, justice hasn't been done. There is no closure, either metaphorically or literally. Agama is still up and running, with the alleged abuser at the helm instead of in a courtroom. The inconvenience of a rape scandal during Swami's quest for enlightenment by penis power was just a short bad dream.

It's not what I had expected. The damage of the cult's shadow is ongoing for those affected, long after the headlines are forgotten. It has messed up women who can't simply rebrand their experiences or pretend they never happened.

Because this injustice perpetuates sexual violence and I have skin in the game, I pick up the baton again.

By now, I've spoken to a dozen people who went through Agama. I've seen the unsolicited 'dick pics' that one of the leaders sent around. I've also listened to a secret recording of a private meeting where Swami compares himself to Jesus, claiming that he has cured students from cancer, and then intimidates a woman – threatening her with bad karma, like breaking a leg.

Many former students I contact are still conflicted, ashamed and confused, but some have gained a more detached clarity since then. Their stories echo every accusation and account I heard three years earlier. They corroborate the evidence against Swami Vivekananda Saraswati and his school that has never been processed legally. So far, it has only been investigated by journalists – and by Helen Nolan.

The Danish HR specialist is the consultant who was hired by Agama for an independent assessment of the sexual abuse allegations. Her report was never released by the school, which has led to speculation about its content. Because the assessor signed a non-disclosure agreement with Agama, I have to jump through a few hoops before she speaks to me on the record. I reach her late at night at the start of the Sabbath weekend in Tel Aviv, where she lives and works. She's a bespectacled woman in her fifties, earnest and concerned, who chooses her words carefully.

Despite earlier claims, Helen Nolan had no personal connection with Agama whatsoever and maintains that her work was done completely professionally and independently. Even for such a seasoned HR practitioner, the project was an outlier in her career. Unfortunately, her hands were tied.

'The investigation wasn't comprehensive,' she tells me. 'But that wasn't down to a lack of trying.'

Only six women contacted her because people suspected the investigation was a whitewash, and there was fear of retaliation. Instead of letting the facts speak for themselves, Helen claims, Agama used a small fraction of her investigation to spin the results. It was 'very disheartening'. She has not spoken to anyone from the school since and is as surprised as I am that Swami is back in business.

Would she send her daughter there?

'No,' she says curtly while her face speaks volumes.

Helen Nolan's reply would have been the perfect ending to my Agama research. But then a door opens that I thought was closed. One of the men who was publicly named and shamed as a sexual abuser three years earlier suddenly agrees to an interview.

Every Agami for Ahimsa I talked to has brought up this person's name with me. They all pointed out that Baz had worked hard to redeem himself after everything blew up.

'He has done more than any other senior teacher to free himself from the indoctrination,' Jenny messages me. 'He took responsibility for his actions.'

It takes a few rewrites of a confidentiality agreement before Baz trusts me with his story. He lives in Israel. When he came out of the army there, he was only 21 years old and bursting to let loose for a while in India, a tradition among his peers. After that, he was going to return home and enrol at drama school. But instead, Baz found Tibetan Buddhism in India.

'I was into martial arts too, a real energy bomb,' he tells me. He's a stocky guy, sprawled on cushions on a mat, hands folded behind his shaved head. 'So I needed something for my body as well.'

That's how he stumbled into yoga and enrolled at Agama,

not in Thailand but in Rishikesh at the time. In a talk which he never forgot, he was told that there are only two ways to evolve as a yogi in regard to sexual conduct: become ascetic and refrain from sex – or become tantric and embrace it. The latter option sounded more 'juicy' to the self-described nerd.

At the end of 2008, Baz visited Agama on Koh Phangan and kept coming back. In the beginning, it was just a calling to go deep in the philosophy and practice. 'I had this intense fervour that you often see in fresh converts,' he admits. Do lots of meditation, all the purifications, become part of the community: this was what he was looking for, especially after the army – an antidote to what he calls 'the merciless culture in the West'.

Baz is still not sure how the bad stuff crept into the teachings he absorbed about 'shiva and shakti'. He points out that tantra is actually a tradition that embraces emotions in all its aspects. Many initiators were women. But as an outsider, new to it all, it was hard to separate what was ancient and authentic from the old-school misogyny that Swami represented.

Sexually, Baz was shy and inexperienced. He had had only one girlfriend in the past. The young student wanted to be part of the game but had too much fear of rejection and failure to be flirtatious.

'I was hiding in my hut, doing tons of yoga.'

The truth was that he was sexually frustrated, jealous of all the other men, and craving intimacy. He sighs with a slight smile. 'Living in a community where it's pretty obvious everyone else is doing it all the time was rubbing it into my face even more.'

Towards the end of his course, he had a private consultation with Swami where they talked about Baz's self-imposed celibacy. The guru challenged him to come out of his shell and get active. It angered Baz a bit. He wanted to prove the master wrong. But then a friend hooked him up with an older experienced Agama woman, and it was amazing.

'Spiritual,' says Baz.

Swami was now grooming him to be a more confident man. Baz needed that encouragement. He had no role models of successful men, so Swami and other senior teachers took that place. Baz learned to overcome his fears and not act out of a loser mentality.

'In that way, Swami was a good father figure.'

After his second year in Agama, 'everything flipped'. The novice became popular with women and started teaching yoga tantra, not just at Agama but across Europe too. Baz had finally found his footing. For the next two years, he only wanted 'high-quality sexual experiences' to compensate for the former drought. It was easy to find them at Agama, no strings attached. He says he often ended up in situations where boundaries were crossed, by women too. They wanted to be with him because he was seen as a hot tantric lover.

'Did I do sexual stuff when I didn't have it in me to say no? Yes, many times,' he recalls. It was the brand and the culture they all had to represent. It wasn't always clear to him when he was crossing boundaries or challenging himself. Everyone was free and open, and he wanted to explore his limits. No one was supposed to be jealous, even if your friend was hitting on your girlfriend right in front of you. He couldn't afford not to appear willing, even if he grew tired of being the 'hired lingam' for a woman in a relationship wanting to try something new. The new persona became his act for a while. Baz describes it to me like doing sales: 'You're always flirty, always on. It's a hype, but very stressful.' Only when it started to feel repetitive and empty, did he get into more serious relationships.

Sometimes he saw other men doing and saying sexist things that made him cringe, but it seemed to work for the cool guys. The women didn't react badly, *So maybe it's not that bad*, he thought. The prevailing attitude was to give everything a try, to do something first and then say yes later. And if it didn't work, try again. In some painful situations within open relationships, Baz could only cope by shutting down his emotions. 'And that is very dangerous, when you override your conscience by trying to fit in.'

It was similar to what he had learned in the Israeli army.

Baz participated in the six-week-long Agama Tantra Initiation. Someone there pointed out to him that he was touching women without their consent and objectifying them that way. He was visibly shaken by this feedback. That had never occurred to him before. But he didn't have the tools or the culture around him to understand what he was doing wrong.

We've talked for almost an hour on camera now. I'm ready to ask Baz about the allegations made in Be Scofield's article in 2018.

'It's not something you ever want your own mother to read,' he told me on our first informal call. According to two anonymous accounts, he had made offensive comments and was also involved in a threesome where a sexually explicit selfie was taken and later shared without consent. When I try to summarise the allegations, Baz pauses the Zoom recording briefly. He is not comfortable going into the details because they also involve two other people who were lovers at the time. He only realised when he met the female friend again later that things were not okay for her.

'I couldn't live with myself until we settled it.'

They had a reconciliation, but his name was still washed up in the testimonials, which hurt – while he says he was rightfully perceived as part of the system. He had a panic attack. It wasn't just the humiliation of the exposure that caused a shock. Baz witnessed in an ATI workshop how another accused teacher reacted to the allegations but didn't take anything on board. That became his biggest transformation, more than the article.

'A few more steps down the path, and I could have been that guy. I would have done far worse things than I did. That scared the shit out of me.'

The curtain was pulled back, but the wake-up call was brutal. Baz left Koh Phangan, stopped all tantra yoga, and returned to Israel. In an instant, he lost the life he had been building for ten years, without a fall-back or a job. He found work as an astrologer.

Losing his community was the hardest. Outwardly, he was functioning, but emotionally, he was in chaos, in a crisis of self-doubt. 'I was afraid that I was blind to how people perceive my actions. Paranoid actually.'

For the next three months, he approached everyone he thought he might have hurt at some stage, to check if they were okay or could give him their perspective. After the shame and self-flagellation, Baz began to sift through everything he had been taught at Agama to understand his actions and conditioning. It was confusing that someone could be a good teacher and still have big flaws. He neither wants to accuse nor absolve those who led him on.

'The theory was great,' he says, 'the implementation obviously not so much.'

Both were mixed in an insidious way and shaped his narrow worldview in an already insular place.

'It was the best of times and the worst of times,' Baz sums up his decade inside the cult, to which he has never returned. 'I regret a lot, but it needed to happen so that I could grow.'

After Agama, Baz started therapy for the first time, whereas before, he only had meditation. It took him two years to regain his moral perspective, an innate sense of right and wrong. He found he didn't know his own personality anymore, and that relationships were a risk he wasn't yet willing to take. On purpose, he stayed single and celibate. Only after a lot of therapy did he slowly re-enter the neo-tantra scene. As a coach, he is teaching tantra for men again with 'rehabilitated Agamis' by his side, but with his own take on masculinity: less poisonous, more chivalrous, and emotionally aware. Baz, now in his early thirties, is also dating again. But he has no desire to be in any open relationship.

His aversion to consensual non-monogamy (or CNM) reminds me of many who left or survived Centrepoint. Some of them became asexual. They had endured years of pressure to be promiscuous, including directives to sleep with someone new every day. Their boundaries were pushed and violated; their instincts overridden. There wasn't much freedom in their 'free love commune', but plenty of coercion and manipulation. Sex became a commodity and a dogma.

In a hierarchical high-control group, open relationships are completely at odds with consensual non-monogamy. Consent can only be freely given between equals, not under pressure. It respects everyone's needs and requires honest communication. Despite the sex gurus' preaching of 'loving', their reign was neither caring nor kind. It's the opposite of what polyamory stands for.

After our interview, Baz writes an email to Helen Nolan, since he learned through me that she also lives in Israel. He thanks her for being part of his process three years ago. While he was facing a social media lynch mob that wanted to see him in prison, the professional investigator did something that he says was 'healing'. She simply treated him like a real person.

I never planned to give sexual abusers a voice or the last word. But the more I've learned about the parts of me that could have easily joined these communities, the harder it is to dehumanise those who did awful things there. I'm wondering where I would have found myself on the sliding scale from bystander to apologist – too caught up to quit, or too compassionate not to?

The blame is often shifted to the 'bad apples' alone. Without excusing any of their actions, I also see these scapegoats as products of their spiritual environment; one which looks down on victims and implies it's always your problem if something feels off. Trainings and teachings can create a psychic split where the student refuses to realise the abuse, where their boundary setting is shamed, and where trauma gets bypassed with bliss and catharsis.

Those men – and women – are the spawn of small but mighty patriarchies in our midst that flourish under the protection of religious freedom. I thought their days of destruction, at least in Aotearoa New Zealand, were over. As I'm about to discover, it turns out I'm wrong.

PART 3

Handmaids on the West Coast

Chapter 19

Fog hovers over Lake Haupiri as the sun sets behind dense bush. Nestled between rivers and hills on the shore of the lake, 30 kilometres into the valley, I can barely make out the large compound in the dusk. A yellow sign at the turnoff from the empty road says 'Concert'. That's all. The only indication that my friend and I have entered the grounds of Gloriavale, after heading west for three hours from Christchurch, is the slow car in front of us. The driver is wearing a headscarf and blue dress. A woman at the wheel? That must be as rare out here as in Saudi Arabia.

The light-grey hostel buildings are double-storey with verandas running around each floor. About six hundred people, the majority children, live there in dormitories, one family to a room. Many residents are second-generation adults who were born into the community. They sleep, pray, sing and eat together, and they work long hours: on the farm, in the laundry, honey factory or childcare centre. Gloriavale also has a communal kitchen and dining hall, sports fields, farmhouses, workshops, hangars, an indoor swimming pool and sprawling lawns.

Although I've never been here before, it all looks familiar. Like millions of Kiwis, I've seen it in the TVNZ series *Gloriavale: A Woman's Place*, which purported to be a documentary but was a highly crafted promotional piece.

The network's most popular programme in 2016 presented the isolated fundamentalist Christian community as a happy, peaceful place of devoted souls: blue washing blowing in the West Coast sunshine and pregnant women gliding about in long robes, softly patting their bellies, and smiling demurely at their men. When I enter this idyll two years later for the first time, it feels a bit like stepping onto a movie set. Or into a strange and foreign country.

We count 24 prams in front of one of the hostels. Next to the car park is the new school and the kids' playground. Wooden military jeeps and a replica World War II cannon are parked between the trikes and slides. War toys are not what I would expect from Christians. But those are only props, stacked next to the hall where the winter concert is taking place. Every two years, the isolated South Island religious community puts on its famous show for free as a gift to the wider community. It runs over a month, sometimes with two events per day, and an overall audience of around 6000. Every guest gets fed a three-course meal. Some spectators come from as far away as overseas, but most are from Greymouth or Christchurch.

The lean old man at the entrance thanks me and my friend for wearing long skirts. His name is Gideon and he's happy to tell us that he's lived in the community for 48 years. Australian-born Neville Cooper – the original name of Gloriavale's late founder Hopeful Christian – was a travelling Christian preacher. He started his first community called Springbank at Cust in North Canterbury in 1969. To outsiders, they became known as the Cooperites. In the early '90s, they relocated 60 kilometres inland from Greymouth where the new compound was named after Cooper's late wife, Gloria.

Its members live according to the description of the early church in the New Testament: no private property, no borrowing or lending money, men in charge. But there are a couple of non-biblical additions. Women promise to be meek, quiet, and never use birth control. Many families have ten children or more. Everyone wears uniforms and no one has possessions because nothing is permitted that allows an individual to stand out. Cell phones are forbidden, and internet access is restricted to a trusted few. The outside world is believed to be evil. The community is run by a group of sixteen men who hold the dual titles of 'Servants and Shepherds' – the SS.

Because most of the shows are sold out that winter, I mention to Gideon at the door that we're lucky to have a ticket. He corrects me: 'Not lucky – you are blessed!' Our modest dress seems to be an invitation for more religious mansplaining.

'What leads to sin?' he asks us as if we were schoolgirls. 'In one word!'

'Uh … mistakes?' I guess. Is this the entry quiz?

'Close!' He fixes us with barely contained anticipation. 'Starts with "D"!'

The devil comes to mind, but again I'm wrong.

'Disobedience,' says Gideon, beaming and nodding.

He carries on with his friendly God-bothering while I browse the church brochures and comic-strip tales displayed on a rack: *Poor Little Lamb, Earnest for the Lord*. Then we're ushered in. No cell phones are allowed.

The dining hall where hundreds of people eat together every day has been transformed into a 1950s Disneyland with elevated rows of candlelit tables, theme-park-like castle walls and colourful murals. My place is framed by a bread roll, chess figures as salt and pepper shakers, and Cheezels in a toy truck. The theme of the night is 'Musical Museum – A World of Adventure and Discovery'.

Adventures and discoveries are not what the repressive world of Gloriavale normally stands for. In this bizarrely decorated place, worldly knowledge and higher education is withheld. Every aspect of life is controlled by the leaders. But today, we get the presentation of an illusion. It's a means for Gloriavale to maintain their tax-free charitable status, just like the Waitangi picnic with music, free homemade buns and ice cream which they put on once a year for the citizens of Greymouth.

Gloriavale is a major player in the West Coast economy and one of its biggest milk suppliers. Annually, it turns over around $22 million in its eleven businesses: midwifery, sheep and dairy, honey production, sphagnum moss, trophy hunting, health-food supplements, an offal farm and West Coast Air that offers scenic flights to Aoraki Mt Cook. At the time of the concert, their assets are $36.4 million and growing each year.

Children attend school until the age of fifteen and join the workforce as 'volunteers' – they don't get paid. A few do further training by long-distance learning. By the age of eighteen, teenagers sign a Declaration of Commitment. In a special ceremony, they publicly relinquish all income and possessions and surrender their personal rights to the community leaders, who also choose their spouse. Special days like Christmas, Easter and birthdays are not celebrated, and funerals or weddings of family members on the outside can't be attended. Women are not allowed to vote in elections.

Our young waiter's name is Zealous. He serves us tomato soup while a large choir enters the stage. Some of the older girls have hair down to their knees. Rows and rows of tiny kids in blue come on, singing and praising the Lord. No one misses a note.

Howard Temple takes the microphone to welcome us. He is the 'Overseeing Shepherd' of Gloriavale. Together with Fervent Stedfast, the septuagenarian American moved to the helm of Gloriavale a few months ago when the 92-year-old founder Hopeful Christian died in May 2018.

After some housekeeping, we get a lengthy rundown about immorality, King Solomon and not denying one another the spousal body. Then Howard Temple introduces 'a man with a vision' who has left 'an outstanding example': 'In honour of Hopeful Christian,' he hollers, 'tonight is for you!'

Christian, aka Neville Cooper, appears on a screen and talks to us. For another ten minutes, we watch a biopic of the late preacher: how he travelled the world, built a community, looked after his flock.

There is no mention of Christian/Cooper's time in prison. He was convicted of indecent assault in 1994 but told his followers that he had been imprisoned for spreading the gospel. To this day, that remains the in-house version at Gloriavale, where a quarter of the community is related to him by blood. Because internet use and reading material is controlled or forbidden, members are heavily restricted in their access to information.

While sweet voices sing 'May all who come behind us find us faithful' over photos of Hopeful's funeral, I'm bracing myself for an excruciating evangelical marathon. But instead of an enactment of biblical tales, we're showered in fairy-tale magic when the curtain opens to an opulent old-school musical themed around different cultures and eras.

The first act, 'All God's Creatures', kicks off with a fast-paced zoo parade of military precision. It's Disney on steroids. Furry animals dance to catchy tunes, including a film song from *Moana*. Cute little penguins waddle along. There's even a life-sized horse. A big burly bear high-fives us on his way out. 'So cool!' I hear from a kid behind me. Everyone is clapping along and fired up. This is top-notch family entertainment, the costumes and props outstanding.

Zealous serves us the second course: meat, rice, peas and croquettes with gravy or white sauce. During dinner, a magician entertains us with juggling balls and dad jokes.

'My wife said to me: "You never take me anywhere expensive anymore." I said: "Right, get your coat on. We're going to the petrol station!"'

It's unintentionally ironic. Gloriavale couples can never go out on a dinner date. They have no money to spend on their own, let alone permission to cycle around a town at night-time to a café, as the next round of performers do. They are acting out a world they don't inhabit.

The same farce applies to Angel Benjamin, well known from the TVNZ series. While tiny cowboys hop out of Wild West coaches, the stunning music teacher sings a song. She is dressed as a Native American, with her long hair down and uncovered. Such frivolous exposure would normally be punished in Gloriavale. That's not the only compromise for a good show. Legs and arms that appear bare in the ethnic costumes are covered in skin-coloured tight fabric.

Another reality TV star of Gloriavale enters the stage: Dove Love, the rosy-cheeked 22-year-old virgin who was about to marry seventeen-year-old Watchful Steadfast after only talking to him for six weeks. 'Pure as a gift', as the narrators told us in the television voice-over, they walked off the stage during their wedding ceremony to 'consummate the marriage' while an elder commented on her 'seal' that only the child-groom was allowed to open. Now Dove and

Watchful are one of the couples dancing on stage. They give each other a sweet little kiss.

During intermission, I spot a group of female visitors in mini-skirts, heavy make-up and jewellery, smoking in the car park. It's hard to tell whether they're just culturally insensitive or deliberately provocative. Mocking Gloriavale in Facebook groups like 'Hopeful memes for Gloriavale teens' has become a fun pastime for fans of the series who treat the cult like a freak show. An eighteen-year-old student even poses as 'Hopeful Christian' on Twitter after the craze started around New Zealand schools. TVNZ now offers Dove Love's schmaltzy wedding song as a singalong video on demand. The 2017 TED talk by Gloriavale leaver Lilia Tarawa is one of the most-watched ever, worldwide. It's not just the free food and show, let alone support for conservative Christian values, that brings some members of the audience here today, but voyeurism.

After the break, Zealous brings us homemade ice-cream sundaes for dessert. We've now been watching for over four hours. The bombastic entertainment effect is wearing off. Coffee and tea have been served and I'm fluctuating between overload, repulsion and compassion. How many challenging months have the self-described sheep of Gloriavale slaved away for this 'sacrifice'? In between rehearsing and performing, they cook and work late into the night, with no release from their usual ten-hour-shifts.

While they're still at school, girls learn how to do laundry, cooking, sewing and childcare. Boys later study farming, engineering and carpentry. They don't get a salary. Their passports, tax numbers and birth certificates are held in an office safe, which they cannot access even when they leave. Most members don't even know they each have a bank account, from which money is automatically transferred into the communal account. Some have walked out straight after the concert season, at breaking point from the countless performances on top of the demanding physical work.

Since 2013, Gloriavale has lost many members, around 20 to 30 a year – people who have either left voluntarily or were expelled. Very few have later returned.

The grand finale has flavours of North Korea. Lovely little girls wave pastel flags in synchronised perfection while hand-animated seabirds, built by the crafty men of the community, meander through the hall. The adult performers appear like an army. No one stands out individually. They don't even get a curtain call at the end; that would be too vain. Only Overseeing Shepherd Howard Temple appears again and takes the microphone, telling us to drive safely in the dark. On the way out, each visitor receives a freshly baked loaf of bread and a piece of homemade butter as a gift.

The main costume maker stands in the foyer, waiting for us. Purity Valor is friendly and welcoming. She doesn't know that I'm a reporter. Her daughter, who is over twenty but looks like a teenager, joins us and listens eagerly while looking down at the same time. Two men in blue walk past and shoot my friend and me a look that I don't get often these days: they're checking us out. The cheerful dressmaker takes us around the back to proudly show us the props and the storage room packed with rows of fancy dresses and fantasy outfits she helped to make. She compliments us on our modest dress. It's an important Christian value for Purity that we 'look like women, not like men'.

I wonder how much her creativity is a compensation for a lack of choice in her own wardrobe. Gloriavale standardised its clothing in 1988 to discourage vanity among women and to economise on fabric purchasing and clothing production.

Every two years, they churn out between seven to eight hundred dresses. The style was developed by the leaders who chose blue because it suited the widest variety of people.

When Margaret Atwood's dystopian saga *The Handmaid's Tale* started screening in 2017, the costumes were inspired by Gloriavale. The dresses have a flap for breastfeeding and function in maternity too. Women swim and cycle in them. They each own a precious pink one as well for their wedding and other special occasions, and two pairs of white sneakers, one for work.

We step into the sinking sun outside the main building and join a group of visitors who stand around Prudent Stedfast. The son of secretary, treasurer and second in command Fervent Stedfast is an engineer – a career path not open to Gloriavale women – and here to answer our questions. His father wrote a 134-page book with a theological interpretation of the Bible. *What We Believe* lays the foundation for all rules at Gloriavale, from what you wear and eat to when you go to bed. This is the best place to raise kids, we hear from Prudent. Women can still be women and don't have to work.

'Not men's work, you mean,' a female visitor challenges him.

He smiles but avoids answering.

I want to know how the cult representative feels about those who escaped overnight or were kicked out. There has been media attention recently on the growing exodus of community members. Prudent is not too fazed by my question and claims that they're all provided with what they need for a new start. Given that they all know how to work hard, they should be fine.

'They're bad apples,' he claims. 'If you allow a sinner in the church and don't deal with it, it gets rotten.'

He's not shy to talk about shunning, which is also common in other sects like the Exclusive Brethren or Jehovah's Witnesses.

'You are not to speak to them, talk with them, eat with them. You cut them off,' he says, describing the punitive practice. If one of his eight children wanted to go, he would have to abandon them in the name of Christ.

'It's all or nothing. My kids know that. If they want the world, they can't have me. That's it.' Prudent says it with a shrug and a smile that makes it sound benign.

Before we walk back to our car, he dashes off to the office to fetch us a King James Bible to take home.

'It's the only one to read!' are the last words I hear in Gloriavale.

I spend the morning in Moana, the small settlement closest to Gloriavale that's popular with holidaymakers. One street down from the pub towards Lake Brunner, Peter Mac is just opening up the Stationhouse Cafe. The hefty publican sees a lot of people passing through during concert season. His village is split between those who like what Gloriavale offers them and those who boycott the performance. Peter would never go himself.

'It's just a con job to show you how great they are,' he grumbles while slowly turning on the coffee machine behind the bar.

His wife, Jan, in a white chef's coat freshly buttoned up, doesn't hold back either.

'I think they are disgusting,' she chimes in. 'Look what they do with the girls there. They don't pay tax and get Working for Families, and they go around all the local businesses and buy everything cheap.'

She places her crossed arms on the table, then shakes herself, gets up and heads towards the kitchen. Her husband shoots me a glance and speaks again.

'They beat their cows. Heard that from one of the farmers.'

He turns back to the bar again with a stern face. 'We don't discuss them much.'

Our chat is over.

A group of locals who sit outside the pub in the sunshine have more to say. Apart from fishing and boating, Moana doesn't offer much distraction. A cult in the neighbourhood that the whole country knows from television always offers something to talk about. Everyone has an opinion on it.

One of the men tells me that he helped a young Gloriavale father get away in a spontaneous rescue action. After a desperate phone call, he met the fugitive by the river and gave him some clothes. Four months later, the man went back in. It's a familiar tale around here.

The others at the table turn to a tough-looking middle-aged woman with wild curly hair and big greenstone pendants. She seems to hold mana (authority or prestige) in their group.

'Guess what happened to me,' says Manaia, tucking into her late breakfast. The self-described hippie owns a piece of land with a house bus down the road from Gloriavale. She recounts how a young Gloriavale man in his twenties visited her unannounced one day. While she was still in her dressing gown, she offered him a coffee – a beverage that's forbidden inside Gloriavale. The young chap came up the steps behind her and grabbed her bottom. Then he told Manaia to take her gown off.

She shakes her mane, stabbing her food. 'I thought I might have to kill this guy with my spade. He was a big boy.'

Manaia managed to get rid of the man by talking him down and playing nice. But she was shaky. After he had left, she informed the manager on the farm nearby, which also belongs to the Christian community, Bell Hill, about what happened. That night, Gloriavale men came up her drive. They brought the young bloke back to apologise. Fervent Stedfast was asking how they could compensate her. He offered to buy her a DVD player.

Manaia pulls a face and reaches for her tobacco pouch. 'I don't even have electricity out there.'

She felt a bit sorry for the intruder, assuming that he would be bashed by the Gloriavale leaders for the transgression. Through the grapevine, other locals mentioned the incident to the local police. Weeks later, Manaia received an anonymous $500 supermarket voucher.

'That was bribery,' she states while her mates outside the pub hang on to every word.

I leave the local gossip mill and head to Greymouth for a coffee with Bronwyn Perkins. She owns the gold mine at Bell Hill, 50 kilometres inland from Greymouth. Gloriavale's closest neighbour has seen the odd runaways from the cult over the years, pedalling along the road in tears early in the morning on a pushbike, or politely asking to use her phone while she is milking the cows.

'They are in puberty and have a snap,' Bronwyn says.

She remembers a teenager in blue clothes standing on her lawn one day, desperately ringing relatives in Australia.

'It's so hard for them.'

But otherwise, she has nothing bad to say about her neighbours. They're always pleasant and polite, even when people in Greymouth give them the finger and swear at them. And they donated $100,000 for the rebuild of the health centre in Moana.

'They're not a freak show but lovely people. We need to accept they are here.'

Bronwyn sounds more protective than defensive, as if talking about an endangered native species. The country woman and business owner is especially impressed with Gloriavale's farming. 'They grow amazing crops, and they have some of the best-run and well-fed herds I've ever seen.'

There's no yelling and swearing, she insists. Certainly no beating. 'It's gentle, with music playing for the cows.'

So many stories.

Chapter 20

Almost no one has joined Gloriavale for decades. The last one was a convicted sex offender who was in prison until 2014 for sexual contact with a fifteen-year-old. He moved to Gloriavale in 2017 and changed his name to Courageous Sojourner. Their population grows each year through reproduction and through Gloriavale's satellite community in India that widens the limited gene pool. After some Indian exchange students were placed at Gloriavale, the West Coast community got involved with an Indian orphanage and finally set up their own place in South India in 2007. Hindus received new Gloriavale names. Some Gloriavale girls were pressured to move there, marry Indians and have children.

Millions who have watched the sugar-coated TV series are fascinated by Aotearoa's most famous cult, more enthralled than repulsed. But only very few New Zealanders get to see the other side, the debris from desperate departures. A network of ordinary Kiwis helping Gloriavale members to get out extends from Auckland to Timaru and from the Waikato to the remotest parts of the West Coast. Most stay under the radar, comparing their selfless efforts to an underground railway or safe houses for Jews back in Nazi Germany.

On a family farm half an hour into the bush from Moana,

I visit Judy and Tom who prefer to remain anonymous. Not even their neighbours know the extent of the quiet humanitarian work that the couple in their forties does in their spare time, with kids at school and long workdays on their farm. The aroma of a home-cooked dinner still hangs in the air of the open-plan kitchen when I enter their spacious house.

'You have to keep a low profile,' says Judy when I sit down.

All she knows is that they're not the only family in the area that helps. 'No one talks.'

Their big dining table has seen many desperate Gloriavale people over the years. The couple insist they're not people smugglers.

'We don't hide people. We go to the leaders and say who's here,' says Tom, a strong man now rolling up the sleeves of his woollen jumper.

If they know the escapee's parents, they will try and ring them. Because they are somebody's son or daughter.

Living so close to the Christian community, Tom often sees young people sleeping in their cars so that they can sneak into Gloriavale to see their families. He usually offers them food and a bed and later rings Gloriavale to ask for permission for them to meet their families. Judy has seen it from both sides.

'To watch mothers spend their final hours with their children that are out here …' She hesitates, her voice dropping. 'It's like an execution is happening. An incredible sense of loss.'

The farmers have had a working relationship with Gloriavale for a decade, hiring staff from the community. Because Gloriavale members are not allowed to walk over a stranger's doorstep or use a phone, they sometimes just sit in the driveway to talk to Judy and Tom. Or they ask the farmers to call someone for them. That way, they are not lying when they are questioned back in Gloriavale.

When Judy is out in the garden in shorts and t-shirt, she feels caught out if one of them pops around. For barbecues she has a longer skirt. For a while, she even wore a headband with it – until she realised that it symbolises submission. Most Gloriavale men who come to their place can look her in the eye, but not the leaders. Hopeful Christian wouldn't talk to her directly, only to her husband.

She shrugs her shoulders. 'It's like being in a different culture.'

They have witnessed the terrible headspace of some heading out into the world. One fellow just walked out of the house in the middle of their conversation, up and down the road, for an hour and a half. Like a pendulum clock: was he doing the right thing or the wrong thing?

'We offer friendship.' Judy sighs. 'It's hard to give advice to people who have been brought up being told that they are better than the rest of us.'

They often don't believe they need CVs or a driver's licence. Judy has the numbers of a policewoman in Greymouth and a youth worker at hand. She knows how to get agencies like WINZ working quickly with the leavers, and she also tries to give some family planning advice to the young girls who exit, like one who appeared on her door a year ago.

'Obviously it didn't work – the girl's now got a wee boy.'

The naivety of the younger ones who come and stay for a while and are suddenly let loose into a world of shopping malls, parties, drugs and dating often means trouble. Judy doesn't want to expose their missteps or mock their behaviour, but Tom tells me about a teenager who stayed with them and made Facebook 'friends' called Chlamydia or Candida.

'He had no idea. None whatsoever.'

The seventeen-year-old celebrated his first Christmas ever with the farmers and was as excited as a little child. The boy had never seen a Santa sack before.

When I get up to leave, I tell Tom that I've been tipped off to check out Kopara Village nearby.

His face is stern. 'I would stay away. But if you go, take a baseball bat. I mean it.'

No further explanation is given.

On my drive back, I pass the lake again. The hostel buildings of Gloriavale are hard to make out in the foggy distance of the other shore. The road soon turns to gravel past the Gloriavale turnoff, leading to where I sat through the impressive concert a few months ago. On the left, further into the remote valley, lies Kopara Village, once an old sawmill settlement and then a backpackers' accommodation. Most of the maroon-coloured cottages with rusty roofs look empty and derelict.

I knock at the first door because there are gumboots and shopping bags outside. An elderly man in Gloriavale clothes and a woollen beanie opens. Behind him stands his mentally disabled son with a sticking plaster on his forehead, also in blue work gear. They both look perplexed. I've been tipped off correctly. The former Gloriavale teacher has been put outside of the community while he is awaiting his trial for sexually assaulting a child. I try to start a conversation. He confirms his name and that he's just come from work but waves me off and shuts the door as soon as I ask about the court case. He is later convicted of indecent assault and avoids a jail sentence in part due to his age and 'physical limitations', being sentenced to community detention and intensive supervision.

When I drive away, a woman in a flannel shirt darts out from behind a cottage and yells 'Fuck off!'

The fog follows me around, rolling in from Lake Brunner over paddocks and empty country roads around sleepy Moana. It's eight o'clock on this drizzly evening and getting dark when I stop in nearby Rotomanu. Most dairy farmers like Judy and Tom are winding down for the night, but Marcus Tuck is heading out the door. A black cat meanders between planting boxes full of lettuce seedlings in the hallway.

'I have to meet this young couple. Sorry, just had a call,' the stocky 54-year-old says to me as if he's only popping out for an errand. But the eyes behind his glasses speak of determination. The son of a missionary who grew up in Papua New Guinea is an elder of a Pentecostal church and on a mission himself. He only hints at the task ahead.

'The guy is that close to being kicked out. They're in trouble. They have a baby.'

He sighs. I don't ask who 'they' are. No names, for safety. Marcus zips up his black fleece jacket and holds up two paperbacks he is taking along.

'If you're a feminist, you won't like it,' he says with a wry smile.

The books are Christian marriage advice, to be handed over tonight in a clandestine meeting in an empty farmhouse 7 kilometres up the road, at Bell Hill. Among the people who still live inside the community under a strict set of rules, Marcus Tuck's religious reading material is regarded as contraband. If found, it could lead to hours of hostile interrogation and weeks of exclusion. But the dairy farmer's approach seems to prove him right. More moderate Christians can break through the faith-based loyalty of

Gloriavale members and reach their heavily indoctrinated minds through the same theological tradition. Meet an ideology with another ideology.

When Marcus, his wife Kathryn and their adult son moved from the North Island to the South three years ago and bought a farm, Gloriavale was 'just a joke', they tell me the next day over coffee in their cosy lounge.

'Did we come down here with a purpose to get involved? Definitely not.'

It started with a community barbecue in Moana at the end of their first spring. A few young men from Gloriavale who work on Bell Hill farm turned up as well. They looked a bit like fish out of water. Two months later, just before lunchtime, a young man in blue clothes walked up to the Tucks' door, sheepishly stuck his hand out and said: 'We met at the barbecue. My wife and I would just like to come in and visit.' It was their 'special holiday' for married couples which they only get once a year: two nights in private together somewhere at another Gloriavale property, like an empty farmhouse or a hunting lodge. During that time, they ate with the Tucks, carefully asking about each other's history – fully aware that it was an absolute no-no in the eyes of Gloriavale to casually sit together and talk.

The couple returned a week later with their children for more conversations.

'They were innocently naive,' Kathryn recalls.

Then a relative of the curious couple wanted to speak to Marcus.

'He was having a few issues and was hurting.'

Not long after, the farmer got a call from the relative's wife. It went on from there, with more pastoral care – not as a form of conversion, but to help them understand the Bible better from a different Christian perspective.

Rotomanu is the first settlement when leaving Gloriavale and heading south to State Highway 73 on the way to Christchurch. People cannot drive outside Gloriavale without going past them, says Marcus. 'We have been put here. God has a purpose.'

In April 2017, John Ready pulled into the Tucks' driveway in his pick-up truck. He had been born in Gloriavale and managed their biggest dairy farm for five years. The Tucks had never met him before.

The father of nine had just dropped off his seventeen-year-old daughter, who had been expelled from the community, in Tīmaru. He was distraught. Tears were rolling down his cheeks. Someone had given him the Tucks' address as a safe place. Half a year later, he returned after he was excommunicated, too.

'He was so lonely,' Kathryn remembers.

She lets her husband do most of the talking. Marcus adds that John was close to slashing tyres. 'There was so much anger.'

Instead of slashing tyres, John Ready moved in with them. He is also employed on their farm now and is around today, but not ready to talk to me yet. It could jeopardise his efforts to get his wife out. Gloriavale despises the media. It's causing enough friction with the cult that Marcus is speaking up about John and other leavers.

In their eyes, Marcus has become their enemy. Not in his. He wants Gloriavale healed. Strengthen the ones who are in there. The last thing he wants is to break up more families. Closing the community would be an absolute disaster, he thinks, because it's the only home they know. He shakes his head.

'We need people helping them, not the law. If you destroy Gloriavale, there are not enough counsellors in the South Island to deal with the mess.'

Tonight, the preaching farmer will head out again. He is going to park at the single-lane bridge that leads into Gloriavale, as he often does. That's where the nightwatchmen normally are. Marcus will just sit there and read out loud from the Bible, spreading its gospel. One of the zealots might come and join him in a prayer. A first step on the long road out of the blue world.

I pull up at the Grey District Council for a meeting with Tony Kokshoorn. The rugged politician has been the mayor of the district town for fifteen years, on the council for 21, and owns a property in Moana where he's about to retire soon. To the locals, he always appeared like a chummy buddy of leader Hopeful Christian when he visited Gloriavale's new honey factory or sat next to the patriarch in a front row at the concerts. He has never officially uttered a critical word about the cult. The local newspaper, which he co-owns, has been reluctant to publish negative reports about Gloriavale so far. Hopeful made himself a friend of the local businesspeople and the Greymouth police, acting as a watchdog to report illegal deer hunting.

Kokshoorn now sits behind his desk, playing with a pen, happy to talk about the place he only refers to as 'the Christian community'. He remembers the Cooperites arriving in the area from Cust and staying well under the radar for almost two decades. He finds it a fascinating place.

'They are in the middle of nowhere, they are very industrious, with incredible workmanship. In terms of helping out in the community, they do a great job and drop everything in an emergency.'

Kokshoorn has no problem with Gloriavale's financial success. At the end of the day, it's employment for the West Coast, 'good luck to them'. When I probe him about the recent allegations, especially their mistreatment of people who want out, he admits that there should be a code of ethics to treat everyone well. Including those who go.

'So why have you never spoken up for the leavers in your community?' I ask him.

'No one has asked,' says the mayor.

Chapter 21

Gloriavale does not have a reputation of harassing ex-members after they have left. Unlike other cults, they don't turn up on someone's doorstep or try to damage their reputation and livelihood. Instead, the leaders have an indirect but powerful stranglehold on members inside. They punish relatives within the community for the actions of family members who have left, or they tell them their loved ones are evil and headed for hell. The supreme control mechanism is the threat of eternal suffering and the grief over the loss of their siblings, children, spouse, or parents for the rest of their lives once they step outside. One ex-member publicly described it as 'torture'.

A secret recording of a two-hour meeting of the Servants and Shepherds reveals how current leader Howard Temple gives a couple and their twenty-year-old son an ultimatum: to totally and completely surrender or be kicked out and be damned. 'Nothing else is acceptable,' he shouts in an angry voice. 'If I hear one whisper among any of these brethren, I will not lie. You'll go. No more discussion. No more debate. No more nothing.'

He tells the struggling family they are 'nobody'. They left immediately. Days later, the father – a hunting guide and trustee – leaked the conversation to outside helpers who had it transcribed. It has since gone to lawyers for the leavers.

The shunning practice goes beyond threatening them that they will never see abandoned family members again. The ones inside are expected to cut them off, speak badly about them and destroy them verbally. Their love is actively turned into hate.

For couples, this psychological combat plays out as an excruciating tug of war. When a married man leaves, then tries to extract his family – it never happens the other way around – then his wife is expected to withdraw her love and loyalty as a form of punishment until he comes back in line. One Gloriavale woman, whose husband was outside and fighting to see her, was put on a West Coast Air plane under false pretences and flown around to different locations in the South Island by the leaders in early 2013. It was a form of kidnapping that went on for weeks to break off the contact.

Because of their subordinate role in Gloriavale, women become the means – or the hostages – through which the leaders exercise control. This form of captivity appears far more effective than any physical prison.

No one from Gloriavale has been trying to knock down those invisible prison walls as persistently as John Ready, to the point of almost collapsing himself. He's not finished yet. That's why it takes months, after my initial visit at the Tucks' house, until he lets me come and see him. I was working on a feature for *New Zealand Geographic* at the time and he feared that anything I published could separate him further from his family inside Gloriavale.

Purity Ready, his wife of 21 years, is only half an hour's drive away but behind a hidden Iron Curtain. John lives by himself in a house just down the road from his saviours-turned-employers in Rotomanu. Not just the Tucks, but everyone with whom I speak, describes him as an excellent farmer and devoted father.

Little pink gumboots stand by the door. Children's plastic chairs are stacked in one corner and baby clothes are drying on a rack. But none of John's kids are currently in his four-bedroom rental home. He's a handsome dark-haired man with a boyish grin, in shorts and a grey t-shirt.

'It feels empty,' he says, looking around after an awkward handshake. 'I've been pretty lonely here.'

The younger kids come for short visits when their mother brings them from the community compound. Not because Purity was withholding the children – the Gloriavale leaders were. They take the superior role of a shadow spouse.

A trampoline stands in the backyard, facing paddocks where cows graze.

'I'm turning it into a bit of a playground,' says John. He bought a set of swings for his younger children and wants to hang them under the large oak tree in the back. If he had his family here, he would get his kids into local sports.

'But I'm in limbo,' he says. 'It feels like the darkest hour before dawn right now.'

I wonder if it's a moral stretch for him being inside the house with me, a female stranger. A picture of the Last Supper sits on the kitchen counter. At 40, John had to learn how to cook a meal. He laughs self-deprecatingly when he mentions how it's 'the worst' when he comes home hungry from work and no dinner is ready for him. Shopping was a challenge at first, standing in front of the supermarket shelves without a clue. He asked elderly women there and they helped him out. The former farm manager also had to learn how to budget and handle money, with pay cheques going into his own bank account for the first time in his life.

When he left Gloriavale on 24 December 2017, excommunicated after solitary confinement, he was given $1000 by the leaders. He didn't want it, he says. It felt dirty to him, like a bribe, so he passed it on.

Self-responsibility has been a major change after all the rules inside Gloriavale. 'You've broken out of this mould, but you're a stunted individual,' says John. 'So you need to develop and grow and become a full person first.'

As long as he's not breaking the law now, he can do whatever he wants. 'But should I do that?'

His biggest enjoyment is to work. He never goes to the pub but has tried the occasional beer. Sometimes he cycles, or goes water-skiing on Lake Brunner. Being able to just drive somewhere – for instance to see his eldest daughter who had been kicked out half a year before him – already means a lot. His focus is solely on his family.

It's an ongoing battle to free or even see his wife. John married Purity – he affectionately calls her Chick — when he was twenty. She was eighteen.

'We actually chose each other when we were young, it wasn't arranged from the top. We've always been in love, very much.'

Nine months later, their first child came along. They now have seven girls and three boys. The youngest one was born only a few months ago. The couple is separated geographically, but not by a lack of love, says John. It's hard to understand why Purity is not with him now even if there is a new-born baby.

'That's the million-dollar question,' he says, scratching his head.

He calls it Stockholm syndrome and compares it to domestic violence – with the Gloriavale leadership, not the husband, as the perpetrator. John moves to the floor from his chair to stretch his sore body after a hard day's work. Sitting cross-legged on the carpet, he talks me through his life inside a cult, the only one he has ever known. It ended too suddenly and not on his terms.

'In many ways, I'm not out of Gloriavale. Because my family is still there.'

John's mother, Sharon, was fourteen when she moved into the Springbank commune with her mother after her father died in a fishing accident. John's dad, Clem, was nineteen when he joined the Cooperites in the early '70s. They had thirteen children, five boys and eight girls. John is the eldest.

He was educated at Gloriavale's school and left with School Certificate when he was sixteen, to cut wood for the community's wood-fired boilers. Later he moved on to deer farming and share milking. Before he turned eighteen, he signed the 'Declaration of Commitment to Jesus Christ and His Church and Community at Gloriavale'. It states that as an adult, he is willingly handing over 'any money or assets which I ever give or help to acquire' to them. That money is 'held in common for the benefit of all its members or given to others in need'. It also says: 'I will never claim anything back for myself, my relatives, or anyone else.'

Lots of things there were great in the early days: the adventure of living alongside each other as pioneers in the bush, going horse riding with friends, fishing in the river. But not everything was like an early settlers' fairy tale.

John and his siblings suffered brutal beatings from their father. Those included their youngest sister Prayer who was born with Down syndrome. She died in 2015 from choking on a piece of meat while she was effectively locked in an isolation room at Gloriavale, after the door handles had been disabled. First responders, like John's younger brother David, had to climb in and out of the window to try and resuscitate her and get further help. But it was too late. The coroner ruled the death a tragic accident.

David was kicked out after he raised questions about the leaders' actions. A later investigation by *Stuff Circuit* revealed that Gloriavale's leaders had been manipulating statements given to the coroner by Prayer's siblings. John's family members have since asked the solicitor-general to order an inquest into her death. Their request was denied.

It wasn't the only public scandal surrounding the Ready family. John's sister Constance left Gloriavale and went to the police with allegations that their father assaulted them, not just with his open hand, but with objects like a shoe, slipper and belt. It was extreme even for Gloriavale standards where corporal punishment is condoned and encouraged. Clem Ready was sentenced to twelve months' supervision.

The biggest catalyst for John's own rebellion was the plight of his eldest daughter. 'She had a pretty tough road. It made me look at the way they treat people,' he says.

From the age of fifteen, the teenager started questioning the religious doctrine and the unfair treatment of girls. She saw the lack of equality, education, freedom of thought and speech. To get her in line, she had sessions with Gloriavale's Servants and Shepherds. They take the role of parents, as the actual parents have very little say in Gloriavale. John sat in one of those SS meetings, listening to his daughter being put down.

'They took her apart. People were mean and sarcastic.'

He was shut down himself when he tried to defend her, too weak and uneducated about what the role of a father is – to protect his children. The guilt still haunts him.

Three times after speaking up, John's daughter was isolated for months at a time, once for a year. No one at her workplace in the sewing room was allowed to talk to her. She often ate alone instead of in the communal dining hall because she felt judged. None of her friends were allowed to come close. Her hair fell out from the emotional stress. Over the course of two years, the teenager became so depressed that she thought it would be easier for everyone if she were dead.

The day arrived when John was ordered to drop his daughter off at the bus stop in Greymouth and never see her again. Instead, he drove her to Timaru to stay with an aunt, his wife's adopted sister who had left the community. All the time, the leaders tried ringing him, wanting to know where John slept, what he ate, who he had talked to on the trip.

'I didn't pick up and they weren't happy about that,' he tells me in his laconic voice.

On the way home, he stopped in Rotomanu, in despair. John was in trouble for returning late to the community that night, but he didn't reveal that he had been at Marcus and Kathryn's place.

His disillusionment grew. He hatched a plan to leave and quietly approached Marcus for a job in case he could get his family out. Soon after, he found a Christian magazine in his truck: *The Gospel of Jesus Christ*. It was left there for him by former Gloriavale members who were sneaking into the community to deposit cell phones and reading material that was challenging the totalitarian community's interpretation of the Bible. When the magazine was discovered, John was taken into a SS meeting and fired from his job as the manager of the dairy farm. They excommunicated him and sent him to Nelson Creek.

Half an hour away, isolated in the bush, the community owns an empty house where they put residents who have misbehaved. Families can also have a holiday there sometimes. It was an awful time for John. 'I had no communication with my family. Elements of the SS would come around to talk at me.'

The longest debate took ten hours. John was there for eight days. 'Then I broke and said what I needed to say: that I was wrong.'

Back in Gloriavale, he worked in the welding workshop for the next six months. The SS did 'insurgency checks'. Workers were asked questions like: 'Do you think you should obey us absolutely and completely?' In one of these spontaneous interrogations, John answered: 'We don't treat one another properly. Including the leaders.'

It was the straw that broke the camel's back. He was isolated at Nelson Creek again and told not to return until he had repented. It was Christmas Eve 2017. A Christian family on a farm down the road took pity on him and took him in for the day. It was the first holiday he ever celebrated, but he felt miserable.

When the SS got wind of the connection he had formed with the neighbours, they moved John to another empty cottage, at Bell Hill – closer to the Tucks' place. They were hoping he would break and crawl back again. Instead, he started dropping in to the Tucks' every night, telling them about the threat of biblical damnation and the coercion that his wife was under.

Now that the SS were losing their grip on John, they put pressure on her. Purity Ready's father is a powerful man in Gloriavale. His daughter needed to conform. Every time John tried to contact Purity, she was condemning him and telling him he was going to hell. When he had to drive her and one of his children back from a hospital appointment in

Christchurch, she told him over the drive of three hours that he was doomed and immoral. She was never going to speak to him again.

'The words out of her mouth were what they made her say,' John claims. Her muted heart spoke another language, as he was soon to find out.

They had to stop at his cottage at Bell Hill on the way to swap cars. While she was briefly inside, Purity sprinkled flour on the kitchen bench. With a finger, she wrote a message in there. It read: 'If I take the wings of the morning and I fly to the highest mountain, I know your love will always be there.' She drew stick figures and hearts next to the sink that meant 'I love you to the moon and back'. John only saw her love message after she was gone.

'It sounds schizophrenic,' he admits, 'but she's not crazy.'

He knew what she was going through – how daunting it is for someone raised in Gloriavale to imagine a life outside, with ten kids but without permanent childcare, guaranteed food on the table, and all the practical comforts of the community. Purity had to override her desire for him because that would be bowing to the flesh. You bow to the leadership instead. She was staying true to how she had been raised. John couldn't fault her for that. He read the Bible that night and then wrote in his diary: 'I have to love my wife unconditionally.'

Then he had an idea. He decided to reply to her flour pictogram with his own piece of art. John asked Marcus for a knapsack, filled it with spray dye and nitrogen, and sneaked into the Gloriavale grounds at night. Outside Purity's window on the lawn, for everyone to see, he painted a love message for her, encircled by a heart. When his wife opened the curtains in the morning, she saw it. John breaks into a cheeky grin.

'I think it made quite an impression on some of the other ladies, too.'

The leaders had it rinsed off quickly. But because of the nitrogen feed, the message grew back weeks later, as grass.

Kathryn Tuck went into Gloriavale to talk to John's wife. It was one of many fruitless attempts to change the dominated woman's mind. John was fighting to save his relationship with Purity while trying to convince her to leave. But for that, he had to be with her. Up to three nights a week, he secretly entered his family's bedroom on the second floor of one of the community hostels by scaling a veranda. Sometimes it would take him an hour to cross the last 50 metres without being seen. He would read biblical storybooks to his children and tuck them in.

Then he changed his mindset. No one could stop him from seeing his children or deny him access anymore. Instead, he just drove up there and walked in, his whole demeanour signalling: 'Don't mess with me. I haven't done anything wrong.'

At the end of 2018, the father's hopes of having his family back together rose when a kind Christian person who heard of his plight offered the whole family a free holiday on Great Barrier Island.

The flights were booked. Purity was going to go to town and buy reef shoes for her children. She seemed excited. John was buzzing. A week with Chick would mean he could turn her around and convince her to leave. The Gloriavale leadership wasn't happy about the planned trip though. They ordered Purity into a series of SS meetings.

'She was in a pretty broken-down state,' says John.

Three days before all the Readys were to leave on 21 December, the Gloriavale leaders took Purity and her children up to Nelson, without telling John. When he wasn't able to find them, he desperately tried to locate his family, even through the police, so they could still go to Great Barrier Island. But it didn't work. The Christmas holiday never happened.

John and his daughter in Timaru also cancelled their flights in the end. 'I couldn't go. I was too gutted.'

On Waitangi Day after the Readys' failed trip, the couple had their tenth baby: Andrew Alexander, who they call Drew. He was the first child conceived by a mother still in Gloriavale with a father outside. It was also the first time for John that he couldn't be there for the birth. Purity secretly sent him a photo of the new-born instead. As soon as John saw it on his phone, he jumped into his car, pulled up outside the hostel in Gloriavale and just walked in. It was past midnight.

'They cannot physically stop me,' he says defiantly.

In the first ten days after the birth, the father went up to Gloriavale for seven nights.

'It takes two hours of sleep out of my night; it's exhausting. I still have to function and get up early. But it's hard for her, not having any help from me at night.'

Hormones and feeding times are stressing his wife, he says, leading to the onset of depression. Purity has copped a lot of abuse in SS meetings for having the traitor's baby.

'It's unacceptable to them that my wife loves me. I'm still here to give her the hugs she needs.'

A message arrives on his phone with an alert.

'That's her!' John is smiling. 'She knows how to get on the Wi-Fi in there.'

Cell phones are not allowed at Gloriavale, and the coverage is minimal. I wait while he types. On Wednesdays, the children visit John for three hours. They eat as a family around the dinner table, and their dad takes them to the swimming pool in Greymouth. They have been to a woodchopping event, traversed the Treetop Walkway in Hokitika, and for one of his daughter's birthdays, they went to a shooting range. The girl pinned her target on her wall in Gloriavale, which was another thorn in the side of the SS and caused trouble.

While the others are in school, John's eighteen-year-old daughter Charity works seven days a week for up to fourteen hours a day in one of the teams that prepare food, clean, and do the laundry.

'Why can't we be with you every day?' his six-year-old asked John.

'I'm working on it,' he told her, his heart aching.

Every other Saturday, the children stay with him overnight. Purity, who is breastfeeding, has been ordered by the SS to stay in a rented house just down the road for the length of the visits and not stay with him. It's another bizarre twist in the saga of their restricted relationship. 'Sick' is what John calls it.

The person who lives in the place where Purity stays wears an electronic ankle bracelet. He is Just Standfast, the recently convicted child sex offender whom I surprised at his remote cottage, before he was sentenced to community detention. It's a small world out here in the west.

'So they'd rather put her up with a paedophile than with me,' John says through clenched teeth. He is seething now. 'Tell me, how does that make any sense?!'

He says that after Standfast was charged, Hopeful Christian summoned the girl who had been molested to a men's meeting where she was told that she had seduced the old man and now had to forgive him.

John's face is tense while his eyes fill up. 'She was a child, you freaks!'

268

—

I meet John and his eldest daughter from Timaru again that year, outside the Christchurch stadium where they're watching a rugby match together. I'm covering his story for the *Herald on Sunday*.

The young woman doesn't like being photographed, and she doesn't want her name used anymore. She's trying to leave it all behind and finds her parents' drama in the public eye a bit embarrassing, her father tells me later. It won't stop him.

'I'm in everybody's ear who will listen. How is it possible that a third party can cut me off from my family and hold my wife ransom – in New Zealand?'

He says he's calling lawyers, checking who might take on his case. But he has no savings and is battling a powerful economic force. David against Goliath. Every time he brings up his situation in the media or with a government agency it feels like another raindrop in the ocean.

The *Herald* publishes the news of the first Gloriavale baby that was conceived outside the cult. It could help John's cause but backfire on his wife. He doesn't show her the story.

Chapter 22

The first person to break free from Gloriavale and talk openly about his ordeal was the founder's son, Phil Cooper, in 2009. He was also frank in outing Hopeful Christian as a predator who fostered a culture of underage sexual abuse.

From the outside, the Christian cult looks like an extremely modest environment. The Gloriavale booklet *A Life in Common* describes that there is no physical contact during a young couple's courtship, which only lasts a few weeks after they have been chosen for each other: 'Couples hold hands for the first time as they make their vows, and then embrace and kiss for the first time with great love and feeling, the prelude to marriage.' Any deviation from the script, like kissing in secret, will be punished.

But there is another side to the chaste appearance. Despite the ankle-length dresses, buttoned-up shirts and strict monogamy, sex has always played a big role at Gloriavale from the early days at Springbank in Cust where Hopeful Christian was determined to bring it out into the open – not that different from Bert Potter. It was never a by-product of the cult, but one of its foundations. As at Centrepoint, the focus on unrepressed sexuality defined the community from the start but was well hidden behind a devout Christian veneer.

The booklet *What We Believe* mentions 'fornication' nineteen times and 'sexual intercourse' fourteen times.

Hopeful Christian talked about it publicly in the same vein as mowing the grass or feeding the calves. Once during mealtime, he encouraged all the men who had had sex with their wife the previous night to stand up and crow like a rooster.

Intercourse is still treated as a natural, God-given enjoyment in a place that doesn't offer much distraction besides work and prayer – a gratification that men deserve at all times. Marital problems are blamed on the women. The patriarch instructed them in special classes how to physically please their husbands, and he sometimes sat in to watch young couples to make sure they were doing it correctly. In group sex sessions at Springbank, under blankets, they were pressured to sleep with their partner to arouse others and demonstrate that they were as natural as Adam and Eve in the Garden of Eden. Those who took part were spoken of more positively afterwards.

Hopeful Christian was a man with a short penis who would measure other men's genitals. 'Short and thick does the trick,' he would tell them. Sex videos were taken of a couple's first encounter on their wedding day and he was known to watch them, before the police confiscated them.

Pornography circulated among the elders, and in the early days of the community, young girls were told to get into the hot tubs with them where everyone was encouraged to touch and examine each other's genitals. Some fathers made their daughters watch the parents having sex, as instructed by Hopeful Christian, so that they would learn what to do as a good wife later on. The leader also thought it was his duty to show teenagers what an erection and male masturbation looks like, while his wife Gloria sat next to him – which he claimed made his indecent exposure proper and legal. She had been dragged all over New Zealand and Australia on his preaching tours, her body wrecked from having sixteen children.

After his conviction, Hopeful Christian pulled his horns in, but the focus on sex continued. Since there is no privacy in the hostel dormitories, with beds separated only by curtains, kids were in the know anyhow. Some of them, usually from puberty, started acting that out with younger ones. It has created an intergenerational chain reaction of victims, including males, who often become perpetrators later. A police inquiry that started in 2020, Operation Minneapolis, uncovered allegations concerning a number of people and multiple locations within Gloriavale, from an old car by the creek, to the hen house and piggery, toilets and bathrooms, workplaces and sheds, and even inside a dinosaur that was used as a prop for the concert.

Phil Cooper endured watching his wife being fondled by his father, the highest authority. He later filed charges against him, as did another woman who had left: Yvette Olsen.

She told the TVNZ *Sunday* current affairs programme in 2015 that when she was eleven, she moved into the Springbank community with her parents but refused to be a meek girl who is only used for kitchen work and producing babies later. Yvette ran away as a teenager with Tim (his real name), a younger boy from Gloriavale who was fifteen. When they ran out of money and returned because of hardship and health problems, they were pushed by the leader to have a registry office wedding, which most of the Cooperites were unaware of. Back at the community, Yvette was called a 'harlot' and kept separate from Tim for two years. They were not allowed to be in the same room together.

Before they could reunite, Hopeful Christian ordered Yvette in for 'special marriage counselling' to 'make things easier' for the nineteen-year-old and her husband. After he locked the door, he told her to lie on the bed and pull her skirt up. If she didn't do this, he said, she would not be allowed to be with Tim. The older man reached up for a glass jar on a cupboard. It had a wooden dildo in it, made in the wood workshop, now covered in oil. Hopeful claimed it was the length of Tim's penis which he had measured beforehand. He pushed her back on the bed and brutally penetrated her with the dildo while she was crying in pain. She thought it was something all women had to endure before marriage. It wasn't the only time she had to go through this torment.

Nine years after the rape with an object, and long after she had left Gloriavale, she contacted police. Five victims, one as young as twelve at the time of offending, had also come forward. Two of the complainants were Hopeful Christian's children. Both Springbank and Gloriavale were raided on 20 July 1993 and Christian was arrested and charged with eleven counts of sexual violation. He was found guilty on ten of them and sentenced to six years in prison in 1994, still claiming he had done nothing wrong. The *Listener* reported of his court appearance: 'The 67-year-old Cooper didn't look like God's representation on earth. Short, his remaining hair oiled back above a short-back-and-sides, his pugnacious chin now sunk into his chest, he looked like just another old colonial boy down on his luck.'

The judge said at the time that it would be difficult to imagine a more serious example of indecent assault. Witnesses have since confirmed that they had been coached by some of the Servants and Shepherds who put pressure on them to be loyal to the cult.

Hopeful appealed and got a retrial in December 1995. The Crown only went ahead with the three most serious charges regarding Yvette Olsen and dropped the rest. Her abuser was sentenced to five years' imprisonment. The preacher spent less than eleven months behind bars, returned to the community and was soon back in leadership. While in jail, he had access to pornography and made friends with a prison worker who later joined Gloriavale for a while.

'He is a man of unbridled lust,' Yvette said in 2015 when she had her name suppression lifted and spoke up on camera. It was a shocking exposé. Eight years earlier, the *Sunday* producers went into Gloriavale for an exclusive interview with Hopeful Christian. Sitting on the stage of the dining hall, he explained that twelve-year-old girls were women, and that the community is an intimate one: 'It's a closer relationship than brothers and sisters in a family.' When confronted with his conviction, he flinched and became agitated. 'Our people are not into it,' he deflected and then angrily claimed: 'They can turn anything good into evil.' It sounded like an echo of the prevailing narratives from Centrepoint.

The documentary was later screened inside Gloriavale, but those questions were cut out by Hopeful. No one there should learn the ugly truth that was now on record.

After Hopeful Christian's first wife Gloria's death, he married a woman in her eighties, who didn't live long. His third wife, Ruth, was only seventeen. He was 50 years older. All up, the patriarch fathered twenty children. Nine of them left the community in the 1990s. Phil, his renegade son, was masturbated by his father when he was eighteen and claimed it happened to his brothers too. Once out of Gloriavale, the 27-year-old wasn't allowed any access to his wife and five children who were still living inside. In a dramatic night-time raid, he slipped back in to kidnap them.

Phil Cooper's book *Sins of the Father* became a bestseller, as did Lilia Tarawa's gripping memoir *Daughter of Gloriavale*. Her mother held the highest rank among the women as House Mother. While Lilia's father still worked within, her family was allowed to transition slowly to the outside world. The Tarawas even managed to transfer $2000 into a new bank account. Leaving her former home was still a culture shock for the eighteen-year-old. It took her years to adapt to a new life.

But this is not how it normally goes. The less privileged who leave Gloriavale on their own, with only the clothes on their back and no one by their side, have no chance to say goodbye or prepare for a new life. A change of clothes and some photos is often all they are allowed to take with them. Some are given as little as $40 and a bus ticket. The amount has increased over the years because of pressure from groups such as the Gloriavale Leavers' Support Trust in Timaru.

The lack of funds and possessions is not the only hurdle. Single leavers, some barely adults, are thrown out on a rocky road into unknown territory, with no friends to call, no cultural compass at hand, no understanding of the wider world – and an ingrained belief that they'll end up in hell.

To overcome all these obstacles, to flee and stand up against injustice, requires an incredible spirit. And to take such a scary step, often born from sheer desperation, requires courage. Those leavers are survivors in every sense of the word. Suicide from trauma and untreated mental health conditions – although an eternal sin in their belief – is a real danger when exiting or inside the cult.

The refugees from Gloriavale are the most courageous and impressive – and sometimes confusing – people I will get to know over the following years.

Theophila Pratt has just come out of a weeklong camp when we first meet. The Rotary Youth Leadership Awards is an empowerment programme. She has recently changed her last name from Faithful to Pratt, her grandparents' name. To be able to see them one day was a driving force for her to leave Gloriavale, she tells me when I visit her at the tidy single-storey house in Auckland that she shares with her boyfriend.

Theo is in her mid-twenties, a thoughtful introvert with long blonde hair and a round face that radiates kindness. She is studying to become an occupational therapist. It pains her that the girls growing up like she did wouldn't have the option of a tertiary education. That they are deliberately kept ignorant, so that they obey.

'I cannot understand how this is even legally possible in New Zealand, and in our school system,' Theo says in a slow, clear voice.

Whatever inner and outer turmoil she had to face in her young adult years, her calmness doesn't give it away. However, even now, the articulate woman is struggling to name the correct date of her exit from Gloriavale.

'It was on leap year day, in … sorry, what's the second month again?'

The word she is looking for is February. Where she grew up, the months and weekdays only have numbers, not names. Theo never knew her siblings' birthdays. Just like Christmas or Easter, those special occasions weren't celebrated. No one got to stand out from the crowd. There were never any gifts.

Theo's original first name is Honey, which she changed at Gloriavale. Despite the charming moniker, her childhood was anything but sweet. She tells me that she was deeply unhappy because her father was abusive and beat her mother. The mother was told by the leaders that this was her own fault.

'It was horrible.' Theo states it dryly in her unpretentious way. 'I tried to run away from it.'

Her brother was beaten up badly by a teacher at school – this harrowing scene is described in Lilia Tarawa's book – and he fled from Gloriavale. His escape was a turning point for Theo. Sometimes she slept in the bush to avoid going back to the dormitory. She wasn't allowed to have a best friend, as a form of control. The group came first. Everyone had to love everyone the same; no one should be special.

Like many girls at Gloriavale, she suffered sexual abuse from a family member, but she couldn't speak up.

'He was good, and I was not. That's how it always goes. Girls and women get blamed for everything.'

From the age of twelve, they had regular meetings where the leaders told them how to behave meekly and dress modestly, down to the smallest details like tying your belt correctly so you wouldn't look seductive.

At fifteen, in her last year at school, Theo began to work. By sixteen, she was making cheese from 5 a.m. until 7 p.m., Monday to Saturday, as well as working in the kitchen on Sundays. The pressure to conform grew, as did her misery. For most of her teenage years, Theo was deeply depressed. She only understands this in hindsight, through her current therapy training. Back then, there was no expression for it, and she would never have received any professional help anyway. Mental health problems are seen as a lack of faith and are ignored even when people are at the brink of insanity.

'You have to pretend,' says Theo.

When she was eighteen, she refused to sign the commitment that gives the Gloriavale leaders the right to marry the young members off and keep their money – a bond of ownership. Lilia Tarawa had spoken the fateful words during a ceremony when she was sixteen: 'I realise there is a place that God has given to women in this life, and I will always keep that place by submitting myself to the men and being a keeper at home and having a meek and quiet spirit.'

Everything in Theo was screaming against submitting to those men for the rest of her life. But freedom of choice was never modelled to her. All good girls did what Lilia did.

When Theo refused to make this statement – her family was much lower in the social hierarchy of the community than Lilia's – she was forced to leave overnight. Instead of saying goodbye to anyone, she received hate letters from her siblings who thought this to be the appropriate farewell. The shunning had already started.

A woman from the sewing room picked an old skirt from the costume department and gave it to the leaders who told Theo to put it on. The girl couldn't get out of her old dress quickly enough. They didn't talk to her directly, only to her brother, like she didn't exist.

Theo managed to go through the family photos and take all her childhood ones. Otherwise, the photos would be destroyed once she was gone, all memories of her erased. She took a book with inspirational quotes of historical figures from the library and an old Bible her mother had owned before she joined Gloriavale. Fervent Stedfast wanted to take Theo's white scarf off her, but she held on to it and hid it in the battered suitcase they gave her.

The next morning, Theo got dropped at the Greymouth bus stop to travel to the airport. She spent the three-hour ride still in shock, which turned into anxiety and overwhelm once she arrived in Christchurch. She had never before been inside an airport or on a plane. A man came up behind her to hand over a trolley. It came as a total surprise to Theo that someone – a stranger, a sinner – would just help her.

The flight was to Auckland. Theo arrived lost and confused at the doorstep of a distant friend of her mother's, a woman she had met briefly once before at fourteen, and the only person she knew outside Gloriavale. The friend thought Theo was only coming for a visit. Theo ended up staying for a year.

Heading to Work and Income in South Auckland to obtain welfare was another shock. The staff member there didn't know or understand anything about Gloriavale. 'Where are your parents?' the person asked, and 'Have you got shoes?' Theo didn't have any.

She cringes. 'They looked at me like, "What's *wrong* with you?"'

Auckland was a strange multicultural melting pot for her. Theo had to learn new social norms like saying hello and goodbye when entering or leaving someone's house. At Gloriavale, where people see each other all the time, greetings aren't necessary. She was guarded because at Gloriavale you hide what you really think and feel so that no one can tell on you. Everyone there is suspicious of everyone else.

Theo had never seen or touched a cell phone. For a long time, she felt awkward not wearing a head covering any more – naked, exposed, and guilty. The condemnation was so ingrained: she would go to hell for that.

Not working every day made her feel lazy, so she got a job as a nanny. Being around small children comes naturally to her. She studied for a certificate in early childhood education.

At first, Theo was quite open to other students about being from Gloriavale, until she realised the stigma that came with it; or she might only get invited along somewhere because of the cult curiosity factor. Music, parties, sports were frightening. She had no reference points with people her own age because she hadn't read the same books or ever watched television. Just to have a conversation with someone she didn't know was a struggle. What to ask? So she just went quiet, unsure of her sudden freedoms. In Gloriavale, girls are not allowed to talk privately to boys, including their cousins. Theo, who grew up believing that birth control is murder and homosexuality a mortal sin, had to relearn a whole new way of being with other genders, not just when it came to sexuality.

'I was always apologising to my boyfriend, for instance, for having an opinion,' she says. It didn't sink in for a while that they were on the same level. She really likes calling him her partner now. 'It's a word that Gloriavale hates.'

At an Auckland church, Theo made friends and tried to forge new ground with her faith where she could have a relationship with God, but without leaders. After a year, the church group had run its course for her. She didn't need a watered-down version of the religious dogma she had escaped from, now with a pastor at the helm. Nature has become her place of solace, inspiration and divinity instead.

'I still believe in a higher power,' Theo says. 'But I don't rely on the Bible anymore.'

The student is slightly hesitant when she calls herself a feminist, clearly avoiding any label or ideology. She thinks for a bit, then says, 'My journey at the moment is just being comfortable with being me and being vulnerable.'

Cult deprogramming is an active process. Theo's has required years of therapy. She builds herself up with books and TED talks and goes on random road trips in her car – a new-found freedom. It's a constant fluctuation between the old and the new. Cheese-making is something she still likes.

'And I love watching people get tattoos!' she says, her face lighting up.

She got her first one the year she went back to Gloriavale. Under the cover of Kathryn and Marcus Tuck, who were picking up a beehive at the community, Theo slipped in for a couple of hours. She walked around between the buildings with an assertive smile, in her own clothes and with her new tattoo. It was an act of triumph. But when she bumped into a close relative carrying a baby, the woman immediately pulled away from a hug and covered her child's eyes instead, so as not to look at the devil. Fervent Stedfast appeared on the scene to chase Theo away. She threatened to call the police.

'They were scared of me,' she says, sounding victorious. 'And my parents, they were scared of Nev [Neville Cooper aka Hopeful Christian] because of me turning up there.'

Two years later, Theo went back in again with a friend and her husband who had also left Gloriavale. They both hoped to see their mothers, but the older women were out working somewhere. Again, Theo ran into the relative who had freaked out. It didn't take long until Howard Temple and Fervent Stedfast approached the visitors to make them leave on the spot. The two said they wouldn't speak to the women, only to the friend's husband, and then the men started filming them with video cameras. Theo didn't get to see any of her family.

On the way out of Gloriavale, Fervent Stedfast followed them in a car. Once they were past the lake, Theo had had enough. She made her friend pull over, then got out of the car and walked to the other vehicle. 'I'll call the police if you don't leave me alone,' she told Fervent – something that no woman in Gloriavale could ever say to a man in power. Later in Moana, they had another car following them.

I begin to understand how unusual Theo's feistiness is. Before I met her, I spoke at length with a woman who cared for many young Gloriavale leavers at her place over two decades, like a halfway house. She told me that most girls who come out of the cult have nothing to say and don't look you in the eye, used to being overcriticised, neither believing in themselves nor thinking for themselves, but only doing what they're told. They are raised to be meek and submissive, not interested in anything else besides bearing children. Some who have only been defined by being objects for men now act that out overtly in their new dress and behaviour. The loss of self is so huge that most don't even know what their favourite colour is. Theo is an exception.

'I always knew it's green,' she tells me with a big smile. It's the hue that surrounded her in the West Coast bush whenever she escaped for the night.

We go to her room. Theo opens her laptop to show me the opening paragraph of the book she has started to write. 'I didn't choose the cult life,' it starts. 'It chose me.'

She takes a folded photocopy of a family photo from a drawer. I glance at twenty people in blue. The picture is a little bit crumpled. Theo had gone through her mother's bag to keep it. She's slightly ashamed of that, but the photo means everything to her.

'She raised me the best she could,' she says. Her voice is emotional now.

'They are all victims of the system there.'

Theo is hesitant to talk about her parents. Her father left Gloriavale three years after her because he was mentally unwell. Then he went missing for days from Greymouth where he still lives. Theo's younger sister was removed from Gloriavale by the police because she also struggled mentally. There are no happy reunions yet. Gloriavale, a place that promotes family values, has destroyed the structure of Theo's own family. She needs to keep a healthy distance from everyone while things are still fraught.

Theo's older brother was kicked out of Gloriavale a few years after her for owning a cell phone. He had to leave the same night that he was found out, despite having seven kids. A leader drove the young father over to the West Coast. 'He told my brother on the way that he's a sinner and might as well kill himself, and that dogs would eat his flesh while he rots in hell.' Theo spoke to her brother a few days ago. She knows what he has to go through to survive out here. He might not last.

She doesn't really mix much with others who left Gloriavale. It can get too intense and gossipy. There is still a lot of judgement of how you should dress and behave. But her closest friend is from Gloriavale: John Ready's eldest daughter, who also suffered depression as a teenager, and who now forges her own path in a law firm. The last time they saw each other, they both got their ears pierced. An unthinkable act for a girl at Gloriavale.

I hesitate to ask Theo about her tattoo, but it's not awkward for her. She takes her boot off to reveal the ink art above her ankle. It's the mountain ridge that she misses. The Southern Alps. She runs her finger over it and looks up at me. Her face is glowing. 'I've come over so many mountains. And I'm going to go over heaps more.'

—

In true Gloriavale style, I leave with baked goods: Theo has made muffins for me. They taste delicious. While I drive through the Waikato to Ōtorohanga to meet another young leaver, I remember the Halloween party I attended the year before the concert. Our group of friends dressed up as Gloriavalites and sang 'Down to the River to Pray', clutching Bibles and wooden spoons. We put frivolous nametags like 'Joyful Threesome' on our hired Victorian frocks. Because I didn't know anyone from Gloriavale back then and have no affinity to any Christian church, it was hilarious, although I cringed first when the idea came up. Now, it's unthinkable for me to put on such a costume. It would be as insensitive and outrageous as wearing a Nazi uniform to Oktoberfest. I'm feeling ashamed. Mocking the world that Theo escaped from means downplaying its problems and making it harder for people like her to fit in and feel accepted.

Chapter 23

Aaron Courage works and lives on a 200-hectare dairy farm. The fresh-faced twenty-year-old takes me around the paddock and past the milking shed on a large quad bike he calls a 'side-by-side', mud splashing up to our boots. Inside his small cottage, he shows me his most treasured possession: Jersey cow catalogues from 1965, three boxes full. An award on the cupboard is for Waikato Dairy Trainee of the Year.

'I won a few merit awards,' says Aaron, looking proud. 'Spent it all on cows.'

He has eight of them now. His dream is to start a herd. Without growing up in Gloriavale, he wouldn't be able to achieve so much at such a young age, he thinks. It's the only positive thing he has to say about his former home. What he tells me over the next hour should be in a social worker's file as serious child abuse. But because Aaron grew up at Gloriavale, none of it was ever reported.

Corporal punishment was the norm at his home. Hopeful Christian used to beat boys with a rubber hose. One father chained his son to a steel post because he didn't know what to do with him. Children who were bedwetting or not working fast enough were often not allowed to eat dinner. They had to sit on the stage in the dining hall with their back to the community.

Every other week, Aaron, a rebellious boy, was hauled into SS meetings for transgressions such as walking around with his cuffs undone. The constant beatings that the then twelve-year old was getting from his father became worse, spurred on by pressure from the leaders to get the unruly boy in line. Not just the adults but also his schoolmates had a vicious go at him, sometimes for hours. The bullying was more traumatic than all the brutal hidings from his dad had ever been.

'I just learned to shut it out,' says Aaron, his hands around a cup, feet in thick socks while his gumboots stand by the door.

After he was kicked out of school one day, he wanted to flee through the gates on a pushbike – his fantasy of a prison escape. But when Aaron asked someone whom he trusted for a secret cell phone, he was reported to the leaders. They brought him into a disciplinary meeting that lasted five hours, telling him he couldn't leave because he was underage. Aaron had made his mind up and told them: 'If you can't find me anywhere to stay, I'm running away. You can't lock me up.' No matter what they were going to do, he was going to go, even if it meant walking for a hundred kilometres.

'I didn't care. I was done.'

I ask him how he felt after that excruciating meeting. He thinks for a moment.

'Dehumanised,' he says slowly, then pulls an apologetic smile. 'I probably shouldn't say this, but if I think back, I want to put on brass knuckles and crack some tooth.'

From there, it got worse. The boy was locked in a room overnight with the windows shut. He was an emotional wreck, alone and exhausted. The next day, his father drove him out to Bell Hill farm, as instructed from above. He didn't say a word. Aaron didn't know what was happening.

Eighteen kilometres away from the community, he was left on his own. He had to work during the day but wasn't allowed to speak to anyone except the farm manager, James Ben Canaan. His father brought groceries around, but Aaron had no idea how to prepare them since he had never cooked a meal or worked in the kitchen. He mainly lived off noodles and a big bag of potatoes, three times a day, without fruit or vegetables. Every night for four weeks he was on his own in an empty house, with nothing to read, nothing to do, no one to talk to.

'It was a form of mental torture. I guess that later had consequences.'

Whenever the loneliness was driving him crazy, he took the pushbike to go up and down the road, sometimes ending up at the gold-mine business a few kilometres away that Bronwyn Perkins owns. Once he was given a meal there: lamb chops, peas, gravy, mashed potatoes. He still remembers how incredible it tasted. Another time, he could use her phone and he called relatives in the Christchurch area who had left Gloriavale a couple of years earlier. A recent Gloriavale leaver with a secret cell phone whose number Aaron had was the go-between. The Christchurch relatives were his lifeline to the outside and contacted distant relatives in Australia who said they would have him.

'I thought I was doing okay at the time, but looking back ...' He shakes his head. 'Total shambles.'

One night, twenty Gloriavale men came over to Bell Hill. They sat around him like in a communist 'struggle session' and threatened Aaron that he would have to live like this for the rest of his life. It didn't affect him anymore. He had a brick wall inside, an armour of scar tissue. Nothing could hurt him now. His only aim was to get out. When they finally let him leave, he had just turned fifteen.

—

Aaron flew straight to Australia to his relatives whom he had never met before. It wasn't the life he had imagined. The public school had 1500 students. He couldn't adjust and felt socially incompetent. No one understood where he had come from. He didn't know a single pop song, only hymns. His uncle asked if he wanted to go to a church service. Aaron's answer was: 'Take me as far away from that as possible!' He hated the religious hypocrisy he had grown up with. They had preached that God was love. But at the same time, God wanted to strike him for every bad thing he did.

At sixteen, Aaron moved back to New Zealand. Like a lot of former Gloriavale kids, he soon went off the rails. The crouching tiger of independence, pushed down for too long, broke free once there was no more supervision. Aaron started smoking and drinking heavily, one pack a day and 60 drinks a week.

His turning point and rescue place was Timaru, where dozens of Gloriavale leavers have settled over the years. He says it saved him. A Baptist family took him in. Aaron, who wanted nothing more to do with religion, reluctantly went along to a few church services. It took him a while to become a Christian again, but of his own free will this time and through a new interpretation of the Bible. It attracted him because it was a completely different approach. He had to learn to trust a faith and its representatives, like someone falling in love again after an abusive relationship. He now prays every morning.

Timaru was also where the former manager at Bell Hill had resettled. Under James Ben Canaan's guidance, Aaron and another young leaver started the infamous night raids that became a part of Gloriavale folklore and the start of its underground resistance movement.

One weekend, they drove across the South Island back to the West Coast where they snuck in through the bush around the back in the dark.

Aaron grins at me. 'Everyone's in bed, you have this freedom and adrenaline rush, and no one can see you – it's a lot of fun!'

Once he walked into his parents' dorm, woke up his dad and had a chat with him. But his mother, more indoctrinated by the leadership, wasn't happy to see her lost son at all.

'They abuse the women differently to the men,' says Aaron. 'They turn the heat on until they crack under the pressure and conform. Like slowly boiling a frog.'

One night, the raiders donned black suits, skivvies and balaclavas and smeared charcoal on their faces. Their drop-off point was an empty ute – John Ready's. They left Christian magazines in there and notes saying to meet them at the dump by the lake. Another time, they dressed up as women in Gloriavale frocks and dropped a hundred copies of books from their Baptist church in the library that way. Two girls walked through at five in the morning but didn't recognise the young lads.

For everyone at Gloriavale, Hopeful Christian was the only authority on religious teachings. He told them that there were no real Christians in the outside world, only sinners. To provide alternative Christian material to those inside would open their eyes to the fact that other Christians take their faith seriously and hold high standards of behaviour. It was the ultimate challenge to the leader – more threatening than any libertarian magazine could ever be.

Those deliveries of contraband gave Aaron and his mates a purpose. It was an outlet for all their pent-up rage and rebellion. The night raiders spent $2000 on cheap pre-paid cell phones which they would load up with contact numbers and leave in a little drop box. A week later they were burnt, but they'd just keep doing it over and over again. He chuckles at the memory while he checks the clock. His morning tea break is over; the cows are hungry.

Before I leave, Aaron wants to show me something. He proudly points to the drawing of a cow's head that is pinned to the wall. His fiancé drew it for him. 'It's her favourite one,' he says, eyes and voice soft with fondness.

He met his girlfriend through a local church only six months ago. Sex before marriage is not an option for them.

'I asked her to marry me last week,' he tells me.

The wedding is in two months. Aaron has yet to ring up his parents in Gloriavale to tell them. He knows they won't be coming.

Cows are wandering along the fence when I walk onto another muddy farm, this time north of Tīmaru. It took a while to get hold of James Harrison, formerly Ben Canaan. Around 50 former members are currently based in Tīmaru, looked after by the local Baptist church, which organises practical, financial and psychological assistance. The Gloriavale Leavers' Support Trust sets up families with housing and community support. Their church group meets weekly for Bible studies at the house I'm standing outside. An overturned baby buggy lies on the grass next to a trike.

I'm still counting the pairs of shoes at the door when James pulls up in his truck. It's the end of a long day, the middle of calving season.

'About fifteen today,' he says, not smiling much, and he lets me inside.

A white puppy jumps up and down, knocking over some

gumboots, while Hope Harrison arrives in a van, bringing the middle ones of their fourteen children back from school. The busy mother still prefers to wear long dresses. 'I don't feel comfortable in anything shorter, and then I'm also freezing,' she says while handing the baby over to a teenager.

She starts preparing food in the kitchen. Since the family left Gloriavale in 2015, she has had two more babies – and her husband has been edited out of the free Gloriavale DVD of their 2014 concert.

'I was the ventriloquist,' he says with a wink.

The Harrisons helped John Ready's eldest daughter and many others to land outside by organising money cards, birth certificates, tax numbers and driver's licences for them. Hope has been trying to teach some of the younger leavers normal social behaviour, like looking directly at people you talk to.

The formalities of normal life were a hard learning process for her, too. While her husband went off to work, she didn't know anything about renting a house or how the rubbish collection worked. Hope had never shopped but suddenly had many mouths to feed. Homeschooling became too overwhelming, as did enrolling half a dozen children in schools and getting them books and uniforms.

'You have your bad days when you cry your eyes out and everything seems terrible.'

A couple comes in from the deck. James's sister and her husband left Gloriavale the week before, a family of eleven. The woman wears a fleece top with a sarong from an op shop. It's not the only thing that looks out of place. Discomfort and fatigue are written all over their faces. They still have culture shock and are exhausted after looking at three houses today.

'How are you doing emotionally?' I ask.

'That's not a good question,' the woman says, turning away.

When they leave, Hope comes back inside, frowning at me. I have freaked them out, she says. 'When you first come out, you have the mindset that the media is evil.'

She puts bowls with chicken thighs and corn cobs on the long dining table, tucking the baby back on her hip.

'We know exactly what these guys are going through. It brings back all the memories, the raw emotions.'

Once on the outside, the women often struggle with running a household and looking after a dozen children all by themselves – whereas on the inside, their food would be cooked, their clothes washed, their toddlers looked after by others. Being on top of each other around the clock takes its toll on the leavers. The young fathers are usually no help because they never had to change a nappy or wipe a nose. On the other hand, many parents have left the community because they wanted to spend more time with their children and not just leave parenting to the collective. But all the mothers that the Harrisons have seen coming out have thought of going back at some stage. Some did, temporarily.

'There are so many things you don't have to worry about at Gloriavale,' says James, half sarcastically. 'You don't have to think. You just have to obey the rules.'

For twenty years he managed Bell Hill farm. Because it's outside the Gloriavale compound, James had to have a phone and was talking to some of the guys who had left before him. When it dawned on him that the horror stories he was being told about the renegades by the Servants and Shepherds weren't true, he began to question whether Hopeful Christian might be lying about the reason for his jail sentence too.

The night the large family left, they stuck a letter under

everyone's door at three in the morning, exposing the leader's hypocrisy about his conviction for indecent assault. It was James Harrison's first partisan action.

'Outside, they met their getaway driver at the wheel of a hired van. He took them over the mountains to Tīmaru. The rescuer was Renè Kempf, an elder from the Baptist church in Tīmaru, which donates boxes of food and whole containers of household items to new arrivals.

I meet him and his wife Bronwyn the next day in their beautifully decorated home in town. The couple own a stone-manufacturing business and have been supporting Gloriavale families for the last five years but are reluctant to make that known.

'They're like family,' says Renè.

Because most volunteers live in Tīmaru, many leavers now start their new lives from there. The services arranged by local churches are similar to those provided to refugees arriving in New Zealand. Although the Gloriavale leavers hold New Zealand citizenship, effectively they were raised in a different country. Where they come from is 'like North Korea in New Zealand', says Bronwyn. Like her husband, she undertook a spontaneous mission to drive someone out of Gloriavale.

It was right after a concert, in broad daylight. As a precaution, she contacted the police in Greymouth to tell them a woman was planning to leave with her children. Bronwyn only knew that they were in the hostel furthest away inside the compound. She pulled up outside the dormitory. Then she waited.

'I have never sweated so much in my life,' Bronwyn says. 'But I would have done anything the moment [the woman] asked, "Will you take me?"'

Chapter 24

At midnight on 25 March 2020, New Zealand moves into alert level four to curb the spread of Covid-19. Everyone needs to stay where they are and follow government rules for the greater good of preventing the pandemic. It's an unprecedented situation for millions around the world, but eerily familiar for some.

'Imagine being born into a world where you were already in lockdown,' Mordecai Courage writes on his Facebook account a day later. He is a father of five and had left Gloriavale with his wife Joy in 2013. They live in Geraldine, an hour from Tīmaru.

> Imagine the virus had gotten so bad that your family and everyone they knew had to permanently isolate. Imagine this is the world you grew up living in. Everyone you knew from the time you were a small child had the same message: 'Stay Inside'. How dare you question what they knew to be true? How could you ever be the one to betray them? There was nothing stopping you just walking out, but why would you? This is what it's like for someone who has been born into and is living in an abusive cult.

Former cult members who have been told all their life to put what's good for the collective above their own needs react differently to imposed health measures than the 'team of five million'. Their distrust of authority is huge and their sense of being manipulated and used always on high alert. The unsettling nature of constant rule-changing is also affecting the leavers' children. In families that are already dealing with various amounts of trauma, lockdowns can get stressful with up to fifteen kids at home and only a few days to organise yourself. How to share one laptop with half a dozen children who all need to zoom with their teachers?

John Ready in Rotomanu does not get to see his family during the seven weeks of the first lockdown. When the West Coast moves to level three again and household bubbles can add a person, he pressures Gloriavale to arrange for his family to be with him somehow. They put Purity and the children up on another farm while John commutes every day to see them overnight.

After ten days, the SS decide that Purity is too far out of their control. They shift her and the kids to a separate place on the community compound, hoping it will scare John off. *Blow it*, he thinks. *I'm not going away.* He has been out from under their thumb for two and a half years by now, but when the leaders come down hard on him one day, he almost caves in and leaves after all. Five of them, who have been authorities all of his life, turn up while he is napping after work. Still sleepy, he steps outside on the balcony of the mezzanine floor. The older men form a half-circle around him, telling him he has been trespassing and needs to leave on the spot. 'The only way I'm going is in handcuffs,' he finally manages to say. The cult conditioning is still there. He's fighting it as much as he's fighting the SS.

John reluctantly starts living at Gloriavale again, driving back and forth to Marcus Tuck's farm every day. His family is still isolated in a separate building, 300 metres away from the main living complex. John keeps a low profile, trying to be as peaceful and inoffensive as possible so he can be with them. But other community members are constantly told what an evil person he is.

That winter, while he's heading back from work one cold evening, he sees his second-eldest daughter Charity and her friend by the side of the road, about 300 metres from the community. He gives them both a lift home.

In the car, the other girl carefully asks him about the leaders. John is honest with his opinion. She later feels guilty about the short conversation that should never have happened and self-confesses to the leaders. In a move that couldn't have been more insidious had it been plotted by Stasi agents in East Germany, the SS then confronts John about picking up a teenage girl at night. They insinuate that he had an ulterior motive, such as a sexual interest, while conveniently leaving out the fact that his daughter was in the car too. It takes John a while until the penny drops. Then he gets angry.

'Really, really angry,' he tells me.

Otherwise, it's business as usual: looking after his kids, looking for a lawyer, and not knowing what will happen next. He says he's been having a lot of flat tyres lately on his commutes. Too many for it to be just a coincidence. Once a Gloriavale boy stood by the road, pretending to be shooting at him. He was only seven or eight.

'The kid was just mirroring what the others think of me,' says John.

Throughout the pandemic, New Zealand succeeds in keeping out the Delta variant of the coronavirus. But the infodemic of misinformation, enabled by algorithms and a distrust in media, politicians and science, can't be stopped at the borders and is harder to contain.

While my husband watches worldwide case numbers rise and prepares for the worst at his public hospital, I watch spiritual communities from Berlin to Byron Bay turn into breeding grounds for conspiracy beliefs. Middle-of-the-road Kiwis who, a month earlier, still thought that the 'New World Order' was an online supermarket shopping option, now send me YouTube links of David Icke, an infamous Holocaust denier and inventor of reptilian overlords. A shamanic workshop facilitator I once respected for his men's work starts hailing Donald Trump. A woman I had joined for her weeklong 'authentic relationship' training – and who later tried to pull me into the gifting circle scheme – is now the local candidate for a New Zealand fringe party that spreads anti-vax conspiracy theories.

I'm in shock and disbelief about what is happening with so many of my former friends and allies. Why is there suddenly such a fundamental gap between our geopolitical and medical views? What on earth – given it's not flat – is happening in millions of minds, and can we ever return to normal once this crisis is over?

Over the following months, I move through my grief and into action. With others from the festival scene, we start the support network Rabbit Hole Resistance and then the grassroots organisation FACT (Fight Against Conspiracy Theories) Aotearoa. The dedicated doctors, scientists, nurses, lawyers and educators in the group spend their free hours pushing back against misinformation.

Some of the worst local spreaders are megachurches like City Impact and Destiny, whose leaders fan the flames with misinformation and propaganda. When the Delta variant arrives, a Samoan church gathering in Auckland with a cluster of cases comes under scrutiny, as did other churches in the first wave of Covid that flouted lockdown rules. Reborn Christians are now copping the same criticism from the pro-science camp as ableist wellness merchants who demonise virologists and peddle supplements. Some of the religious objections to the Covid-19 vaccine are incorrect claims that it contains foetal cells.

We try to stop the grifters and influencers whom we know are causing harm – while we try not to blame those who have fallen for their spiel and under their spell. It's a fine line to walk. I'm alienated by the position that people I still hold dear are now taking. My heart sinks further when I learn that they join the angry mass protest in Wellington on 9 November 2021, where gallows and swastikas are displayed. They in return see me as polarising in my stance. I'm not welcome in their circles anymore, especially as a journalist, and neither would I feel safe among fervent anti-vaxxers, some of whom refuse to wear masks and still claim that Covid is a hoax after six million deaths worldwide.

The extremists remind me of cult supporters who defend their warped belief system at all costs. But I still have compassion for those who hesitate to trust medical authority and vaccinations for many complex reasons and now feel discriminated against by the public health measures. When the vaccine mandates force some of them to give up their jobs for their conviction, the division is painful – a dilemma that I have no easy answer for. I pull away from the exhausting debates and stay on my side of the fence where I do volunteer media work for FACT.

The last place I would have imagined myself, in the conflicting climate of early December 2021, and as an agnostic, is at an evangelical service with anti-mandate protesters.

But the weekend that the new 'traffic light' system kicks in, I'm on the road to Tīmaru again. Liz Gregory, the driving force behind the Gloriavale Leavers' Support Trust (GLST) has invited me to join her Baptist church group on Sunday. Over 60 Gloriavale leavers have by now become part of the South Canterbury congregation. Many more started their journey there and moved on.

The address I'm given is not a church in town but a rural property in Milford. I was there over two years ago: it's James Harrison's farm. We haven't been in touch since then, but I've seen him on camera. The outspoken anti-Gloriavale activist showed up at an anti-government protest in October, where he said: 'I'm here today because I grew up in Gloriavale under a very strict controlling system, and we wanted freedom for our kids, and now I see the same thing happening in our country where our freedoms are taken away.' James is the first person to greet me as I pull in at the gate. There is none of the tension that I feel around former friends who now think of me as the enemy. Some counterculture festivals that I loved to attend for years are a no-go zone for me. Again, it comes with a sense of loss similar to when my tantric endeavours ended. I had become a workshop junkie, trying to recreate the intensity of my first 'fix'. Instead of chasing the drug of radical transformation, I had to turn to simpler, more grounded pleasures like family trips, yoga classes, old friends and time in nature – a safe zone after what felt like a break-up. Since then, I've been cautious about who I mix with socially, wary of new 'tribes'. The festival people I now feel closest to tend to gather at Kiwiburn – the New Zealand Burning Man event that supported the government's call for vaccinations early on. It's a creative, geeky, playful scene – with no hierarchy, no leaders, no monetisation, and a strong emphasis on consent. But I keep my enthusiasm for this new community in check.

It's a muggy morning, rain is in the air. Folding chairs are set up in an open-face barn overlooking empty cow paddocks. The floor is divided by a row of straw bales. On each side, only the officially allowed number of 50 people under the orange traffic-light restrictions can mix and mingle without a vaccine pass.

'It's legal but creative,' Liz Gregory says half apologetically as we sit down.

A fair number of worshippers haven't had the jab. Not a single person is wearing a mask. Some families on the other side of the barrier have come out of Gloriavale, one only weeks ago. A young woman still wears a head scarf. The kids and teenagers – too many to count – sit on straw bales in the back, chatting to each other. The ones from Gloriavale only saw a live band for the very first time the night before when Liz's husband celebrated his birthday.

The pastor, a jovial South African in a checked shirt, welcomes his congregation to this 'open air revival meeting', which elicits some appreciative chuckles. Standing on a raised wooden platform, he launches into his sermon. While a summer shower starts drizzling down, he preaches against wicked leaders, their failure to punish criminals, and what he calls the 'promotion of perversion'. If it's a dig at Gloriavale, I'm down with that, but it seems to be his take on current politics.

At the end, the pastor urges everyone to pray for 'the persecuted church' in a hostile environment and godless country. We stand up to sing 'O Come, All Ye Faithful' and 'All Glory Be Forever'. Liz – in colourful leggings, sleeveless blouse, and blue-rimmed glasses – sings with full devotion. Her beautiful voice drowns out the patter of rain on the tin roof.

After the pastor announces the Lord's table, everyone gets up to receive a small cup of grape juice from the front. Gloriavale practises the Communion ritual too, but their weekly service lasts up to four hours. For me, who grew up around liberal Protestants strumming peace songs on the guitar, this is new religious territory – as it is for the recent leavers who come from the other end of the Christian spectrum. Here, we all meet in the middle. What seems conservative to me is progressive for them.

We finish the open-air gathering with packed lunches on the straw. Liz and her helpers clean up afterwards while the boys refrain from a task that is women's work where they come from.

The rural excursion is more than a fascinating cultural immersion. It's humbling to meet people I have so little in common with, from their views on abortion, evolution, euthanasia to sex education, but I still appreciate their gentle humanness. I embrace their heroic efforts to fight the place that oppressed them, despite our differences on other topics. It gives me hope that this can be possible with everyone on both sides of the current divide, not just either side of the straw bales.

Immunisation was always demonised at Gloriavale, an act that would take you straight to hell. After the Sunday meetings, Hopeful Christian would sometimes put on anti-vax documentaries for the community to watch. As a result, the vaccination rates in their district were alarmingly low until recently, when the previously staunchly anti-vax leaders did a sudden 180-degree turn just in time for the mandates. No 'legal but creative' solution would allow such a large community of the unvaccinated to gather under the current rules.

Initially, the community ignored all restrictions until the Gloriavale Leavers' Support Trust blew the whistle on them. Each hostel floor is now a bubble of under a hundred people who eat together. Their teachers and midwives are since vaccinated, as well as the majority of the SS. Liz sees their vaccination roll-out as purely strategic.

'They would lose over two million dollars a year for their preschool if they had to close it,' she says while she rummages through a lost property box from yesterday's party.

Without a preschool, mothers would have to stop working, which would hurt the Gloriavale businesses that rely on their labour. And with homeschooling, the leaders would lose control over the curriculum. Now, those afraid of the vaccination are worried they are going to hell if they refuse it. 'It's twisted. And coercion. Some are really upset about it, but no one feels safe to express an opinion. Unity is the Holy Grail.'

Liz knows my opinion on vaccinations, but she's diplomatic – and empathic. 'Let's remember to be kind while people still process what's happening at the moment.'

Liz Gregory is a force to be reckoned with – not just because her team of staff and volunteers can organise houses, cars, food parcels and childcare for a family with a dozen kids overnight. It's been a huge year for them with over 70 people coming out of Gloriavale in the last fifteen months – 10 per cent of Gloriavale's population in one year alone. Since they started the trust, they've arranged over 2000 bed nights, lent out a rotating fleet of five vehicles, set up dozens of houses and helped to clothe over 120 people.

Liz says that they first help people to leave the property, then to leave the ideology, 'with love and care'. The trust runs cultural education sessions with government departments and social services, from the police to Oranga Tamariki. They've raised $40,000 through Givealittle to help with leavers' resettling and also printed a booklet that helps with cult departures. The former teacher in her forties has been interested in cults since school but never thought she would be instrumental in challenging one. Like Barri Leslie in Auckland, who led the fight to close down Centrepoint two decades ago, Liz Gregory is on a similar mission in Tīmaru, in the truest sense of the word.

'It's missionary work for us. Absolutely. They're being fed the wrong gospel in there, that their salvation only comes from obeying their leaders and living at Gloriavale. I want them to be set free.'

I get it. Liz is passionate about Christianity and therefore offended that Gloriavale misrepresents it – whereas I don't care much about churches but about sexual healing and authentic relationships. Yoga and therapy is part of my world; praying isn't. The distortion at Centrepoint and Agama was always closer to the bone for me than Gloriavale because those communities sprang from a field I also moved in. It won't be long before that changes.

Liz's missionary focus on Gloriavale was never planned. Others usually go to places like China. It all began when Rosanna and Elijah Overcomer showed up in Tīmaru in 2013, the first Gloriavale leavers in the area; two lost souls with five kids, among 30 Baptists. Over the years, family members who had also left joined them. Rosanna's sister Joy and her husband Mordecai were shouted a belated wedding by the generous Tīmaru church. In Gloriavale, the couple was denied a proper ceremony because they had broken the rules and been secretly meeting. They, the Harrisons and many more are now supporting a concerted legal approach.

The GLST did a survey to find out which changes should take place at Gloriavale. The responses from young and old leavers all said the same thing: get rid of the leaders and remove their control over the money. A team of lawyers offered to set to work and the GLST filed a Teacher Council complaint. The school principal, Faithful Pilgrim, was suspended for not providing safety for the children by letting a known sex offender teach. Ten teachers were temporarily stood down during the investigation.

There have been or are multiple cases, from allegations of abuse to employment issues. Police and Oranga Tamariki visit Gloriavale regularly now, family uplifts have occurred, and people are coming forward to lay charges. Things are moving. Gloriavale likes to appeal and use name suppression to keep everything out of the media while they drag out the proceedings, says Liz.

'It costs the victims more while they wait and wait. It's painful.'

Because of name and location suppression, the cases have sometimes stayed under the radar. The people inside Gloriavale don't know about them yet because their leaders won't tell them.

'I don't believe they're capable of change,' is Liz's verdict as she rushes to her car, long hair flying. She is weary of the lack of action by government agencies for so many years.

Lawyers are waiting at her house. Her face is misted by warm drizzle and glowing with determination. The activist shoots me a last look that I wish the Servants and Shepherds could see. 'We're not giving up. The leaders need to be held accountable for their failure to care for their people. The harm needs to stop.'

Chapter 25

The church meeting in the barn ends with a surprise. While everyone is packing up, I'm introduced to a woman in a long purple skirt. Virginia Courage – dark hair, round eyes, full figure – has an openness and curiosity that I didn't expect from someone in this setting. Gloriavale leavers are usually too shy or suspicious to talk to media. My attendance was kept quiet.

Virginia, who many call Ginny, is John Ready's younger sister, closest in age. The 42-year-old only left Gloriavale two years ago with her husband, David, and their ten children. Not a long time in cult exit terms, I point out.

She laughs. 'The only regret I have about our life is not leaving there sooner!'

She's an extrovert, eager to talk after a life of staying mute.

Earlier in 2019, while still in Gloriavale, Virginia periodically dropped in at John's place in Rotomanu. Her eldest daughter had left the community, but the parents decided they wouldn't cut her off. They had legitimate reasons to visit their girl. Seeing her expelled brother John, who was fighting to get his wife out, would have gotten Virginia into trouble, though.

'It broke my heart when they kicked him out,' she tells me. 'I cried for months and could not imagine a life where he is not a part of it. He's the most amazing and important person for me, next to my husband.'

Because John was so well liked at Gloriavale before he left, some of the leaders started a smear campaign against him to destroy any sympathy people might hold. They ranted about him in meetings and during mealtimes, with his wife and children sitting at the table: he was not a man of God, they said, but full of sin and pride. Virginia asked two of the leaders to explain to her which crimes he had committed according to the scripture. She got no answers.

When she had some access to the internet, she found news reports where John was quoted directly. She knew she could trust his words. Nothing he said in there lined up with what the leaders claimed he had done. Virginia felt angry. It was a switch. Her heart was telling her to stand by her brother, even if she had to hide that from others. 'That was me first standing up, just in a really small way.'

Not in her wildest dreams could she have imagined that three years later, she would be standing up in a really big way.

John's house was where Virginia saw the *New Zealand Geographic* issue that also described his plight. She read it three times. It made her cry.

'I didn't realise how common other people's pain was,' says Virginia, 'the horrible things that were done to them. My free thought was so restricted. I only knew the propaganda we were told.'

I'm teary too. I don't know yet that I have a wahine toa in front of me, a brave warrior who has seen things that could change the course of Gloriavale in the same way that Centrepoint fell. Someone who woke up to what was happening and made the decision to leave. Virginia is Māori, her mother is Ngāti Porou. She was never allowed to identify with her culture in Gloriavale. One of her sisters doesn't even go into the sun so that her skin stays pale.

Weeks later, I'm back in Timaru. Virginia is seventeen weeks pregnant with baby number eleven. For the first time, she will be giving birth in a hospital after a lot of previous birthing trauma.

When Liz Gregory and I pick her up at her place, she is nibbling on a pie to beat the morning sickness. Her two youngest daughters, blonde and bubbly, jump around us. A teenage girl works at the computer. Virginia and David's wedding photo from Gloriavale is in a frame next to a stack of board games on the bookshelf. It feels like a happy home.

Since it's the school holidays, we retreat to Liz's house at the other end of town. It looks out over sheep paddocks and has a swimming pool in the garden, put in specifically for Gloriavale families who come and stay. A shipping container has been converted into an office for the Gloriavale Leavers' Support Trust. I have a peek inside. Photos of men with their names adorn the wall – a who's who of the key players at Gloriavale. 'Howard Temple. Change is coming?!' is printed in bold letters on a piece of paper.

'Our mantra,' Liz explains with a laugh.

We leave the cult busters' headquarters to join Virginia in the living room. Over the next two hours, I'm taken down a rabbit hole of darkness and distortion. It starts to resemble Gilead, the dystopian setting of *The Handmaid's Tale* where enslaved women are breeding machines for their owners. It's a timely reveal. A year earlier, says Virginia, she wouldn't have been able to speak about anything to anyone, let alone go public.

—

Virginia Courage's earliest memory of molestation is in her first year at school.

The old teacher, who was sentenced at the end of 2019 for other offences, slid a hand up her dress and touched her bottom. No one said anything. He did it to many of the girls, and in such a way that they weren't freaking out. Years later, when Just Standfast sexually assaulted a nine-year-old girl, whose parents confronted the school, the principal Faithful Pilgrim didn't contact the police but just moved the teacher to a boys' class. Hopeful Christian was in India at the time, so the current leader Howard Temple was in charge of all major decisions.

Virginia always had plenty of unwanted attention from the community's men. Comments were made about her, like 'Oh, she's far too pretty', which implied more than just a compliment. Before the child could even read or write, she learned that she was prey. It was her duty alone to stay untouched and modest so that one day she could be married off as a spotless bride – the principal achievement for a Gloriavale girl.

According to Virginia, the dominant father figure of her childhood who acted as the voice of God was 'a sexually perverted predator'. Hopeful Christian set the precedent for all that happened to her – and to many other girls in her age group. He required all of them to have long flowing hair to make them more attractive. If they secretly trimmed it, their parents would get in trouble.

When Virginia was ten or eleven, the community was building and selling water beds. The kids were helping with sanding the frames. One Saturday, when the others had left, Virginia stayed on, giving Hopeful a hand. He started telling her about a sanding machine the young men had been using in the wood workshop for sexual experimentation. Virginia played dumb. Hopeful carried on with more explicit detail. She looked at him with big eyes, pretending she didn't understand so that he would stop. When he couldn't engage her further, he told her: 'I think you need to go home and talk to your dad, love.' She knew that her father would be growled at by Hopeful if his daughter didn't have the kind of knowledge she should be having. It was a dilemma. She didn't want to get her dad into trouble because in Hopeful's view she had prudish hang-ups that the parents should fix.

They were still at Cust at the time, where her family lived on one floor of the Big House at Springbank, when she became aware of an adult community member preying on teenage girls. At first she didn't believe the stories: he had a wife, so surely this must be a mistake. During the day, the man acted like nothing had happened. There was no embarrassment, no recognition. Maybe the girls had just dreamed this up? They told no one. All girls at Gloriavale learned that if something inappropriate occurred, it was because they were too flirtatious, too frivolous or in the wrong place at the wrong time. But how could their bed be the wrong place for them to be in at night? It was so confusing. Virginia secretly kept a knife under hers for years, but felt guilty about it – 'such an unchristian thing to do!'

Some of the men, she says, were 'calculated and extremely practised at what they did'. The abusers were good at grooming and laid a subtle foundation of friendship. Because everyone thought these were nice and disciplined men, the only people who could be wrong in these scenarios were the victims. She says it was clear that other members knew what was going on and did little to stop the hurt.

It all came out when Virginia was sixteen. Her friend's father admitted he was worried his daughter had been abused. 'The Lord spoke to him and said: "Something happened to her." So he asked her.'

'Knowing the truth wasn't a relief,' Virginia remembers. This shameful secret could ruin her chances of marriage. How to even disclose this to your parents when you can't find the right words because you spent so long trying to pretend it never happened?

Hopeful Christian was in jail for the indecent assault of Yvette Olsen at the time, so her friend's father approached one of the leaders. In the community, you don't handle things yourself as a parent but give the power to the person above you. More girls were outed as victims. It should have been enough to bring the community down at the time, or at least have a proper police investigation, says Virginia. But that never happened. Instead, the girls were summoned into the dining room – the main area where people were coming and going, doing jobs and using the main bathroom next door. The community had by then shifted from Springbank to Gloriavale.

The girls sat there, crying. Virginia remembers how they were told it wasn't their fault. But because it was handled so publicly, the story quickly made the rounds and the girls felt guilty about all the anger that erupted. In the end, everyone was assured from the top that they were still virgins. They were okay for their wedding days. Nothing was taken from them, the leaders said.

Virginia erupts in angry tears as she remembers those words. 'Nothing was taken from them – really?!'

It seemed this was the most important thing.

It wasn't the end, but the beginning of a death. It was even worse than before because so many knew it now. Girls who had been sexually abused would be outcast and stay single.

Bringing in the police was not an option. Never. They all knew that from when they were little. You just don't go to the police. Instead, the abuser was put in a hut outside Gloriavale for a while. His wife wasn't told anything.

He came back supposedly repentant and was made to apologise to his victims. Virginia says that the leaders never dug into his history. They explained his crimes away with excuses, making him sound like the victim in the scenario. His wife was to blame for his moral failure.

When Hopeful Christian was released from prison, he was in charge again. Virginia says he should have never been allowed to return to the community, which had by then doubled from its original size. Hopeful called a meeting with the victims, without their parents, to make sure none of them would ever speak to the police. He even did a trial interview with them. What would they say if someone asked them about it?

'Oh, I would say I'm not thinking about it anymore,' one of the girls said.

Hopeful corrected her. 'No, no, you have to say that you've got nothing to say.'

In the meantime, another woman who had left Gloriavale had gone to the police and told them about the issues inside the community. Everyone was on high alert. Hopeful told all the dads to instruct their daughters to say nothing. Virginia was out shifting cows with her father when he passed on the instructions from above. Someone from the police turned up, but Hopeful managed to assure them that the offender had been dealt with. No parents or victims were interviewed. Case closed.

I ask Virginia what she had believed, back then, was the reason their late leader had gone to prison.

'Oh, that it was an attack from people trying to destroy the church ...?' she says with a self-deprecating grin.

She had no other choice but to believe it. If you spoke up against Hopeful, you were acting against God. There were whispers – only from women – about what he had been up to at Springbank with young girls. He encouraged couples to take teenagers from other families into their bed for 'marriage education'. Both the wife and the single girl had to endure these arranged sessions. Hopeful also had sleepovers at his house in Cust for underage members, male and female, putting them next to him in the bed and describing in detail what he was doing with his wife at every moment. A young boy was instructed by Hopeful to hide under his parents' bed, then report back to the patriarch.

The penny only dropped for Virginia weeks ago that Hopeful Christian was into exhibitionism or what she calls 'reverse voyeurism'. She thinks the vain man got off on others watching him have sex. 'Helping people and their marriage' was just the cover story. Virginia tells me that Hopeful Christian's obsession might have come from his own inadequacies: he wanted to be seen as having sexual prowess.

With the move from Springbank to Gloriavale and into blue clothes, the beliefs shifted and became more rigid. A real spirit of arrogance set in, says Virginia. When she was little, they accepted other Christians' views. Now they were taught that they were the one true church, and obedience to its representatives was the only way to heaven. Hopeful Christian was just hiding his perversion behind stronger religious ideals. It became all about the look. The overblown concert and the Mormon-like uniforms were intended to distract from the gruelling reality.

Optics are also important inside Gloriavale. Women and girls have to stay slim and are openly criticised for any weight gain from an early age. After giving birth, the wives are expected to have their previous body shape back within months, no matter how old they are.

Virginia married David Courage at age twenty. It was arranged, but they did eventually fall in love. She was terrified on her wedding day, though, because of Hopeful Christian. He hovered around outside the 'love suite', which has a spa and is only used for the defloration, making an appearance before and after. Hopeful was known to check out a bride's lingerie or hand the groom some lube. Virginia tried to block out the old man's intrusions because the big day was overwhelming enough: the enforced display of love for a person she hardly knew, then being carried away in a red sedan chair withs kids dancing around them, all building up to the collectively anticipated 'consummation'. Others would often be public about their quota afterwards, what they had been doing when and where, but David didn't succumb to these expectations. The young couple kept their first intimate experience private and respectful.

Not everyone was so lucky. A young woman confided in Virginia that the night before her wedding, Hopeful took her aside for a prep talk that she found disturbing. It shattered her romantic notion about what the wedding day and her marriage was all about. She hardly knew the young guy she got married off to. On the day, he struggled to contain himself. While still on stage during the wedding, performing their big kiss to a special song for the occasion, he let his hands wander over her pink dress, greedily claiming her like a trophy in front of everyone. From then on, for the week of their honeymoon, the bride was at the groom's beck and call in the bedroom. It was a shock to her system. She would have to spend the rest of her life fulfilling his demands, whether she was sick or tired.

Across the years at Gloriavale, Virginia got to hear more awful details. Another friend confided in her about the undignified sexual experiences on her wedding night. She was crying.

'She had never even held hands with someone before. It broke her.' Breaking girls in and breaking them down are ways the cult controls them. 'Sex was the only important thing going to happen for us.' Virginia's tone is dry. 'It was almost as if you didn't need any other skills.'

According to their marriage vows, it is every Gloriavale man's right to sleep with his wife at any given time. In the booklet *What We Believe* it says: 'Husbands and wives do not have the right to withhold themselves sexually from one another.' Refusal on her part is unbiblical. This dogma is openly preached, and I remember it from Howard Temple's introduction at the concert. Virginia explains to me that the women truly want to love their husbands because they've been taught their whole lives that this is what they should do. 'This is their calling. And these fellows actually think that they love their wives, even if they treat them poorly. They honestly have no idea.'

She says there are no other means that men in Gloriavale can show their wives they care. 'There is so little friendship. There is so little the couple can experience together.'

People have no money to buy presents, cards, flowers or tickets to a concert. They can't go on trips together and stay in a hotel, or invite friends around for a surprise birthday. There is nothing available to them except sex.

Despite all their pubescent 'sex ed', Gloriavale men are not taught how to consider their wives. The women don't know that, under New Zealand's law, they have the right to say 'no'. For them, it's not God's law.

Soon after giving birth, women are expected to function sexually again.

'How soon?' I ask.

'Within days,' says Virginia with an expression that fluctuates between pain and exasperation. 'And if not, maybe if they had bad tearing – well, for many, there's always the back passage.'

She mentions a friend who birthed her baby in the morning and the same evening was penetrated by her husband. 'She thought it was a sign of his love. But that's not love. It's dominance.'

In the hyper-sexualised cult culture, sodomy between older and younger boys has become so common that it is just referred to as 'mucking around'. When someone's 'mucking around' became too rampant or public, Hopeful Christian quickly married the boy off, who would then continue in the same vein with his wife.

An eleven-year-old boy was sexually assaulted by an older teenager. When his mother found out, she only said: 'I don't think it hurt him that much, he didn't go all the way in.'

For Virginia, it was the most awful excuse she'd ever heard. The abuse is so entrenched that people have become desensitised. No one feels responsible for it. If 'stuff happens', the leaders put it on the parents, who feel powerless.

Virginia's father, Clem Ready, once approached a leader, saying that he had heard too many disturbing stories. The leader dismissed Clem's concern. His answer was that every girl should expect to eventually get fiddled with – it was a part of life in Gloriavale, like everywhere.

Virginia's history seemed to repeat itself a few years ago. A married man was stalking one of her teenage relatives. His father had also been making sexual comments to Virginia since she was nine, right up until her adult life.

When Virginia noticed what was going on with her relative, she felt utterly helpless. She couldn't just walk up to a man and tell him that this was unacceptable, and to keep away from the kid. Because of the hierarchy, parents are not the first line of authority in Gloriavale. There are always three levels above you. It depends on who the accused person is, who they're married to, what family they belong to and what story they're going to tell. In this case, it could backfire on the girl's family, especially the mothers, for 'not keeping her in order'.

Just Standfast, the old teacher who had touched Virginia and other kids at school and whom I had surprised at Kopara Village, was in court during this time. The police were running a course at the Gloriavale school, 'Keeping Ourselves Safe'. Its message landed, and a young victim came forward. Virginia says the leaders then called a meeting, claiming the stories from the victim and the man she accused weren't lining up. The offender, they said, had since repented and had become a changed person overnight.

'They wanted to shut her down,' says Virginia.

She claims some of the leaders perpetrated a slander campaign against the harassed child and encouraged anyone to come forward with proof that she wasn't a good girl.

'It was character assassination and worse than the actual transgression,' says Virginia, enraged and tearing up again. 'They wanted to break her amazing happy spirit to make sure she stays quiet and doesn't talk about it. I've seen it too many times and it breaks my heart.'

It was time for Virginia to leave Gloriavale.

—

'Were you a happy person in there?' I ask Virginia.

She thinks for a moment. 'Back then, I thought I was,' she replies slowly. She married a good man, and she loved her kids. But looking back now, she was miserable. 'I was so exhausted most of the time.'

Since she had left school at fifteen, she had been working from six in the morning until eight at night, cooking and cleaning, with one day off per week. Her older daughters and younger sisters did the same. Three of them were burnt badly from carrying a large kettle filled with boiling water that tipped over. They weren't given time off to let their wounds heal properly.

Boys were woken up at 3.30 am to do milking before their regular jobs such as rock-picking or gardening – they worked up to seventy hours a week, as unpaid 'volunteers'. Virginia's son Hosea worked in the moss factory when he was six years old, without earmuffs or any safety equipment. There he was hit by a supervisor with a shovel handle and had bruises for days. A ten-year-old's arm got stuck in a conveyor belt in the factory, and another boy almost lost his eye in an accident in the moss swamp where kids were working in freezing conditions, with no gloves and little food, soaked to the bone. Instead of being taken to a doctor, the injured seven-year-old was beaten with the pitchfork that he had stepped on by mistake.

Gloriavale teacher Vigilant Standtrue also grabbed, shook and pushed boys who didn't handle produce carefully. For an urgent honey order of tens of thousands of jars, some members only got a four-hour break on a three-day shift. Hosea's cousin Levi, who was fifteen at the time, was one of them. His hands were bleeding afterwards. Another teenager lost three fingers while working at the bee box factory.

Most adults never received dental care. Even if they had been in pain for weeks and couldn't sleep due to their rotten teeth, they were told there was no money for treatment. The amount Gloriavale spent on each member's food was less than four dollars a day – while in New Zealand's prisons, the daily budget per inmate is $5.60. To punish someone, labourers often went hungry. *What We Believe* states that 'those who will not work hard at what they are capable of doing should not be given anything to eat'. Workers only receive six days of leave a year, and pregnant women work until the day they give birth. Virginia was having physical issues from all the wear and tear – for years she'd suffered a twisted pelvis from an untreated hip joint, without any resting or recovery between babies. She went back to work in the crèche weeks after the deliveries.

Despite the toll it takes on their bodies, Gloriavale women gain an unspoken status by having as many children as possible. Ten or more is the benchmark to aspire to. After giving birth, Virginia tried to starve herself to lose her baby weight so that Hopeful wouldn't make disparaging comments. To get her figure back and keep it, she would have to avoid getting pregnant again – which was also wrong and evil. 'I had a constant war going on in my mind and couldn't win it either way.'

By the time she was pregnant with her eighth child, she was about to collapse. Three weeks before the baby was born, Virginia just sat on a chair in her room for the entire time, in a stupor. She didn't even have the energy to move or read a book. In the depth of her depression, she thought about taking her own life. She had been struggling with suicidal thoughts since her sexual abuse had started. It was unthinkable to ask anyone for mental health support. Her dark desperate thoughts became just another secret she had to hide.

After she left Gloriavale, she only learned through the GLST how many others had struggled with suicidal ideation as well. There have been numerous attempts, mainly by teenagers: strangulation, starvation, wrist-cutting. Overdosing on pharmaceuticals or natural supplements. Disappearing into the bush. Men thought about jumping off buildings, women were praying to die in childbirth. They never told anyone.

Virginia thought it was just her. The year before she left, a young worker who had been badly bullied was airlifted to Grey Hospital after he hanged himself. He died a few days later. Gloriavale referred to it as a 'work accident'.

The Courage family's first landing place was Tīmaru, then Christchurch. After leaving, Virginia's nightmares stopped immediately. She gave a number of victims the confidence to speak to police. Some thanked her for helping them to finally tell the truth. It took some of her friends, now adults, months to realise what someone had done to them when they were young, and just as long to have the guts to let the police know. They thought it was all their fault and they would be absolute traitors to speak about it.

One devastated woman came all the way to the police station – 'a grown woman with a family, who had never been allowed to process this' – then turned around without speaking to anyone because she couldn't bring herself do it. A week later, she returned to give her statement.

Virginia's voice breaks into a sob. The dam has burst. The guilt and shame she carried all her life has transmuted into passion and anger.

'Someone has got to open their mouth about this. Someone has to say it's true,' she spurts out. 'It's been going on for fifty years, and you people know about it, and you've hidden it. You blamed victims, you silenced them. If you want to hate me forever, here it goes!'

She grabs a tissue from a box on the table. It hurts her that there are still girls in there who think it's their fault, and parents who would blame their daughters. She wants them to be able to say that what happened was totally unacceptable. To say their child did nothing wrong.

Typical for sexually abused children, some of them felt guilty that they didn't fight back, scream or push away the abuser. It makes them feel complicit somehow because at Gloriavale a thirteen-year-old is considered an adult. Only when Virginia left did she realise that the girls she knew had still been children back then. And that it was adults who knew better who had been assaulting them.

Speaking up often feels lonely. Some women – even victims themselves – still defend the cult leaders, saying the SS didn't know about all these cases. Virginia challenged them and asked, 'But what have they done about the stuff they *did* know about?'

When another woman from Gloriavale learned about the harassment of Virginia's teenage relative , her only comment was: 'Oh, that was always going to happen – she's far too pretty!' It was like déjà vu. Nothing had changed in thirty years.

Liz Gregory has been sitting in on our conversation. Gloriavale, she says, has become a dysfunctional family, hard-hearted and without empathy. The love has vanished; the people are broken. Not just the leaders are callous. Members also keep each other in line. After a lifetime as spiritual prisoners in a toxic culture, those who come out don't suddenly become a happy bunch. Old patterns, like the fat- and slut-shaming, the judging, the snitching, the hierarchy, can carry on. Adjustment takes time.

We talk about whether people change when they leave the cult.

'Do they really?' Virginia asks herself. 'Or are they finally allowed to be their real self?'

Chapter 26

'Do you want to go to war with me, brother?' Virginia asked John when she was still inside Gloriavale. Neither had any idea what it would entail: how it would drain them, how long it would take, how many oceans they would cross and ships they would burn until the only way out was forward.

In a dramatic turn of events, 2021 became the year of John Ready's biggest battle. A team of lawyers finally took on his case, and three years after he was expelled, he launched a civil claim against Gloriavale. With his sister and mother as additional plaintiffs, he is asking for the trustees to step down and end the alleged physical, emotional, sexual and spiritual abuse. It's his way to redeem himself because he failed his teenage daughter. Back then, he didn't have the power to push back. The defendants are the most powerful men of Gloriavale: Howard Temple, Fervent Stedfast and Faithful Pilgrim – Purity's father. They stand accused of slave labour and breeding predators.

The Gloriavale Leavers' Support Trust calls it a 'historic battle' and is fundraising for it. From a business perspective, 2021 turns out to be a good year for Gloriavale. Covid hasn't impacted on their major industries. Its annual revenue in 2020 was $18 million. According to one of the witnesses in the landmark case, a former trustee, $100,000 is spent on legal fees every month.

The week before *John Ready v The Christian Church Community Trust* gets its first hearing in front of a judge at the High Court in Christchurch, Gloriavale makes a surprise move. They wait until John is at work in Rotomanu, and then give his wife an ultimatum: you either get rid of your husband, or we'll get rid of you. They order Purity Ready to call the police and take out a restraining order against John for trespassing on the property. It's not the first demand of this kind. But this time, Purity doesn't fold.

She turns around to go and pack. Then she calls John to tell him that her Gloriavale life is finally over. She's crying. Her children have to leave their home overnight and don't know if they will ever see their cousins, uncles and aunties again. It's daunting, overwhelming, stressful and sad. John rushes back from the farm and stands guard so that no one hurls abuse at his wife.

The turnaround doesn't come as a relief. John is in disbelief that the leaders are finally letting Purity go and wondering what game they're playing this time. Is it just a manoeuvre so that he drops his case? But since there are more Gloriavale leavers trying to extract their wives and children, he wants to set a precedent that could lead to a class action suit. To help those who are in the same boat and can't help themselves. He needs to see it through – while he also has his large family to feed and help settle in. There is no celebration for this historic moment of Purity's exit. She is pregnant with their eleventh child.

Charity, the second eldest, is already an adult and can stay on by herself after her family has left. She wants to come to her own decision, and sits down with Howard Temple to ask him pointed questions about things like the handling of the molestation of a young family member and her older sister's expulsion. When the twenty-year-old receives only unsatisfactory answers, she quits, on her own terms.

Charity is the first one to take off the blue frock. She doesn't want to represent Gloriavale anymore. While she now looks like everyone around her, she is catching up on practicalities like getting a driver's licence and running her own finances. The other adjustment for her and her sister, after shifting to what they've been told all their lives is a terrible place, is doing 'men's work'. Working on Marcus Tuck's farm along with their brothers is a good change, though. The girls prefer being outdoors with animals to slaving in the hot community kitchen.

The transition has been easiest for the youngest children who had no concept of the outside world, or the frightening tales that came with it. But because they're homeschooled until the next semester starts, they haven't made new friends yet.

I see them in early 2022 when my husband and I drive through Moana. It's only a brief stop to drop off afternoon tea from the Greymouth bakery. The Readys have moved to another house. Three-year-old Andrew, whose birth made national headlines in my piece for the *New Zealand Herald*, plays in the yard with two dark-haired siblings. I can see bunk beds through the windows and the older girls in the kitchen. They shoot me a quick glance and look away.

Purity steps outside holding a baby. She's a delicate woman with freckles and glasses in a short-sleeved flowery summer dress. We both smile down at her tiny son who is only a month old.

'His name is Ian,' she says softly. It means 'God is gracious' in Scottish Gaelic and was her father's name before he changed it when he joined Gloriavale. Ian is their first child born outside the cult. It's not a word I would use around Purity since she might recoil at any criticism. 'Home' is what she still calls Gloriavale while she is slowly adjusting to the new.

We only exchange a few sentences; I don't want to probe or linger. She tells me that her little ones write cards and letters to relatives inside. But the last time they turned up at Gloriavale, they weren't welcome anymore.

We then go to the Tucks' farm, where everything started. John pulls up in a truck. It's a hot summer day, so we sit inside. The black cat is there again and brushes past our legs.

Purity is not participating in any media interviews or the highly publicised court case, but she's not undermining his efforts either, John explains. It's a positive for him that she can express what she wants even if it's not always what he wants.

'She's finally left that abusive relationship where she feels she can't say anything. That's been drummed into her from childhood and really hard to undo.'

Her healing process entails that no one is having any more power over her. Every 'no' from her is a win, says John. It's one day at a time for them at the moment. John has a job offer on a farm near Timaru. They're moving south in May and need to just quietly live their lives for a bit, after all the upheaval. Things can always change and it's going to be a grind. He looks emotional when he says that you can't get out of Gloriavale without a degree of damage. 'So let's just get on with it.'

I have a surprise, which I've only told Marcus Tuck and Liz Gregory about. They both wished me luck. Since I'm in the area, I've decided to go into Gloriavale again. John flinches, then catches himself.

'Just rock up there,' he advises me. 'Tell them how much you liked the concert. They'll want to sell their best impression to you. But don't mention that you're a journalist.'

There is no fog over Lake Haupiri this time. The dense bush around the shore has flowered, the empty road is dry and dusty. We pass two teenagers who are standing next to a station wagon in the afternoon sun. They can't be from Gloriavale because they're in denim shorts. And pashing.

'No hunting without permission' says the sign at the turnoff to the community. The last time I drove past, I hadn't met Virginia and John, or Theo and Aaron. I didn't know the extent of pain that a few men and their rigid beliefs can inflict on so many people.

We drive across Gloriavale land, my husband at the wheel. The sky is blue, no cloud in sight. The paddocks and farm tracks stretch out towards the wilderness, framed by the dark ridge of Mt Alexander in the distance. It could be a film set, the Kiwi version of *The Sound of Music*, but we're entering a Christian gulag.

In its 30 years, this place has never been confronted with social media boycott groups, picket lines, arson, or 'rape cult' graffiti and faeces on their walls like Agama Yoga. Instead, it has benefitted from positive prime-time coverage on national TV, and its tax-free status.

When the grey hostels appear, I'm sweating not just from the summer heat in my high-collared long dress. We overtake three boys in blue on a small electric vehicle that looks like a cross between a Chinese rickshaw and a tractor.

Children are everywhere when we pull up at the main building. Some are playing in the cardboard remains of concert decorations. It says 'Willy Wonka's Chocolate Factory'. Because of Covid, the concert I attended in 2018 was their last one. Two young women carry a white baby cot across the yard. The hostels are still lined with prams. Nothing has visibly changed.

The women in the office, most of them behind cubicle walls, give us an alarmed look when we walk in. I'm expecting to be turned away within seconds. But instead, a receptionist takes us outside on the lawn where Howard Temple, the cult's leader, is talking to a younger man.

Temple was still Howard Smitherman, a mechanical engineer in the US Navy, when he first came to New Zealand. After becoming a Christian, marrying, and joining the community at Springbank, his wife became the head of the school and he the principal of one of their early childhood centres. The late Hopeful Christian made him his successor before his death. He is now 81 years old, short and wiry. In his working uniform, he looks like a friendly elderly gardener, not the despot who allegedly intimidates and punishes his flock in the name of the Lord. Despite his unthreatening look, I'm nervous.

Introducing my husband as a doctor who has treated some of their elders at Grey Hospital serves as an icebreaker. Someone brings us chilled apple juice and chairs to sit on while I reveal that I'm writing a book about religious communities. This could spell the end of our flying visit. But Howard seems equally flattered, amused, curious – and barely suspicious, because in his world, women hold no power.

'You have a faith of any sort yourself?' he croaks with a southern drawl, squinting under his blue sunhat.

We don't have a clear answer.

He's happy to chat for a bit before he needs to head into a meeting. I ask if I can take notes, and ease gently into my questions. Although my husband stays quiet, Howard mostly looks at him while he answers me. His jovial tone becomes patronising when he tells me that I just 'went down a couple' for working in the media. He is not happy about the attention Gloriavale has had in the news recently.

'It's a nuisance, it's annoying!' He sighs. 'We've got a pretty strong faith. God's gonna see us through.'

We nod politely. It's my segue to address their problems with the law without going into specifics. He first thinks I'm referring to Covid regulations.

'We're bound by the Bible,' says Howard. 'The Bible tells us to put ourselves in subjection to the higher powers.'

But still, 'people have rights' in this place.

'We're not trying to force our beliefs on anybody. We are positive people.'

God sees things 'a little bit different', and salvation is offered to those who obey him. He quotes a Bible verse.

At the risk of blowing my only chance with the preacher, I bring up the child sexual abuse at Gloriavale. 'It sounds like it has been going on for a long time,' I suggest carefully.

Howard doesn't miss a beat. 'Not for a long time; we weren't conscious of it at all,' he claims. 'I know of some instances that we have dealt with it.'

I want to know how. Did they go to the police?

He shakes his head. 'The spirit of Christ that the Bible teaches is to forgive. It's a difference to the law, they don't have forgiveness.'

He admits that this approach didn't help because 'they' – the sexual predators – were 'still there'.

'It should have been dealt with differently, but we didn't know. We didn't know to what extent it had become. Once the police came in and uncovered it, we had to deal with it.'

The leaders didn't see it as a serious problem, he admits – but it was more serious than they realised. What sounds like accountability at first turns out to be deflecting: it happened out of their sight and was out of their hands – and nothing unusual. He waves his hands a bit.

'There was wrongdoing in Gloriavale, but nothing that's not going on out there. It's common in boarding school situations.'

In boarding schools, sexual abuse victims are usually not brought before a dozen men who make the child forgive the perpetrator. When I mention the girl who the old teacher had touched indecently, I expect Howard to deny the outrageous procedure I heard about. But he confirms it.

'Yes, that was expected.' He is firm, not apologetic. 'That's what the Bible teaches.'

One of the apostles had asked Jesus how many times he should forgive his brother. 'Seven times?' Howard quotes from the scripture. Maybe it's 70 times; he is difficult to understand. I say that it made girls think it was their fault.

'No, it wasn't their fault,' he comes back straight away. And contradicts that in the next breath when he makes child molestation sound like an adult affair.

'A girl can be as seductive as a man. Two people get together, and it ends up in sex.'

I want to know what changes have been made at Gloriavale to prevent these issues.

'No, no change,' he states, telling me it was all in the past. His tone is confident. 'We're just more conscious of what has happened. Now, we will be a little bit more thorough. The ones who have done it before will be a lot slower to do it again,' he reckons. But the temptation is the same because 'the devil is not going to give up'.

Speaking of giving up: what about the Gloriavale leavers trying to get their wives out? Again, Howard is not fazed. A divided family is 'an ugly, horrible thing', he says, but that is their choice. He says it happens everywhere in society when a husband walks away.

'A couple who was married here, raised their children here … I tell them if you want to go, you're free to go.' His creaky voice turns up a notch. 'There's five hundred of us, if you want to go, you can go!'

The Bible tells him to withdraw himself from them.

'If any man teaches any other doctrine than what you've received from us, we put him out. A heretic. Reject him. It's cut and dry. You can get all emotional about it, but it's either me or Satan.'

There's one topic left while I still have his ear: the role of women. With a sarcastic laugh and a wink to my husband, he throws in that I'm 'liberated', making it sound like it's a pain they both have to put up with.

'The Bible says it's not permitted for a woman to speak in church,' he explains. 'If she has any question, it's answered by her husband at home.'

'That's in the Bible?' my husband asks, not convinced. He read the Bible from front to back while we sat through long, hot church services on a Tokelauan atoll twenty years ago.

Howard nods and quotes Ephesians, chapter five: 'Wife, submit yourself to your own husband in everything.' God has put the man over the woman, he explains.

'You've heard of Adam and Eve's business in the Garden of Eden? They shall not eat the fruit of that tree. Then she gave up on that and he dealt with the devil first.'

It's time to challenge him more. What if he were in a subordinate position in society just because of how he was born – say, because of the colour of his skin?

He laughs at my question, then gets serious. 'Okay … these women here, they have a place. And they're happy with that place because it's the place God gave them, and they accept that.'

He denies with a sneer that they're under anyone's thumb. It doesn't bother him either that many people want to see Gloriavale closed. 'No, no, let it go!' He waves it off. 'That's been happening since the beginning of Christianity. What did they do to Jesus? What wrong did he do?'

The world is getting worse, he laments, and God's judgement day is going to come, no matter what. 'All we can do is do the best we can to survive.'

It's getting busy on the lawn when we get up to leave. People are carrying picnic tables outside and setting them up in rows. Tomorrow is their 'celebration day'.

Gloriavale bought a 2365-hectare waterfront station at Lake Brunner in 2019 where they plan to house more members. A few families have already moved there. The new expansion to their four properties was described as a 'trophy' with a cattle farm, native forest, exotic timber plantation and building consent for tourism lodges. That year, The Christian Church Community Trust made a profit of almost $2.8 million. Since the cult doesn't borrow money according to their beliefs, the tax-free charity had to pay the purchase off over time, helped by the total of $4.5 million it receives in government subsidies and funding each year – and by tightening the food budget and holiday time. Their assets have now grown to $50 million.

To celebrate this financial milestone, everyone gets a day off and the leaders a chance to lift the morale with fast food and fun games. They've hired bouncy castles and hydroslides for the kids. It will be a glorious day.

Epilogue

It is July 2022, and I'm taking a break from researching cults – while processing my own involvement in what I was once so passionate about. My perspective keeps changing.

Other lives have changed too: Angie Meiklejohn is a devoted grandmother and teaches self-defence to girls, after her story was turned into the documentary *Angie*. Louise Winn had her name suppression lifted, left Auckland, and started therapy in 2021. She stopped writing poems but still makes art.

Theophila Pratt graduated with a Bachelor of Health Science, the first woman from Gloriavale with a tertiary education, and now works at a special needs school. Aaron Courage became a father and is learning to parent without corporal punishment. Virginia Courage had a healthy baby boy called Jonas. John Ready's civil suit reached a temporary settlement, but it's not the end of his battle. In another landmark case, the employment court ruled that there was exploitation of workers, including children, at Gloriavale. More slave labour, human rights and sexual abuse cases against the Christian community are underway, while it has issued a lengthy public apology to the people it harmed, promising change. It's a first in their 40-year history.

Last month, an international group of concerned neo-tantra and sex educators started collecting reports about ISTA and the adjacent 'mystery school' Highden Temple in New Zealand. Earlier this year, Osho from India was exposed, posthumously, as a sexual abuser. He had a hit list: those who would speak out about it should be killed. On Koh Phangan, Agama held a special day to honour their guru 'Swamiji' while the community group Safe Phangan tries to stop Agama's re-emerging influence on the island. Thailand finally extended the time limit for reporting rapes from three months to twenty years. Anti-cult agencies across Europe are still investigating allegations against MISA guru Gregorian Bivolaru.

Unlike many Western countries, Aotearoa New Zealand does not yet have a government agency specialised in cult prevention and exit counselling. It is desperately needed. So are media outlets that report about the spiritual and therapeutic sector as much as they do about sports, movies, real estate and cars – not with ridicule, but discernment. The rapidly growing self-help market deserves the same scrutiny as other businesses. Cult journalism needs space for nuance, not just clickbait when terrible things happen.

The years of the Covid-19 pandemic have highlighted how vast cultic belief systems are, how they can lead to political extremism, and how easy it is to get sucked into them. The mental-health impact of death and sickness, of isolation and hardship, on millions of people around the world makes them more prone than ever to fall for charismatic leaders or retreat to idealistic and isolated communities. Canada, Mexico and Paraguay have had an influx of European Covid deniers, some of them from the far-right, who have started their own colonies to escape the 'matrix'. In Aotearoa New Zealand, spiritual festival organisers involved in the anti-government protest have bought communal land together with their supporters.

—

To understand cultish dynamics, we need to look at ourselves and not just at the questionable gurus. What makes us admire someone so much that we let them tell us what is good for us, without an inquiry on our part or qualification on theirs? What mental gymnastics do we use to reframe the kind of subjugation that breaks the human spirit as 'tough love' or 'growth'? How often have we stayed silent in the presence of an emperor with no clothes, afraid to stand out in the crowd? And if we truly believe we can create a better world, or help others to be better versions of themselves, can we safely encourage them to join our path?

There's a very fine line between passion and manipulation, between being a good student or an infatuated follower. It's easy to blur it. If spiritual idols go unchecked for the sake of keeping peace, not losing friends or upholding an ideology, then I wonder how much we're also at fault for putting them on a pedestal in the first place. Adulation eventually corrupts.

Growing up in Germany, the question of collective guilt and redemption has haunted me since I first learned about the Holocaust. The silence of the bystanders disturbed me as much as the atrocities. When do the oppressed become the oppressors, or just complicit to save their own skin in a totalitarian system?

My father, a child during the war and a refugee from the East, was in a Christian–Jewish reconciliation group in his forties. At the age of twelve, I told myself that I would have been as brave as Sophie Scholl, who was executed for her peaceful resistance to Hitler. Or at least I would have been hiding Anne Frank in our basement. Now in my fifties, I can't say with certainty what I'm capable of, good or bad, when put in extreme circumstances. It's easy to act like a hero from the sidelines, or judge after the fact. But it's also a cop-out for the other side to say: 'You weren't there.' Not everyone was just following orders.

After years of exploring the minds of once-loyal Centrepoint, Agama and Gloriavale members, I'm less interested in the role they played back then. I want to know what they did after the downfall. Are they still holding on to their old ideology, making excuses for it? Or are they involved in a restorative process that helps the victims' recovery, instead of whitewashing their own actions?

My 2015 feature 'Bert's Labyrinth' in *North & South* motivated Christchurch doctor Caroline Ansley to start the Centrepoint Restoration Project. Together with two other survivors who also appeared in the TVNZ documentary *Heaven and Hell – The Centrepoint Story*, she launched an open letter to the former adult members of Centrepoint in 2021. So far, only a few of them have shown commitment to a reconciliation process.

'Vergangenheitsbewältigung' is a German post-war term that means 'coming to terms with the past': uncovering and repairing the horrors of the Third Reich. The same honest investigation, not only in a judicial context but also psychologically, is needed for cults. Too often, politicians, police and social services are oblivious, naive or ignorant. Or even complicit, as in the case of Centrepoint. Justice is rarely done in a timely fashion. Former members of a group that harmed them, or where they harmed others, require counsellors who are specialised in cultic abuse, and expert witnesses in court who can explain the coercion and indoctrination that keeps so many silent. There aren't enough of these professionals around, while for every person finally coming forward about their suffering, there are hundreds of others not able to speak up. The girl in the caravan is not alone.

Acknowledgements

This book feels like a miracle baby after a miscarriage – one that I was anxious to birth.

In 2012, I set out to write a book about Centrepoint. The commissioning editor left the publishing house soon after and I was on my own when the project became overwhelming. Two years into it, after legal threats made against me, the death of a friend, and PTSD from vicarious trauma, I pulled the plug. To stay with the baby metaphor, it was more a termination than a miscarriage. A relief at the time, but also a defeat that was hard to accept for my professional ego.

If it hadn't been for Holly Hunter at HarperCollins, there would never have been a second attempt. She blew enough wind under my wings to get me going again and over the finish line. Her care and competence made her the perfect midwife. I'm honoured to have ended up in such good hands and with an incredibly dedicated publishing team, after feeling like a failure.

While I was in the thick of it on my first round, Nicky Hager came to my rescue as a mentor and Ali Romanos as a defamation lawyer. Some friends and colleagues helped me selflessly during that difficult time in big and small ways: Jules Barber, Tracey Bradley, Paul Elsner, Anders Falstie-Jensen, Julie Hill, Lynley Hood, Felix Ihlefeldt, Rebecca Lee,

Slavko Martinov, Jeffrey Mason, Jared Savage, Courtenay Stickles and Anja Striepke. Apologies if I've missed some names – I had to put a lid on it all back then. Thanks to David Fisher for letting me drag it up again at the Investigative Journalism conference in 2017, and to Emma Hart for being the best transcriber ever.

All my advisors and experts in the background have my gratitude for their fact-checking and generous input: Gemini Adams, Caroline Ansley, Chris Cooke, Uma Dinsmore-Tuli, Georgia Duder-Wood, Liz Gregory, Brian Gruber, Jenny Hale, Christopher Jones, Janja Lalich, Barri Leslie, Renate Mayalila, Cat McShane, Jazmin Metzger, Matthew Remski, Lorraine Taylor, Marcus Tuck, Cecilia Tiz and Abhay Vaidya. The editors and documentary makers who took my sometimes-botched efforts seriously – Costa Botes, Sarah Daniell, Virginia Larson, Natalie Malcon, Toby Manhire, Rachel Morris and Rebekah White – made a difference and were a joy to work with. The New Zealand Society of Authors has also been a great support, and Joanne Naish's court reporting for *Stuff* a reliable resource. David Farrier's fearless cult-busting inspired me.

I'm extremely lucky to have friends who get my work and helped in many ways, like Uleshka Asher, Henry Bersani, Matthias Blattner, Rebecca Brosnahan, Michelle Duff, Kate Evans, Kyle Greenwood, Kit Hindin, Honalee Hunter, Jan Jeans, Kirsty Johnston, Kati Lindenberg, Gitta Mayer, Sören Mund, Laura Reinger, Breeze Robertson, Zoe Rose, Anna Schäfer, Andrea Solzer, Wilrieke Sophia, Tyler Stent, Kerry Sunderland, Marianna Tomarelli, Ondra Veltrusky, Roger Boyce, Jaya Gibson, Lucy Matthews and Camia Young. Special thanks to Naomi Arnold for wielding the scalpel, to Paul Baakman and Mareile Stoppel for the therapy, and to FACT Aotearoa for having my back.

I wouldn't have made it through my cult crashes without the love of the three men in my life: my sons, Quinn and Jasper, and my husband, Frank. Throughout this long and challenging project, he showed up as a listener, a lover, a first reader, a soother and a gourmet cook. His generous spirit and sound bullshit radar got us through the ups and downs of our personal growth adventures.

More than anyone, every survivor and whistle-blower deserves immense respect for coming forward and seeing it through. Without their courage, there would still be silence. Many I interviewed I couldn't include. You know who you are, and your stories matter too.

Kia kaha.

Further resources for cult awareness, intervention and recovery

Books

Take Back Your Life: Recovering from Cults and Abusive Relationships by Janja Lalich and Madeleine Landau Tobias (Bay Tree Publishing, 2006)

Terror, Love and Brainwashing: Attachment in Cults and Totalitarian Systems by Alexandra Stein (Routledge, 2016)

Combatting Cult Mind Control: The #1 Best-selling Guide to Protection, Rescue, and Recovery from Destructive Cults by Steven Hassan (Park Street Press, 1989)

Opening Minds: The Secret World of Manipulation, Undue Influence and Brainwashing by Jon Atack (Trent Valley, 2016)

Wounded Faith: Understanding and Healing from Spiritual Abuse by Neil Damgaard (International Cultic Studies Association, 2022)

Practice And All Is Coming: Abuse, Cult Dynamics, and Healing in Yoga and Beyond by Matthew Remski (Embodied Wisdom Publishing, 2019)

Cultish: The Language of Fanaticism by Amanda Montell (HarperCollins Publishers, 2021)

The Guru Papers: Masks of Authoritarian Power by Joel Kramer and Diana Alstad (Frog Books, 2012)

The Anatomy of Illusion: Religious Cults and Destructive Persuasion by Thomas W. Keiser and Jacqueline L. Keiser (Charles C Thomas, 1987)

Cults in Our Midst: The Continuing Fight Against Their Hidden Menace by Margaret Thaler Singer (Jossey-Bass, 2003)

Disrupting the Bystander: When #metoo Happens Among Friends by A.V. Flox (Thorntree Press, 2019)

The Art of Receiving and Giving: The Wheel of Consent by Betty Martin and Robyn Dalzen (Luminare Press, 2021)

Sex In The Forbidden Zone: When Men In Power – Therapists, Doctors, Clergy, Teachers & Others – Betray Women's Trust by Peter Rutter (Tarcher, 1989)

Betrayal Trauma: The Logic of Forgetting Childhood Abuse by Jennifer J. Freyd (Harvard University Press, 1989)

Organisations and useful websites

In New Zealand:
centrepointrestorationproject.com
gloriavaleleavers.org.nz (Gloriavale Leavers' Support Trust)
sexualabuse.org.nz

Internationally:
Igotout.org
tbylr.com (Take Back Your Life Recovery)
icsahome.com (International Cultic Studies Association)

openmindsfoundation.org
cultrecovery101.com
Instagram.com/cultawareness
redflagsinworkshops.com

Podcasts

General:
Conspirituality
A Little Bit Culty
Generation Cult
IndoctriNation
Decoding the Gurus
Let's Talk About Sects
Sounds Like A Cult
Everyday Cults. Everyday People
Armchaired & Dangerous

About specific cults (including some in this book):
The Commune
The Orgasm Cult
Bikram
Guru: The Dark Side of Enlightenment
The Gateway: Teal Swan
Transmissions from Jonestown
Dear Franklin Jones
Escaping NXIVM
Building Utopia: Bhagwan Shree Rajneesh